Identity and Strategy

'My vision is not what's important to you. The only vision that motivates you is your vision.'

Bill O'Brien, *Hanover Insurance*, quoted in Senge (1990, p. 211).

Identity and Strategy

How Individual Visions Enable the Design of a Market Strategy that Works

Olaf G. Rughase

Schindl Rughase Partners, Landsberg/Düsseldorf and the Zollverein School of Management and Design, Essen, Germany

Edward Elgar

Cheltenham, UK • Northampton, MA, USA

Published by
Edward Elgar Publishing Limited
Glensanda House
Montpellier Parade
Cheltenham
Glos GL50 1UA
UK

Edward Elgar Publishing, Inc.
136 West Street
Suite 202
Northampton
Massachusetts 01060
USA

A catalogue record for this book
is available from the British Library

Library of Congress Cataloguing in Publication Data

Rughase, Olaf G., 1968–   .
    Identity and strategy: how individual visions enable the design of a
market strategy that works/Olaf G. Rughase.
        p.   cm.
    Includes bibliographical references and index.
    1. Strategic planning. 2. Corporate culture. 3. Organizational change.
4. Marketing. I. Title.
    HD30.28.R843   2006
    658.8'02—dc22   2005052089

ISBN-13: 978 1 84542 310 0
ISBN-10: 1 84542 310 0

Printed and bound in Great Britain by MPG Books Ltd, Bodmin, Cornwall

Contents

Figures

Tables and boxes

TABLES

BOXES

Acknowledgements

This book is the result of a five-year project. Many people have helped me along the way. I cannot mention everyone by name who shaped the writing of this book in one way or another but I would like to address particular thanks to some individuals.

First of all, I would like to thank Franz Liebl, Anne S. Huff, and Birger P. Priddat who encouraged, helped and supported me in innumerable discussions during this whole project. These productive discussions have helped me to sharpen my ideas and concepts. It is no understatement to say that this book would not exist without their thoughtful and guiding suggestions, comments and recommendations.

I must express deep gratitude to Michael Schindl who has been working with me on the subject of strategy for several years. He provided immense help for this book by sharing his practical process experiences with me and by giving critical feedback. I am especially indebted to him for taking the main burden of running our joint business partnership during the period of this project.

I am grateful to Gerhard Linke, Ulrich Rieger, Thorsten Voigt, Holger de Vries, and Hiltrud Koslowski for their significant help.

Finally, I would like to offer special thanks to Sandra Hengstermann for encouraging words, understanding and good humor when I deeply struggled with this project – you kept me going.

Olaf G. Rughase

Foreword

Anne Sigismund Huff

Scholars/practitioners shaped management disciplines and helped system-ize practice until about 50 years ago. Unfortunately, from my point of view, the double agenda is not seen as often today. But this book shows why it is important, and how it can be achieved.

Olaf Rughase draws on his experience and academic training to develop a new approach to designing strategies that are likely to be successfully implemented in the marketplace. This topic has been central to strategic management from its inception and is of increasing interest in many other fields. Still, most observers are likely to agree with Michael Tushman's presentation of the current situation: 'Inertia is so, so, so strong that few companies are able to succeed in their attempts to move away from current technologies and current customers.'[1]

It is generally agued that 'stress' motivates organizations that try to find new ground. Most of the literature, both academic and practice oriented, tends to emphasize the negative impact of competitors' success, declining revenues, eroding customer bases, and other disappointments, though galvanizing opportunities from changing technologies, customer demographics and the like are also recognized. A few argue that positives within the organization, such as strong returns, are also potentially stressful and likely to lead to strategic change.[2] Olaf Rughase makes a similar point, but his positive position is the 'desired future identity' of the organization, initially articulated by individuals and then melded into a mutually agreed ideal.

Though it is not framed in these terms, I am interested in this book first of all because it contributes to positive organizational scholarship.[3] There is a compelling argument, recently expressed by Sumatra Ghoshal,[4] that theory and practice have been stunted by initial assumptions of self-interest and other human limitations. In contrast, Rughase assumes that most enduring strategies must be fashioned from within, by those who not only know the organization as it is, but have already thought about what it can be. That is a very refreshing starting point.

The subsequent argument draws on and contributes to theory in several areas of contemporary interest. The key role of organizational identity, and individual identification with that image, is described in detail as the first move in designing strategy. One distinctive feature of the case study is that it shows how identity brings emotion into the design process. Rughase argues that external analysis, and in particular the needs of customers, are more likely to be uncovered when energized by a possible future, even though his process is designed to then facilitate a critical review of initially desired identity.

Perhaps it will be surprising to those who are engaged in contemporary work on identity, emotion, design, and customer-based strategy to discover key contributions from older references as well as more recent citations in this book. Rughase uses, for example, details from Russell Ackoff's work on strategic design that began in the 1950s. He reminds us that Kenneth Andrews's influential description of strategy from the 1960s is rooted in values. He draws on Derek Abell's 1980 definition of the enterprise, which is rooted in customer configurations.

However, as already noted, this book is not just an academic treatise. Its insights grow out of facilitating strategy making, and one of these experiences is described in some detail. There are many practical observations to be found here. Political realities are acknowledged. Alternative paths anticipated.

It all sounds complex, and it is. But I finished reading this book thinking that it provides a genuinely fresh voice on compelling management issues. New approaches to understanding and changing organizations are needed. The ideas advanced here are, in combination, a genuine departure from past efforts. The theoretic development, which moves back and forth from experience to academic explanation, is convincing.

These achievements are clearly the result of Rughase's considerable personal abilities. In addition, the book's interest and success, in my opinion, are also due to its point of departure and its objectives. Rughase's desire to improve his practice proves to be a useful compass for finding key references in an ever-growing academic literature. And the literature in turn is a powerful tool for highlighting and making sense of practical experience. The results of weaving both strands of thought together are much more engaging than if he had pursued a Mode 1 (academic) or a Mode 2 (practical) objective alone.[5]

European scholars, and especially Germans I have learned, are still likely to gain considerable experience moving between research and practice. I believe a globalizing world makes their approach to knowledge production increasingly necessary. Though inertia characterizes our efforts in the US, as all others, I hope to see inter-Mode scholars establish a middle ground between theory and practice. You hold an exemplar of this promising strategy in your hands.

NOTES

1. Michael R. Tushman, presentation at London Business School, 24 June 2005.
2. Huff, A.S. and J.O. Huff with P. Barr (2000), *When Firms Change Direction*, Oxford: Oxford University Press.
3. Cameron, K.S., J. Dutton and R. Quinn (eds) (2003), *Positive Organizational Scholarship*, San Francisco: Barrett Koehler.
4. Ghoshal, S. (2005), 'Bad management theories are destroying good management practices', *Academy of Management Learning & Education*, **4** (1), 75–92.
5. *British Journal of Management*, special issue, 2001, volume 12.

Resurrecting the future of strategy consulting

Franz Liebl

The road towards a successful and workable strategy is strewn with a host of obstacles. This does not only include the many strategy papers devised by consultants which are quietly shelved by management and never acted upon. Even strategy processes which are ostensibly based on the principle of participation and which involve the relevant stakeholders also have their inherent weaknesses.

The conclusions that can be drawn from this history of failure may be formulated in this way: first, organizations are evidently incapable of implementing strategies which are not in tune with their identity, however attractive and well thought out those strategies might appear to the impartial observer. Second, unless these identity issues are clarified at the very outset of strategy development, they crop up uncontrolled and often invisible during the strategy making process, say, for example, in the way people think about the future developments likely to face the company. Third, tedious strategy processes which seriously hamper the creative development of novel strategic options are the inevitable outcome, not to mention the (intended and unintended) distortions in future scenarios that result from these omissions.

Two fundamental questions have to be asked. First, what role does identity play in the different phases of the strategy making process? And, second, can we unleash the power of identities by making them transparent and by ensuring a proper alignment? What, therefore, are the creative potentials of a strategy process which makes sufficient allowance for identity, and what is the procedure for reaching this desirable goal?

With these questions Olaf Rughase has addressed a field that is highly significant for strategic success but where there has been surprisingly little research hitherto. Hence, his book contains some pathbreaking ideas which will impress both the practitioner and the academic. All the more so as Olaf Rughase – unlike many others writing on strategic management topics – does not proceed ahistorically. Particularly for those who have followed the development of strategic management over the last 20 years and more, it is fascinating to see how Rughase extracts potentials for his central question from classic works by authors such as Ackoff, Abell and Andrews, which clearly have not been given the recognition they deserve in the scholarly discussion or which have inexplicably fallen into oblivion.

What Olaf Rughase's brilliant book conveys is the indissoluble alliance between strategy content and strategy process – a realization which, as I see it, will very much be the shape of things to come in strategy consulting. The future will not belong to the classic, content-driven 'recommendations' which, we're told, just have to be implemented by a top-management team 'with a strong hand'; nor will it be sufficient simply to 'irritate' an organization systemically in order to bring a viable strategy about. Olaf Rughase's answer here is closer to strategic practice because it is more complex. He highlights two issues pertaining to the relation between content and process which have to be addressed simultaneously. First, how must a strategy process be designed in order to be able to generate goal-oriented and innovative contents? And second, what contents have to be fed into strategy making in order to fuel the process? It is only when both these aspects are taken into account that the preconditions are in place for strategic innovation which (at the same time) has a realistic chance of being implemented.

Introduction

This book is about strategy making. Over the last 50 years, academics, consultants, and practitioners have been thinking hard about strategy, providing many – often powerful – analytical tools, frameworks and processes. And for many years, the academic discipline of strategic management had an impressive impact on organizational practice. But times have changed. When I talk to managers about strategy and strategy making today, they often roll their eyes and their body language waves this topic aside. Asked for reasons or underlying experiences that cause their refusal, they often answer in the form of a question: 'What about strategy implementation?' When inquiring further it turns out that this question actually refers to their practical experience – many strategies are not realized. Even more dramatic, this experience is becoming a truism. As a result, strategy has become a term that has fallen into disgrace for many practitioners and dramatically lost practical relevance in recent years (see Huff, 2001).

This is a paradox because, at the same time, practitioners as well as academics see that creative and customer-oriented strategies are increasingly indispensable to organizations in times of hypercompetition and rapidly changing business environments (see Magretta, 2002; Porter, 1996; Ford and Gioia, 1995). In accordance with other strategy researchers my sense is that these times of rapid change require substantial modifications in strategy making. In such an uncertain environment, 'the key to success moves from the "optimal strategy" to the "most skilful strategy process"' (van der Heijden, 1996, p. viii). Instead of being the strategic decision makers they used to be, top managers become strategic architects, designers and coordinators of a skilful process which involves people at many levels of an organization. Thus, strategy making has become radically decentralized in an organization, involving many people (Floyd and Wooldridge, 2000, p. xiv; Hamel, 1996).

Despite this shift towards decentralization, strategic management research and practice still tends to overly emphasize the more rational aspects in strategy making that focus on the best economic solution. By dismissing other important factors, such as the aspirations, feelings, emotions and values of involved organizational members, strategy making may produce a logical or even an optimal economic strategy, but its outcome is very often far from being received as an attainable and realistic strategy by organizational members. In effect, strategies are frequently not realized due to the fact they cannot successfully connected to the existing mental concepts and desires of organizational members (see Liebl, 2001a and 2001b; Mezias et al., 2001).

As a strategy consultant I can draw from many practical cases which confirm these shifts and their effects for strategy making. However, I have also been involved with and influenced by the academic field of strategy as a scholar for many years, and I have become more and more theoretically intrigued by the changing nature of successful strategy. This book is the product of five years of academic research that was guided by the practical question: How can organizations develop creative strategies that are desired and attainable in the eyes of the many organizational members who must be involved?

When I started this somewhat ambitious research project a pragmatic and problem-oriented perspective offered me a different view on the contributions of available literature in management theory. While the field of strategic management provided only limited sources with regard to the practical problems I saw confronting strategy, other fields in management theory, such as organization theory, organizational development and change, and managerial and organizational cognition offered many relevant theoretical insights which are closely linked with strategy.

One of these research areas that offered especially relevant findings focused on organizational identity, which refers broadly to what organizational members perceive, feel and think about their organization (Whetten and Godfrey, 1998). The organization's identity reflects what members think about 'who they are as an organization' as well as 'who they should be as an organization'. This research area provides strong empirical evidence that indicates that identity has significant impacts on strategy making (see Dutton and Dukerich, 1991; Dutton and Penner, 1993; Dutton et al., 1994; Gioia and Thomas, 1996; Glynn, 2000; van Rekom, 2003).

However, these remarkable findings have not attracted the attention of strategy researchers adequately. In fact, it seems that research in strategic management does not pay enough attention to relevant findings and contributions in other fields of management theory that are likely to question their still dominant rational mind-set and economic focus. Thus, it is no surprise that the impacts of value-laden and identity-related factors have not been considered in strategic management, prolonging the existence of the striking blind spot in strategy that initially led to my academic studies.

Responding to this blind spot, I consequently focused my research on organizational identity and strategy, explored their relationship and developed a theoretical dynamic framework that puts organizational identity in a strategy context. But working with companies in practice, theoretically linking two streams in management theory is not sufficient. Especially, strategists and consultants need to find a procedural answer on how to design a strategy – they need to develop a skilful strategy process in practice. From that practical perspective, strategy making is about process-embedded actions. When taking this seriously, theoretical findings in strategy need to be taken further down the road – down to the practical work of strategy making which needs operational steps and concrete procedures. This is what this book tries to do.

Based on theory and theoretical findings, it is the aim of this book to propose a practical strategy making process that can help organizations to evolve creative strategies that are desired and attainable in the eyes of organizational members. I argue that individually *desired* organizational identities which refer to the future – and which can be seen as individual visions – not only have a strong impact on strategy making but can be practically used in a strategy making process. These individual visions play an important part for the whole strategy making process. But these visions are only one aspect that enables the design of a desired and attainable market strategy that works in practice. Understanding the critical needs of current and potential customers is the other important condition to design a successful market strategy. This book shows how customers and their needs can be closely connected to organizational identity in practical strategy making.

During academic research my consulting profession ensured that I was constantly able to assess how newly gained theoretical findings can be turned into practical process steps in strategy making. In effect, many parts of the whole strategy process design and its operational steps and procedures proposed in this book are a result of my daily work with private and public organizations.

By offering a concrete and also theory-rooted strategy making process which has been tested in practice, this book contributes to the development of a 'most skilful strategy process' – as van der Heijden has called it. It demonstrates that relevant findings in other fields of management theory are worth considering and can be used to modify strategy making in practice. It is my personal solution to preventing strategic management from losing relevance in practice.

In summary, this book offers three main contributions in the field of strategy:

- developing a theoretical dynamic framework that puts organizational identity into a strategy context;
- proposing a practical strategy making process that can help organizations to evolve creative strategies that are desired and attainable in the eyes of organizational members, and

- showing how the organization's customers can be closely connected to organizational identity in strategy making.

Audience
This book is meant for academics in strategic and organizational management, researchers, leaders and managers as well as consultants and students who are searching for new and innovative processes in practical strategy making that are also grounded in management theory. It addresses both 'practice-oriented academics' and 'reflective practitioners' who seek academic work that does not – in their opinion – remain theoretically abstract and detached from important practical questions or who do not want to rely on practitioner books that give – again in their opinion – too simplistic answers to complex issues.

Overview of the book
This book is organized into eight chapters that move from identifying a specific blind spot in the field of strategy to exploring theoretical foundations for an alternative, developing a theoretical framework that fits the practical requirements for strategy making and finally to designing a practical strategy making process which is tested in a real case study and discussed afterwards.

Chapter 1 establishes the intention of this book in more detail by substantially identifying the critical blind spot in contemporary strategy making theory. Drawing on relevant literature, it describes the missing link between organizational identity and strategy.

Chapter 2 provides an overview of the concept of organizational identity, its theoretical foundations and links to other management concepts by briefly reviewing the relevant literature in organization theory.

Chapter 3 relates organizational identity to the concept of strategy. It clarifies that strategy is an exceptionally customer-oriented concept before developing a theoretical framework which considers two different temporal aspects of organizational identity in the context of strategy – current (present) organizational identity which is separated from desired (future) organizational identity. This chapter shows that a dynamic framework can be created by merging these two temporal perspectives. Even more, it indicates that desired organizational identities are strong active drivers and motivators to guide organizational change.

Chapter 4 analyses the impacts of desired identities on strategy making in practice and formulates four substantial new requirements for a practical strategy process. To support new requirements theoretically this chapter explicitly draws on topics such as appreciative inquiry and system thinking in management theory and beyond.

Chapter 5 briefly describes how these new requirements can be methodologically integrated into a general strategy making process design. This short chapter also identifies another blind spot in the field of strategy – the actual design of a practical strategy process which covers many operational actions that are key to successful strategy making.

Chapter 6 describes what a concrete, designed strategy making process can look like and how it can craft a creative market strategy that is desired and attainable in the eyes of organizational members. This is done in the form of a real case study. At certain points in the case study, further theoretical and practical background is provided that helps to clarify and further reflect on methodological or theoretical questions with regard to the processes and steps proposed. As this chapter represents an important contribution by describing the proposed practical strategy process in detail it takes up a substantial part of the book.

Chapter 7 briefly reviews the case study and highlights selected lessons learned. In addition, it describes further practical experiences gained with the impact of desired organizational identities, in particular in larger organizations.

Chapter 8 concludes this book by discussing the central function of weighing and balancing rational and analytical with value-laden factors when designing practical strategy making processes.

1. Identity as a blind spot in strategy making

The term 'strategy' is used extensively in management literature and has lost meaning in the process. In 1996, Porter shed some useful light with his highly regarded *Harvard Business Review* article 'What is strategy?' Porter argues that strategy is about being different. It is about unique positioning in a market by creating and using the most sustainable competitive advantages. 'It means deliberately choosing a different set of activities to deliver a unique mix of value [to customers]' (Porter, 1996, p. 64).

But how can such a strategy be brought about? Strategy separated from strategy making is academic at best (Voigt, 2003). In practice, the concept of strategy and the process of strategy making are inseparable and managers encounter their most difficult problems at this particular interface. Therefore, this book focuses on the process of strategy making because I constantly see difficulties in bringing a strategy about and realizing it (compare Eden and Ackermann, 1998). Strategy making deals with the process of *how* a strategy can be designed (also known as strategy formulation) and realized in practice.

Reviewing the existing literature, it is interesting that Andrews's concept, which was developed in the 1960s (Learned et al., 1965; Andrews, 1987 [1971]), is still the most prevalent in strategy making (Mintzberg and Quinn, 1996, p. 46). Andrews suggested that a successful strategy is the outcome of a process that creates an essential fit between internal strengths and weaknesses and external threats and opportunities. This prescription is associated with the 'design school', as Mintzberg calls it (Mintzberg, 1990; Mintzberg and Lampel, 1999, p. 22).[1]

There was a fairly broad consensus for many years that strategy formulation using this and many other ideas was followed by implementation in a sequential process; however, in recent years the strategic management field has made a considerable change. Whereas the 'design school' gave the impression of being highly rationalistic and was clearly a top-down approach, Mintzberg, amongst others, introduced an evolutionary paradigm to the strategy making process. He proposed that strategy is often developed as the result of an emergent process rather than a process that is rationally planned and subsequently implemented – therefore strategy formulation and implementation cannot be separated from each other (see Mintzberg, 1990; Ansoff, 1991; Mintzberg, 1991; Mintzberg, 1994).[2]

This fruitful strategic management debate in the early 1990s paved the way for other important schools of thought about strategic management – such as the 'learning school' (Braybrooke and Lindblom, 1963; Mintzberg and Waters, 1985) or the 'cognitive school' (see Walsh, 1995) – and has consequently led to new developments in strategic management.

Today, many strategy researchers try to integrate different schools of thought, applying a cyclical approach in order to highlight the idea that strategic management consists of permanent learning loops that spiral on different levels within a continuous process (see Eden and Ackermann, 1998; van der Heijden, 1996; Hampden-Turner, 1993; Mintzberg and Lampel, 1999). 'Rather than preferring one school of thought over another, it is more productive to see these as different aspects of the same complex journey to strategic achievement' (Eden and Ackermann, 1998, p. 33).

Strategy making is a deliberate intervention for reconfirming or redesigning strategy

When strategy is conceived as a continuous learning process, it is neither purely deliberate nor purely emergent – it is in-between both extremes. Or as Chakravarthy et al. (2003, p. 1) put it: 'Strategies, as we all know, are in part planned and in part emergent.' This development makes the process of strategy making even more important in strategic management. In effect, strategy making – in particular how a strategy is designed – still plays a key role in strategic management (Eden and Ackermann, 1998; van der Heijden, 1996; Bryson, 1995; Liebl, 2000b).

Strategy making is understood here as a *deliberate* intervention into a continuous learning process which enables organizations to reconfirm or redesign an existing strategy. Almost all strategy researchers and practitioners agree upon the need to explore distinctive competencies and external opportunities in a controlled and conscious way. Thus, strategy making remains responsible for ensuring competitive advantages and finding new business opportunities, as well as new business models which support the organization's activities (see Liebl, 2000b, p. 19; Porter, 1996; Huff, 2001).

Although some premises of Andrews's original concept have fallen away – for example, that formulation and implementation are sequential and independent activities or that the manager who is at the peak of the hierarchy is ultimately the only strategist – others are still in place and should be considered in strategy making (Mintzberg and Quinn, 1996, p. 46).

A particularly complicated development involves Andrews's (1987, pp. 18–19) assumption 'that strategists are analytically objective in estimating the relative capacity of their company and the opportunity they see

or anticipate in developing markets'. Abell (1980) is among those who have
questioned analytical 'objectivity' as a starting point for strategy making.
He hypothesized that an underlying definition of the business acts as a reference point which influences strategy making enormously. This draws the
attention of managers towards limited aspects of the environment and away
from others. Since 1980, cognition researchers in the field of strategy have
undertaken many empirical studies which indicate that this focusing effect
not only exists but is also quite strong (see Gripsrud and Gronhaug, 1985;
Walton, 1986; Reger, 1990; Reger and Huff, 1993; Porac et al., 1989; Porac
and Thomas, 1990; Porac and Thomas, 1994; Farjoun and Lai, 1997;
Johnson et al., 1998). These perceptions provide subjective constraints for
strategy making by limiting the amounts and types of opportunities and
threats that a firm will consider (Porac et al., 2002, p. 128). Nevertheless,
reflecting on these constraints helps organizations to be analytic and as
precise as possible. In effect, a business definition creates a perceived space
of self-positioning against competitors and should therefore be the starting
point for strategy making, even if there is an ambition for significant change
in the current way of operating.

An undervalued factor in strategy making: what people 'want to do'
Next to the important finding that current business definition serves as a
cognitive anchor, there is another interesting observation to be made:
while the more rationalistic part of Andrews's strategy making process has
been widely accepted within the limits of bounded rationality, which
implicitly or explicitly dominates the world of pedagogy and practice
(compare Mintzberg, 1990; Mintzberg and Lampel, 1999; Farjoun, 2002),
there is another aspect of Andrews's work that has been given much less
attention by strategy researchers. Andrews (1987, pp. 18–20) summarizes
four factors which are essential in strategy making: what a company *might
do* in terms of environmental opportunity; what a company *can do* in
terms of its abilities and resources; what the people in the company *want
to do* in terms of their own personal values and aspirations; and what the
company *should do* in terms of broader ethical and societal considerations
(Figure 1.1).

What a company 'should do' in terms of ethical and societal considerations is a factor in strategy making that has notably changed over the
years – differing from Andrews's (1987) apparent expectations. Freeman
and Liedtka (1991), for example, have recently come to the conclusion that
the stakeholder concept has actually been substituted for corporate social
responsibility in many definitions of strategy.[3] Building on this idea it might
be said that what a company 'should do' is related to the purpose (mission)
of a company, which cannot be determined without an understanding of

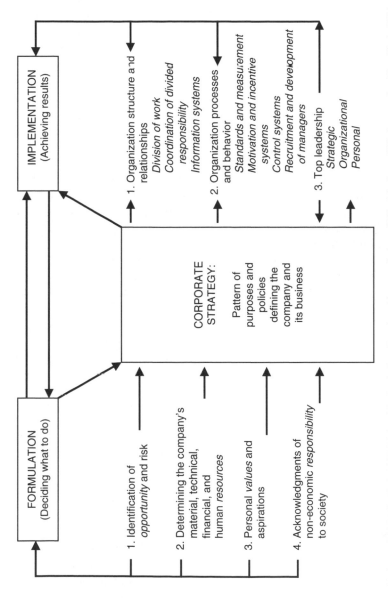

Figure 1.1 Andrews's concept of corporate strategy

stakeholders' impact, especially those stakeholders who are critical to the company, such as customers.[4]

The purpose of an organization is also inherently tied to an understanding of what organizational members 'stand for' (Freeman, 1984, p. 90). In strategy making, this points to the need for an explicit and deliberate attempt to answer the question: 'What should we stand for?' It reinforces the need for considering the role and function of an organization as a whole and its relationships to important stakeholders.[5] But an organization does not exist as an entity *sui generis*. Rather, it consists of its organizational members. Only due to the fact that organizations have a choice of purpose can these organizational members decide what the purpose of the organization 'should be'. However, this meaningful decision is closely related to what people 'want to do'.

As Andrews (1987, p. 19) says: 'Personal values, aspirations, and ideals do, and in our judgement quite properly should, influence the final choice of purposes. Thus, what the people in a company *want* to do must be brought into the strategic decision.'[6] Andrews must have been aware that his focus on value-factors might offend colleagues in the field then called business policy because – by explicitly departing from the stereotype of the single-minded economic man – he strongly argues that it is not only inevitable but also desirable for those involved in strategy making to have a voice in organizational direction (Andrews 1987, p. 57). Today, strategic management focuses primarily on theories of rational action in strategy making. Taket and White (2000, p. 56), who studied decision making in strategic and multi-agency settings more specifically,[7] come to the conclusion that management science has been dismissive of value-factors, manifesting in various ways: 'a) a tendency to ignore them (bracket them out of consideration) . . .; b) a tendency to regard . . . [them] as interference, something undesirable to be minimized; c) a view of . . . [them] as . . . tool[s] to be manipulated in the service of "rational" ends'. That is not to say that researchers did not recognize the important role that value-factors, for example emotions, feelings, beliefs, and aspirations play in organizational life on occasion (see Pratt and Dutton, 2000; Gabriel, 1998), but rather that they do not yet systematically consider them in strategy making.

The missing link: organizational identity and its impact
What people in a company see that their company '*should* do' and what they '*want* to do' is closely linked to the concept of organizational identity, which is a quite young research area in organization and strategy science. Organizational identity refers broadly to what members perceive, feel and think about their organization. It is primarily presumed to be a collectively shared understanding of the organization's central, distinctive

and enduring characteristics. Since Albert and Whetten's highly regarded article in 1985, a growing number of strategy researchers have become interested in the topic of organizational identity (see Stimpert et al., 1998). 'Research on dominant logics, interpretive frames, strategic vision, and so forth, indicates the importance of coherent and shared cognitive schemas regarding the organization . . . for the formulation, acceptance, and implementation of strategic plans' (Ashforth and Mael, 1996, p. 32).

The notion of identity and identification has a long pedigree in organization science. Yet only in recent years has it become widely deployed, including an interest in identity at the collective level (such as organizational identity) and not only at the level of individuals (see Brown, 2001, p. 113; Hatch and Schultz, 2004). Albert et al. (2000, p. 14) suggest a reason for the increasing interest in this subject just now:

> The momentum to study identity and identification . . . comes from a rediscovery of the importance of meaning and emotion in organizational life. The beauty of the identity and identification concepts is that they provide a way of accounting for the agency of human action within an organizational framework. By internalizing the group or organizational identity as a (partial) definition of the self, the individual gains a sense of meaningfulness and connection. Identity and identification explain one means by which individuals act on behalf of the group or the organization. Thus, theories of identity and identification are infused with motivation and feeling. They help to explain the direction and persistence of individual and more collective behaviors.

In accordance with Abell's (1980) challenge of the assumption of analytical 'objectivity' in strategy making, as discussed above, empirical studies in the field of organizational identity by Dutton and her colleagues have shown that identity guides and activates the individual's interpretation of strategic issues, thus influencing which environmental issues are noticed and which are not (see Dutton and Dukerich, 1991; Dutton et al., 1994; also Gioia and Thomas, 1996). These researchers find that identity shapes and directs strategic change through its links to a strategic agenda building process because identity determines which strategic issues are perceived feasible to resolve (see Dutton and Penner, 1993; Dutton and Duncan, 1987a). Dutton and Penner (1993) show that identity also heavily influences the individual's and the group's motivation to invest and act on strategic issues. In addition, Glynn (2000) uncovers in a qualitative field study that identity influenced organizational members' opinion about distinct competencies of their organization. Different identity claims, which were made under organizational crisis, accounted for variations in the perception of organizational core competencies. Also, Reger et al. (1994) as well as Gioia and Thomas (1996) found that organizational members claim ideal and desired future organizational identities. Their research also indicated that these ideal and desired concepts guide strategic behavior (see also van Rekom, 2003).

Identity appears to be 'critical to how and what one values, thinks, feels, and does in all social domains, including organizations' (Albert et al., 2000, p. 14; see also Haslam et al., 2003b). Andrews (1987) similarly recognized: 'The assumption that strategy is essentially a value-free appraisal and choice of economic opportunity and evaluation of results without reference to company capability, personal values, and entrenched cultural loyalties has often led to strategic recommendations by staff departments and consulting firms that companies were neither able nor willing to carry out' (Andrews 1987, pp. 82–3; see also Ansoff, 1988, and Eden and Ackermann, 1998, pp. 15–16). Although Andrews's quotation dates from 1987, it appears to remain valid to the present day. A recent study shows that from the perspective of managers, in most cases employees are neither willing nor able to implement change programs (see Cambridge Management Consulting, 2001). It has become a widely accepted belief that designing and formulating a strategy is the easy part and strategy implementation is the hard part.[8]

But as Liebl (2001a, p. 133) points out, many problems that arise during strategy implementation may be symptoms of previous shortcomings in strategy analysis or in the design of the strategy making process. As outlined in the introduction, strategy making has become decentralized in organizations (Bartlett and Ghoshal, 1993; Hamel, 1996). To overlook the fact that much of the organizational members' past thinking is not only embodied in rules, routines or programs, but also in institutionalized values and formed beliefs about 'their' organization, is a common but unnecessary mistake in strategy making (Andrews, 1987, p. 59; see also Mezias et al., 2001, p. 74).

The empirical findings in the field of organizational identity confirm a significant impact of identity on strategy making. Identity appears to act as a mental constraint during the evaluation of external opportunities as well as internal organizational capabilities. Identity also heavily influences the motivation of people on which strategic issues they will invest and act. So far, these impacts of identity on strategy making have been a striking blind spot in the field – one that is not yet been systematically incorporated into a practical process of strategy making.

What about creativity in strategy making?
It is important that strategy making continues to be defined as a creative process (see Große-Oetringhaus, 1996, pp. 155–6). Empirical findings in the field of organizational identity point toward an involuntary or unintentional restriction of creative ideas during strategy making, and members' shared beliefs about 'their' organization may lead to creative

ideas that are seen as unrealistic. Eden and Ackermann (1998) state: ' "brainstormed" ideas tend to be rejected because, after the social event of the brainstorming session, they cannot connect with existing mental schemas and so do not persist as an actionable idea' (Eden and Ackermann, 1998, p. 70; see also Sappington and Farrar, 1982).

Obviously, in strategy making, there is a need for achieving realistic, attainable strategies which have creative potential for organizations *and* are also desirable to organizational members. But taking all the considerations just reviewed into account makes strategy making a challenging and complex process. Considering value-laden factors is especially difficult because they may lead to conflict, emotion and critical tensions between participants during a strategy making process.

The use of facilitators in strategy making
For that reason, internal or external facilitators are often employed to guide the strategy making process. Despite this, there is hardly ever an understanding of the task and potential roles of facilitators in contemporary strategy literature (see for instance, the critique of Taket and White, 2000, p. 57). This assertion is based on the opinion that the task and potential roles of facilitators are especially important as a means of methodologically reintegrating identity-related factors into strategy making, since these factors are connected to emotional domains and the feelings of organizational members. With regard to Andrews's four factors in strategy making, a facilitator should enable participants to explore, weigh and balance *all* four factors: what the company *might do*; what the company *can do*; what the people in the company *want to do* and what they think the company *should do*. As Abell (1980, p. 18) concludes: 'The weighing and balancing of these factors is at the very heart of strategy formulation.'

These observations have shaped the aims of this book, which are:

1. To highlight the strategic context of the organizational identity literature and link it to existing literature on managerial and organizational cognition, creative cognition, inertia, and strategic management. In addition, this book will reflect on creativity in the light of perceived attainability during the strategy making process.
2. To develop a dynamic theoretical framework of organizational identity within the strategy context that can generate a practical process for strategy making.
3. To use this practical strategy making process to integrate the idea of organizational identity, its significant impact on strategy making and new requirements for effective strategy making that were revealed by means of a real case study.

4. To pay careful attention to the task and potential roles of facilitators during such a practical strategy making process. Facilitators seem to be very important for reintegrating influential identity-related factors into strategy making, a role which has been largely ignored by strategy researchers.

As a first step, Chapter 2 provides a more in-depth overview of the concept of organizational identity and its relationship to other management concepts.

NOTES

1. The 'design school' is also often connected with Selznick (1957) and Ansoff (1965).
2. In contrast to strategic planning researchers, Andrews qualified his model in 1987 (3rd edition) where he admits with regard to the processes of formulation and implementation that they are: 'interrelated in real life but separable for the purposes of analysis' (Andrews, 1987, p. 18).
3. For a brief summary about the relationship between the stakeholder concept and social responsibility see Liebl (1996, pp. 99–101).
4. Thus, the stakeholder concept positioned itself on the level of constitutional decisions and corporate policy (see Liebl 1996, p. 100).
5. Which does not necessarily require that an organization is 'socially responsive' in a certain way or would need a particular set of values (see Freeman, 1984, p. 91).
6. See also Freeman (1984, pp. 89–90).
7. Taket and White (2000) reviewed several methods such as the 'strategic choice approach', 'strategic options development and analysis (SODA)' or 'SSM – soft systems methodology'.
8. See Huff (2001, p. 125). See also Hamel (1997, p. 78). Hamel thinks that this belief is 'deadly wrong'.

2.   What is organizational identity?

This chapter provides an overview of the concept of organizational identity, its foundations and its links and/or relations to other management concepts. As Hatch and Schultz (2004, p. 5) observe, current organizational identity research embraces an amazing diversity of theoretical perspectives, orientations and emphases – 'a field that is in a state of continuous disintegration and reintegration as it struggles to incorporate ideas from many academic disciplines and numerous empirical cases'. It would exceed the aim of this book to provide a comprehensive scientific outline of the nature and impact of organizational identity. Nevertheless, this chapter briefly reviews the existing (and steadily growing) literature about this subject.

2.1   THEORETICAL FOUNDATIONS

Organizational identity is a quite young research area, mainly shaped by Albert and Whetten in 1985. Albert and Whetten (1985, p. 264) describe organizational identity as 'a self-reflective question' asked by organizational members, capturing the essential features of an organization. As summarized by Gioia (1998, p. 21) Albert and Whetten define organizational identity as follows: 'Organizational identity is a) what is taken by organization members to be *central* to the organization; b) what makes the organization *distinctive* from other organizations (at least in the eyes of the beholding members); c) and what is perceived by members to be an *enduring* or continuing feature linking the present organization with the past (and presumably the future).'

Organizational identity has its theoretical foundations primarily in research on identity in the social sciences. While Albert and Whetten (1985) originally referred to symbol interactionists, social scientists and psychologists, such as Cooley (1902), James (1890), Mead (1934), Erickson (1959) or Goffman (1959), many organizational researchers (see Dutton et al., 1994; Sarason, 1996; Ashforth and Mael, 1996; Schultz et al., 2000; Ravasi and van Rekom, 2003) now draw increasingly upon social identity theory, which offers a social-psychological perspective. This perspective was mainly developed by Tajfel (Tajfel, 1972; Tajfel and Turner, 1986)[1] and Turner (Turner, 1982 and 1985). Social identity theory is intended to be a social-psychological theory of intergroup relations, group processes, and the self. Identities are created through interactions between individuals and/or groups in social context – they are socially constructed (see Czarniawska, 1997, p. 44; also Weick, 1995, p. 20). 'The basic idea is that a social category (for example, nationality, political affiliation, sports team) into which one falls, and to which one belongs, provides a definition of who one is in the defining characteristics of the category – a self-definition that is a part of the self-concept' (Hogg et al., 1995, p. 259).[2]

The social identity concept addresses the psychological processes involved in translating these social categories into human groups. It describes creating a psychological reality from a social reality – examing the 'group in the individual'. For that reason, it mainly elaborates the sociocognitive generating processes that underlie the operation of identity: categorization, self-enhancement and uncertainty reduction (see Hogg and Terry, 2000a).

A concept of self-categorization specifies the operation of the categorization process as the cognitive basis of group behavior in social identity theory (Turner et al., 1987). This is the process which transforms individuals into groups. Members of groups are no longer seen as unique individuals, but rather as embodiments of relevant prototypes. Prototypes are fuzzy sets that contain the context-dependent characteristics of group membership. These prototypes are often described in the form of exemplary members (who best embody the group) or ideal types (an abstraction of group features) (Hogg and Terry 2000a, p. 123). As Turner et al. (1987, p. 50) conclude, social identity entails a *depersonalized* sense of self, 'a shift towards the perception of self as an interchangeable exemplar of some social category and away from the perception of self as a unique person'.

Levels of analysis

Social identity theory provides strong and powerful theoretical support for the concept of organizational identity (Dutton et al., 1994, p. 256; Sarason, 1996, p. 28). But social identity theory, as well as theories of organizational identity, deal with several levels of analysis of self-representation (Hogg, 2000a, p. 414; Brewer and Gardner, 1996).[3] On the one hand, the images that individuals hold about their group or organization are unique to each individual – they see the entity *as* a group member or *as* a member of that organization. On the other hand collectively shared images of individuals of groups and organizations are seen as a reality *independent* of any given individual (see Scott and Lane, 2000, p. 43; Brewer and Gardner, 1996, p. 83).[4] Both perspectives can be taken as descriptions of collective identities. The individual image of his/her social context is collective in the sense that the person shares the *source* of his/her identity, and therefore – to some extent – the ensuing identity, with other people (see Simon and Klandermans, 2001;

Simon, 1999).[5] Group or organization identities (as entities *sui generis*) are collective in the sense that they are *consensual*, or *collectively shared* by their members. Their 'significance depends on a collective audience, among whom there is some level of consensus – albeit how much remains in question' (Scott and Lane, 2000, p. 43). As a result, an individual's image of his/her social context may or may not match a collective identity of a group or organization (see Dutton et al., 1994, p. 240).

Identity and identification
Whetten and his colleagues make another important distinction between researchers who are concerned about 'identification with' the organization and those who are interested in the 'identity of' organizations (see Whetten and Godfrey, 1998; Whetten, 1997; Hatch and Schultz, 2000, p. 15).

The first group of researchers is interested in the question of identification which asks 'How do *I* come to know who I am in relation to *"my" organization*?' (Pratt, 1998, p. 171; Brewer and Gardner, 1996, pp. 86–7). For instance, Dutton et al. (1994, p. 239) define identification as follows: 'When a person's self-concept contains the same attributes as those in the perceived organizational identity, we define this cognitive link as organizational identification.'[6] Theory and research propose that members' self-concept (personal identity) and organizational identity are closely linked (Brown, 1997; Elsbach and Glynn, 1996; Elsbach and Kramer, 1996; Diamond, 1993). What individuals perceive, feel and think about their organization as members is important to them (see Stapel and Koomen, 2001). Organizational identity serves as a basis for identification. Insofar as an organizational identity accords with personal needs and attributes, individuals tend to include themselves in a process. Over time, for example, members may regard themselves as an exemplar of the organization and act, think and feel accordingly, internalizing the mission and by extension, the strategy of an organization (Ashforth and Mael, 1996, p. 44). The 'individual not only acts on behalf of the organization in the usual agency sense, but he also acts, more subtly, "as the organization" when he embodies the values, beliefs, and goals of the collectivity. As a result, individual behavior is more "macro" than we usually recognize, and organization behavior is more "micro" than generally acknowledged' (Chatman et al., 1986, p. 211). Organizational identity in this case provides individuals with an emotional and cognitive frame of reference (Pratt, 1998, pp. 180–84) that is able to reduce uncertainty (Hogg, 2000b; Hogg and Mullin, 1999), provide affiliation (Baumeister and Leary, 1995), and support self-enhancement (Turner, 1975; Hogg et al., 1995; Ashforth, 2001).

Researchers who are interested in the 'identity of' organizations, focus on how organizational members collectively understand and perceive the organization's central, distinctive and enduring beliefs, thereby answering the question, 'Who are we as an organization?' The three characteristics of organizational identity first offered by Albert and Whetten in 1985 (central, distinctive, and temporal continuity) suggest that the nature of organizational identity has a strong cognitive factor (see Reger et al., 1994; Fiol and Huff, 1992). It operates as a shared organizational schema that influences attention and decision making (see Dutton and Dukerich, 1991; Prahalad and Bettis, 1986). Research on organizational identity from this perspective is closely connected to research on managerial and organizational cognition (compare Kemmerer and Narayanan, 2000; Walsh, 1995), which can provide additional insights for identity research.[7]

The claim of centrality has a self-referential character that consists of pivotal beliefs, values and norms. As Ashforth and Mael (1996, p. 24) note: 'This character often reflects the needs and preferences of organizational powerholders.' In contrast to this internal reference, claims of distinctiveness involve comparisons with other organizations (see Tajfel and Turner, 1986; Oakes and Turner, 1986). When making an intergroup comparison, there is a tendency to maximize intergroup distinctiveness and to differentiate as much as possible on as many dimensions as possible – typically castings one's own group in a more positive light (see Hogg and Abrams, 1988). While Martin et al. (1983) found that claims of comparative uniqueness are in fact not unique, Dutton et al. (1994) note that it is more important that organizational members *believe* that they are distinct and therefore act accordingly to promote that identity. Thus, categorization generates accentuation only on those perceptual dimensions which are believed to be associated (or correlated) with the comparison (see Hogg and Abrams, 1988, p. 23; for empirical evidence see Elsbach and Kramer, 1996).

Static or dynamic organizational identity?
The idea of enduring continuity has been more of a topic for debate in the literature than the other two characteristics of organizational identity. Albert and Whetten (1985) seemed to assume that identity was fairly static, but other researchers in the field have discussed how enduring organizational identity actually is. Gioia et al. (2000, p. 65) differentiate between an enduring identity and an identity having continuity, suggesting that a continuous identity can shift in meaning and interpretation while retaining the labels of core beliefs and values. 'There is a reassuring continuity for members . . . in saying that their mission or central values stay the same, but the representations and translations into action take different forms over time. Thus . . . [organizational identity] is effectively in flux because of its practical ambiguity (allowing for flexible interpretations . . .) and its complexity (allowing a repertoire of values to fit many instances . . .)'

(Gioia et al., 2000, p. 65). From this perspective, which is in keeping with the definition of identity to be used in this book, the concept of organizational identity is inherently dynamic – it has an 'adaptive instability' as Gioia et al. (2000) call it (see also Sveningsson and Alvesson, 2003).[8] As a result, it is very likely that multiple organizational identities can be found within an organization (see Albert and Whetten, 1985; Ashforth and Mael, 1996, Golden-Biddle and Rao, 1997; Pratt and Rafaeli, 1997; Pratt and Foreman, 2000a).

Identity as narrative
Another perspective on dynamic organizational identities takes a narrative or storytelling approach (see for example, Humphreys and Brown, 2002), mainly influenced by Czarniawska (1997). From this perspective, identity is created by a self-narrative (Bruner, 1990; Ezzy, 1998). Thus, organizational identity, like individual identity, is characterized by a 'narrative quality', utilizing the capacity to narrate one's life and to express stories about one's life (D. Taylor, 1996; McAdams, 1993). These autobiographical narratives make sense of 'who we are' by remembering experiences in detail (Baumeister and Newman, 1994, p. 677; Conway, 1996). Due to the narrative quality of organizational identity, organization and strategy researchers have recently attempted to conceptualize organizational life, change and theory as story making and reading or as narrative discourse (see Boje, 1991; Barry and Elmes, 1997; Gabriel, 2000; Dunford and Jones, 2000; Hardy et al., 2005).

Different time-bases of identity
There is one other important aspect of organizational identity that has received hardly any attention from organization and strategy researchers: organizational identities can differ due to their time-base (see Corley, 2002, p. 117). Next to present organizational identity claims (which are the main focus in organizational identity research), organizational members can also claim past identities that are still salient for them, or indeed, they can claim organizational identities they hope for in the future. As a result, organizational identities can differ in their temporal states and refer to present identities as well as to past or future ones (see Pratt and Foreman, 2000b, p. 142).

2.2 ORGANIZATIONAL IDENTITY AND RELATED CONCEPTS

As can be seen from the brief description above, the concept of organizational identity is not only a complex phenomenon, but also tends to overlap with and/or to relate to other known management concepts such as corporate identity, organizational culture and organizational image. By linking or contrasting organizational identity with each of these manage- ment concepts one can sharpen the somewhat fuzzy boundaries of organi- zational identity.

Corporate identity

Many practitioners as well as academics would refer the concept of organi- zational identity primarily to corporate identity. That is probably because the concept of corporate identity was created by practitioners in the mid- 1970s and has been widely adopted in theory and practice ever since (see Selame and Selame, 1975; Margulies, 1977). Corporate identity is concep- tualized as a marketing function of top management that is made real through visible graphic designs such as logos, company house styles, and so on. Corporate identity plays a role in communicating an organization's strategy (Olins, 1989). This understanding of corporate identity has grad- ually broadened, becoming more of an interdisciplinary paradigm as the influence and creation of identity through behavior and communication, is shown to be symbolic to internal as well as external audiences (van Riel and Balmer, 1997, p. 341).

Even though organizational and corporate identity does indeed overlap to some degree, there are still considerable differences. Hatch and Schultz (2000, pp. 17–21) distinguish these concepts in terms of perspective, recip- ients and communication channels. Corporate identity takes (and needs) a managerial perspective for a conscious communication through chosen symbols, whereas organizational identity takes an organizational perspec- tive because it is created by an informal and unplanned agreement between organizational members about what the identity of their organization is.[9] In addition, corporate identity mainly targets external stakeholders and audiences. On the other hand, organizational identity is a self-reflective question of organizational members about 'who they are' and therefore is internally created and held. As described above, corporate identity nowa- days also considers internal audiences, but these efforts are driven from a functional, managerial perspective, a way of doing 'PR' to yourself (see also Elsbach and Glynn, 1996). Finally, corporate identity is expressed through traditional communication channels such as television, print media, the internet, and so on, whereas organizational identity is directly experienced in everyday organizational life and language. Exchange of a perceived organizational identity to third parties would therefore require direct interpersonal interaction (see Hatch and Schultz, 2000).

Despite these differences, Hatch and Schultz (2000, p. 19) promote a combination of both concepts: 'Instead of choosing between corporate or organizational identity, we advocate combining the understandings offered by all the contributing disciplines into a single concept of identity defined at the organizational level of analysis.'

Organizational culture

Until recently, comparisons between organizational culture and identity led to vague and nebulous distinctions (see Fiol, 1991). Sarason (1996, p. 28) noted that it is important to supply an added value to organizational identity that has not already been provided by culture studies in order to prevent the presentation of 'old wine in a new bottle'. Since this observation, there have been further efforts to compare organizational identity with culture. Organizational culture is now seen to be a contextual frame (among others) that shapes answers to the question, 'Who are we as an organization?'(see Hatch, 1993; Fiol et al.,1998). Hatch and Schultz (1997, p. 360) see organizational culture 'as a symbolic context within which interpretations of organizational identity are formed'. Similarly, Fiol et al. (1998, pp. 56–7) state:

> An organization's identity is the aspect of culturally embedded sensemaking that is self-focused . . . Identity is affected by organizational culture and also by other meaning-making systems with which the self interacts . . . Although culture provides the system of rules that defines a social system, identity provides the contextual understanding of those rules that govern people's understanding of themselves in relation to the larger social system.[10]

Another distinction made by Sarason (1996, p. 31) is that organizational culture focuses on shared values, whereas organizational identity focuses on shared beliefs. Beliefs take place at a more conscious level because organizational members are explicit about their perceptions and interpretations of 'their' organization in describing what they think, feel, and so on (see also Hatch and Schultz, 2000, p. 25). Beliefs about self-identity 'may be described as subject to continuous self-reflection' (Sarason, 1996, p. 32; see also Giddens, 1991, p. 52). In contrast, organizational culture refers to deep and tacit levels of values and norms. Symbols, physical artefacts, and overt behaviors cannot be directly interpreted as identity-defining or identity-expressing elements (see Schein, 1985 and also Rindova and Schultz, 1998, p. 49). Further, organizational culture does not necessarily need or incite explicit reflexivity (Hatch and Schultz, 2000, p. 26).[11] However, values and beliefs are directly linked, as can be seen in the contextual character of culture; in other words: organizational identity beliefs have value-based foundations (compare Barney and Stewart, 2000, p. 38).

Organizational image

The concept of organizational image is also of specific importance to organizational identity (Whetten and Mackey, 2002; see also Alvesson, 1990).

In marketing, strategy, and communication literature, organizational image (as well as reputation) is a perception and/or judgement of organizational actions, products (brands), services or achievements by external audiences (for example, customers, stakeholders, investors, television, and so on). This perspective, recently summarized by Cheney and Christensen (2001) and Dowling (2001), suggests that an image can be founded in a current identity and/or strategy of an organization, but it remains a perception and/or judgement by others of the considered self.

In that sense, organizational image is the externally interpreted counterpart of organizational identity, functioning like a mirror (see Hatch and Schultz, 2002, pp. 998–9; Dutton and Dukerich, 1991). Whereas image is concerned with the question, 'How are we perceived by others?' organizational identity deals with the question, 'Who are we as an organization?' Organizational identity is a relative and comparative concept, which means it is created only through interaction with others. However, images of 'how others perceive us' can have a strong influence on organizational identity and image.[12]

This significant impact has been described in many different research areas (for an analysis of 345 studies see Rosenthal and Rubin, 1978). For instance, the Pygmalion studies, carried out in classrooms with children, have shown that the influence of images can be enormous (Jussim, 1989, 1986). Teachers were told that some of students in their class tended to perform poorly and were not well behaved, in short, were not very smart. Others were said to be intelligent, hard-working and successful. The teachers behaved differently in regard to these two groups. Whereas they were supportive and tolerant when they thought a student was smart, they interacted in a much more brief and dismissive manner when a student was thought to be less competent. Although the students had been separated into these two categories randomly by researchers, after a short period of time and almost without exception, these randomly attached labels came to represent the actual performance of the individual students. It has been shown that these images affected them far into the future, and were a more powerful predictor of performance than IQ scores or performances before the experiment. The obvious conclusion is that 'who we are cannot be separated from the perceptions others have of us, just as our perceptions of others are influenced by who we are' (Hatch and Schultz, 2000, p. 23).[13]

It is very important to note that image is defined here as the external perception of the self; the self considered from the position of the other (Hatch and Schultz, 2002, pp. 994–6). Of course, individuals or groups in organizations may ask themselves the other-reflective question, 'How do I/we think *others* perceive us?' But the answer is an imaginary construct of an image, telling only what they *think* others think about them.[14] Dutton et al. (1994, p. 248) define this form of image as 'construed external image'. While we will see that this and other closely related questions about images are of central value for an organization during strategy making, it is essential to make the distinction between self- and other-reflected questions by the self (Leary and Kowalski, 1990; Whetten and Mackey, 2002, p. 400).

Concluding the review of links and contrasts between organizational identity and other known management concepts, Figure 2.1 shows the relationship between organizational culture, image and identity as described above.

Up to this point, a brief overview of the concept of organizational identity, its foundations, and its links to other related management concepts has been given. However, due to the complexity of research on organizational identity and the multiple perspectives developed in the theory, several important aspects of organizational identity should be clearly stated before exploring the relationship between identity and strategy. I will follow Pratt and Foreman's (2000b, p. 142) advice to be clear about the following aspects with regard to research on organizational identity:

- Delineating the origin of the identity;
- Naming identity claimants and identity targets;
- Delineating the identity audience;
- Being aware of time.

The *origin* of identity has been described in section 2.1. The theoretical perspective which will be taken in this book is based on social identity theory. Identity from this perspective can be evolving and dynamic, shifting in meaning and interpretation. I will focus on two (closely related) *identity claimants*: organizational members (individuals) and organizational collectives (groups of organizational members, up to the whole organization). While individuals claim what is central, distinctive and enduring about the organization (*identity target*) they are a member of one or more organizational collectives that can hold consensually shared beliefs about what is central, distinctive and enduring about the organization characteristics (*identity target*). In other words: both identity claimants share the same target and identity dimensions, but differ in their 'level' of identity. The *identity audience* is by definition solely organizational members (individuals) and collectives of organizational members, because identity is a self-referential concept. On the other hand, images and reputation are external perceptions of the self, not necessarily matching with the claimant's perceived identity. Finally, being aware that identity claims can differ with regard to the time-base, this book will focus on present and future organizational identities.

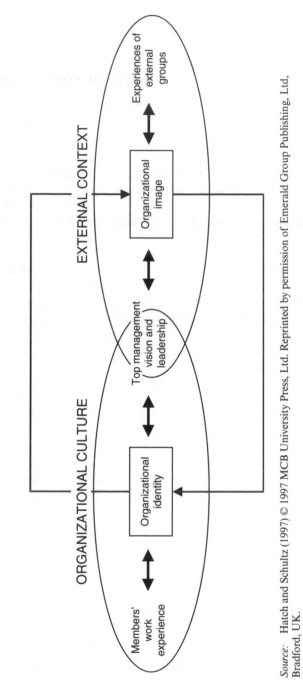

Source: Hatch and Schultz (1997) © 1997 MCB University Press, Ltd. Reprinted by permission of Emerald Group Publishing, Ltd, Bradford, UK.

Figure 2.1   *Hatch and Schultz's model of the relationship between organizational culture, identity and image*

NOTES

1. Social identity theory has its roots in Tajfel's perceptual overestimation and judgemental accentuation research of the late 1950s and early 1960s, and his analyses of stereotyping and cognitive aspects of prejudice of the late 1960s. Together with Turner, who joined him as a graduate student in the early 1970s, Tajfel integrated his research topics (for example, social categorization, intergroup relations, and so on) around the concept of social identity theory. He died in 1982.

2. Social identity has been described in detail by social identity theorists elsewhere. See for instance Hogg (1992); Hogg (1993); Hogg and Abrams (1988); Tajfel and Turner (1986). For historical accounts see Hogg (2000a); Hogg and Abrams (1999); Turner (1996).

3. Brewer and Gardner (1996) outline three different levels of self-representation – from the individual up to the group level. These different levels refer to different levels of inclusiveness of conceptualization of the self, which means the shift from 'I' to 'we' as the place of self-definition. The extension of the concept up to the levels of organizations and even industries was initially made by organizational researchers (see for example, Ashforth and Mael, 1989) and has recently drawn the attention of social psychologists (see Hogg and Terry, 2000a; Hogg and Terry, 2001). However, all levels have many direct parallels of conceptual features – differing mainly in their collectively-shared character (see Albert, 1998, p. 10 and Ashforth and Mael, 1996, p. 21).

4. As Hogg (2000a, pp. 411–12) said: 'self-conceptualization, feelings, and behaviors are governed by the in-group prototype'.

5. See also Hogg and Terry (2000a, p. 124): 'Because members of the same group are exposed to similar social information, their prototypes usually will be similar and, thus, shared'.

6. It should be mentioned that there is a dispute about the 'internalization' of organizational values and beliefs into the personal concept. Whereas social identity theory defines identification as part of an individual's concept (see Tajfel, 1972), Ashforth and Mael as well as Pratt try to clearly distinguish identification from 'internalization'. I take the view that social identities involve to some degree a change of the self-concept ('internalization') and should therefore not be completely separated from identification (see Pratt, 1998, pp. 175–6; Ashforth and Mael, 1996).

7. For instance, how a shared organizational schema can be made more visible through cognitive mapping (see Fiol and Huff, 1992; Langfield-Smith, 1992; Huff, 1990; Huff and Jenkins, 2002).

8. This dynamic view is entirely consistent with social identity theory (see Hogg and Terry, 2000b, p. 150).

9. It is worth noting that these perspectives may correspond to each other, as managerial identity communication efforts can become part of an organizational identity.

10. Accordingly, Dutton and Penner (1993, p. 95) state: 'organizational identity is a subset of the collective beliefs that constitute an organization's culture'.

11. Hatch and Schultz (2000, p. 26) importantly acknowledge that 'there may be aspects of identity that run as deep or deeper than the tacit levels of culture . . . just as some aspects of culture may be made explicit'.

12. See the process model of identity-image interdependence by Gioia et al. (2000) or see the model in Hatch and Schultz (2002).

13. See also Swann (1987).

14. See also Hatch and Schultz (2002, p. 995).

3. Identity and strategy: a dynamic framework for connecting the past with the future

Having an impression about the concept of organizational identity and how it is defined in the current literature still leaves an open question about how organizational identity is related to strategy. In the course of this chapter two different temporal perspectives of organizational identity and their relation to strategy are reviewed: current organizational identities, representing past experiences in the present, are separated from desired organizational identities for the future. These relations are key to integrating organizational identity into conscious strategy making which in turn should result in desirable and attainable strategies for organizations. However, before illuminating these relationships between organizational identity and strategy, it is important to briefly clarify how 'strategy' is defined within this book.

3.1 STRATEGY: A CUSTOMER-ORIENTED DEFINITION AND ITS LINK TO ORGANIZATIONAL IDENTITY

Strategy has become a catch-all term that is used as a single noun, a prefix or an adjective, to mean whatever one wants it to mean (see Hambrick and Fredrickson, 2001, p. 49; also Markides, 2004). This book will define strategy as the way in which an organization will achieve deliberately chosen competitive advantages. A similar definition can be found in Hanssmann (1995, p. 256), who says: 'Strategie ist die Schaffung und Nutzung möglichst dauerhafter (verteidigungsfähiger) Konkurrenzvorteile' [Strategy is the creation and usage of the most sustainable (defendable) competitive advantages].

Influenced by the works of Porter (1980 and 1985) in particular, the notions of competitive advantage and strategic positioning have become widespread in theory and practice.[1] Porter strongly emphasizes the importance of unique and superior performance (Porter, 1997, pp. 50–60). More explicitly he says: 'Competitive strategy is about being different. It means deliberately choosing a different set of activities to deliver a unique mix of value' (Porter, 1996, p. 64).

An important consequence of emphasizing that the aim of strategy is to enable an organization to gain sustainable competitive advantage, is that strategic innovation becomes crucial (see Johnston and Bate, 2003). For example, strategists might consider introducing new rules of competition in the market, creating new business designs, and creating new markets (Liebl, 2002b; Yip, 2004; Mitchell and Coles, 2003 and 2004; Ramírez and Wallin, 2000).

However, the work reported in this book was initiated with the recognition that the value of uniqueness created by strategists is exclusively determined by customers. Any quality or feature of a product or service that is for any reason not noticed by the customer will not create any value leading to competitive advantages (Liebl, 1996, p. 41–2; Coyne, 1986; Magretta, 2002, Chapter 1). In other words: competitive advantages are only created in the mind of the customer (Rughase, 1999, p. 37).

It is worth noting that this perspective has only recently become axiomatic in management science. As Magretta (2002, pp. 23–4) states: 'One of the most powerful insights of modern management . . . is that there is really only one test of a job well done – a customer who is willing to pay for it . . . Only by meeting the needs of customers, as customers themselves define those needs, can an organization perform.'

Unfortunately, this important insight in strategy is still threatened by dominant, manufacturing-minded management tools, such as those developed for achieving total quality management, business re-engineering, or change management, all of which still tend to take the place of strategy in managerial practice (Porter, 1996, p. 61). While these improvement tools are important for internal operational effectiveness, this book will clearly draw on a strategy definition that is based on deliberately chosen competitive advantages that are in effect determined from the outside-in.

Consequently, strategy is an exceptionally *customer-oriented* concept of how competitive advantages can be achieved by allocating resources which are available to the organization (Liebl, 1999a, p. 8). Hambrick and Fredrickson (2001, pp. 50–54) introduce five elements of strategy in order to make the 'how' as concrete and useful as possible. These five elements give answers to the following questions/topics:

1. How will we win in the marketplace? (Competitive advantages from the viewpoint of the customers: which deliberately chosen set of activities will deliver a unique mix of value?)
2. Where will we be active and with how much emphasis? (For example, product categories, markets, or geographic arenas.)

3. How will we get there? (For example, internal development, joint ventures.)
4. What will be our speed and sequence of moves? (For example, speed of expansion, sequence of initiatives.)
5. How will we obtain our returns? (What is the business model: what products/services do we sell and at what pricing?)

To underline this customer-oriented perspective of strategy, the term 'market strategy' will often be used within this book and should be understood as a synonym for strategy.

A strategic dimension: organizational identity defines the mission of an organization

Even before the concept of organizational identity was introduced in 1985, Freeman (1984, pp. 90–91) proposed a very similar idea to define the mission of an organization[2] as an answer to the self-reflective question: 'What do we stand for?' Freeman argued that this level of strategy involves the role of an organization as a whole, and its relationship with other social institutions.[3] He chose the example of Bell Telephone, legendary in its attention to service (from the viewpoint of customers), to underscore the importance of this self-reflecting question (Freeman, 1984, p. 84):

> As Bell moves toward the break-up required by the recent settlement with the Department of Justice, and towards being more responsive to changes in the marketplace and new technologies, one of the critical questions for its management is what happens to the traditional values such as 'service' and 'universal service', the very foundations on which the company was engineered. What does Bell now stand for, and what are or should be the dominant business values of its managers and employees?

About ten years later, Sarason (1996) employed the concept of organizational identity to shed some light on Freeman's important question.[4] In addressing the issue of 'Who are we as an organization?' she suggests that an organizational identity defines the mission and seminal beliefs of an organization (see also Ashforth and Mael, 1996, p. 32). Despite their common history and shared beliefs, Sarason (1996 and 1998) describes how the seven so-called 'Baby Bells' began to evolve in different strategic directions, developing different identities, after they were separated from AT&T. She especially investigated the history of US WEST and how organizational identity and strategy were linked during several key episodes. 'Understanding strategy in the context of organizational identity allows an understanding of why US WEST chose the alternatives taken among a larger feasible set of options' (Sarason, 1996, p. 159). In short, because of its strategic dimensions, the concept of organizational identity has a close interdependency with strategy (see Barney et al., 1998; Große-Oetringhaus, 1996).

This close interdependency will be discussed in the following subsections from two temporal perspectives. First, from the perspective of current (present) organizational identity and, second, from the perspective of desired (future) organizational identity. A desired identity is different and separable from a current identity, yet they are intimately connected. This separation will improve the understanding of their distinct functions (Pratt and Foreman, 2000b, p. 142), providing a theoretical basis for a methodological integration of the organizational identity concept into practical strategy making.

3.2 CURRENT ORGANIZATIONAL IDENTITY WITHIN THE CONTEXT OF STRATEGY

Ashforth and Mael (1996, p. 33) note in an emphatic way that organizational identity does not determine strategy. As already stated, a current organizational identity is connected to the seminal beliefs of an organization, whereas strategy refers to the organization's competitive advantages and the (intended and current) activities used to achieve them. By this, strategy and organizational identity are reciprocally related (Ashforth and Mael, 1996, p. 33). The relationship between a current market strategy and a current organizational identity is mediated by actions and interactions (see Figure 3.1).

It is important to note that this framework can be used for both identity claimants, individual organizational members and larger groups within the organization. Organizational identity is the collectively 'shared' version of individually perceived organizational identities (see Figure 3.2).[5] With regard to the collective version, I am aware that a transformation from individual identity perceptions into a collectively 'shared' version is simplified here and more difficult by far in practice (see Dutton and Penner, 1993, p. 104; Jelinek and Litterer, 1994; Langfield-Smith, 1992; Daniels et al., 1994; Gedi and Elam, 1996, p. 47).

Organizational members act and interact strategically within their organization and with other individuals, groups or institutions. Actions and interactions are in a continuous flow, closely connected with experiences. As Schütz (1967, p. 39) states: 'My *action as it takes place* presents itself to me as a series of *existing* and *present* experiences, experiences that are coming to and passing away. My *intended (intendiertes)* action presents itself to me as a series of *future* experiences. My *terminated completed act*

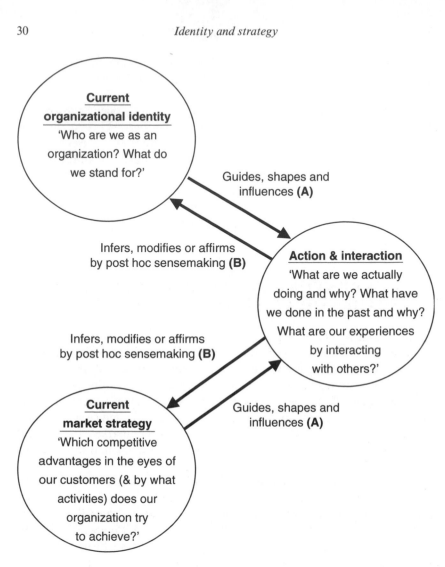

Figure 3.1   Current organizational identity within the strategy context

(which is my expired action) presents itself to me as a series of *terminated* experiences which I contemplate in memory.'

Within this continuous flow of actions and interactions, with the present as an interface, *intended actions* are influenced by current organizational identity and/or strategy (arrows labelled with (A) in Figure 3.1) and *terminated completed acts* infer, modify, or affirm a current organizational identity, and/or strategy by retrospective sensemaking (arrows labelled with (B)

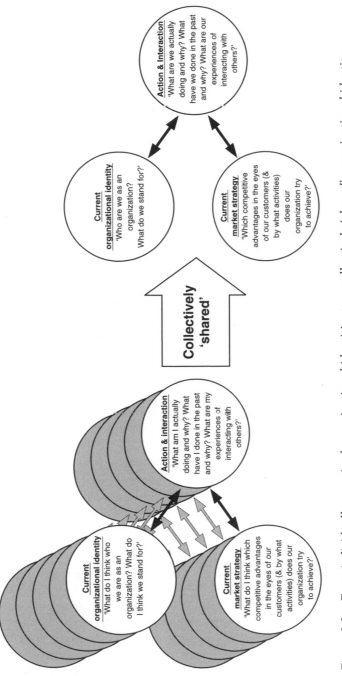

The circles contain the following text:

Action & Interaction
'What are we actually doing and why? What have we done in the past and why? What are our experiences of interacting with others?'

Current organizational identity
'Who are we as an organization? What do we stand for?'

Current market strategy
'Which competitive advantages in the eyes of our customers (& by what activities) does our organization try to achieve?'

Collectively 'shared'

Action & interaction
'What am I actually doing and why? What have I done in the past and why? What are my experiences of interacting with others?'

Current organizational identity
'What do I think who we are as an organization? What do I think we stand for?'

Current market strategy
'What do I think which competitive advantages in the eyes of our customers (& by what activities) does our organization try to achieve?'

Figure 3.2   From individually perceived organizational identities to a collectively 'shared' organizational identity

in Figure 3.1). This flow of strategic actions and interactions is an emergent process of going back and forth between both concepts, identity as well as strategy, as a precursor and product of sensemaking (see Barney et al., 1998, p. 111; Gioia and Thomas, 1996, p. 398). Each of these links (see Figure 3.1) is described in more detail in the following subsections.

3.2.1 Influences on Intended Strategic Actions and Interactions

Intended strategic actions and interactions can be influenced by organizational identity and/or strategy ((A) in Figure 3.1). How both concepts guide, shape and influence intended actions and interactions is discussed below.

Organizational identity shapes intended actions and interactions
To begin with, 'You have to know who you are before you can take action' (Barney et al., 1998, p. 113). A current organizational identity guides, shapes and influences intended strategic actions and interactions in several ways on (a) an individual and (b) an organizational level of analysis.

(a) The individual level of analysis   On the individual level organizational identity influences the perception of strategic issues with regard to their legitimacy, importance, and the feasibility of resolving problems with these issues (see Dutton and Duncan, 1987a; Liebl, 2000b, pp. 108–13). By this it influences microprocesses of strategic agenda building in an organization, meaning the creation and prioritizing of a limited array of issues and actions (Dutton and Duncan, 1987b, p. 115; Dutton and Penner, 1993). A good example to describe the influences of identity at this level is the widely recognized study about the Port Authority of New York and New Jersey (PA) by Dutton and Dukerich (1991).[6] The PA, being in the business of public transportation, had to struggle with homelessness as it began to impinge upon their transportation facilities. Their current organizational identity served as a reference point for judging that this issue was not a legitimate strategic issue because the PA was not in the social service business – with the result that no initial actions were taken. It is easy to image that all organizations are likely to recognize only a limited number of issues in their environment as within their scope.

Issues gain perceived legitimacy for an organization when individuals perceive them as organizational identity-relevant (see Dutton and Penner, 1993, p. 99). But an individual's sense about a current organizational identity also affects a strategic issue's interpretation. In the beginning the PA took no action on homelessness because it was not perceived to be relevant to their main business. This changed when central elements of the PA's identity were threatened; PA members feared a spread of homeless people to their other, higher class facilities (such as the World Trade Center or the airport), they began to contemplate action. Employees saw themselves as members of a highly professional and first-class organization, and this identity became a critical reference point for perceiving that homelessness was indeed of importance to the organization. This importance increased even further when actions were considered by the management that were inconsistent with the current organizational identity. These threats may also affect the individual identification with the organization.

These threats also tended to affect individual identification with the organization. Those with a strong identification with the organization reported that threats to the Port Authority potentially compromised their self-concept, which also escalated the importance of the homeless issue (see Dutton et al., 1994; Ashforth and Mael, 1989). In consequence, the importance of a strategic issue increases when members perceive that it may (a) induce actions which are inconsistent with their current view of organizational identity, and/or (b) affect valued characteristics of the current identity (Dutton and Penner, 1993, p. 101).

Organizational identity also influences the perception of the feasibility of resolving strategic issues at the individual level. Once PA members saw the homelessness issue as strategic and important they were able to resolve it relatively quickly (with the necessary expenditure) by establishing drop-in centers. The positive internal result was that PA members were able to reaffirm that their organization was able to 'get things done'.

Another important point is that identity influences the individual motivation to take action on strategic issues. First, when 'strategic issues are identity-consistent, individuals are more likely to believe that *they* have the skills and competencies for dealing with the issue' (Dutton and Penner, 1993, p. 102, emphasis added). Equally, resolution of strategic issues seems feasible when members perceive a strategic issue as organizational identity-relevant (Dutton and Webster, 1988).

As already mentioned, the concept of member identification is closely linked to organizational identity. This cognitive connection further motivates members to strengthen valued parts of the current organizational identity or to revise unattractive elements of the identity (Dutton and Penner, 1993, p. 104). The overall conclusion to be drawn is that current organizational identity heavily influences, guides and constrains an individual's perception of motivation to work on strategic issues.

(b) The organizational level of analysis   On the organizational level, the collectively shared (depersonalized) version of individually perceived organizational identities (see Figure 3.2), organizational identity 'activates routines and programs that shape the processes and create the outputs of

agenda building' (Dutton and Penner, 1993, p. 97). Collective beliefs about a current organizational identity tend to be embodied in rules, routines and programs, as well as in human capital (compare Simon, 1947; Cyert and March, 1963; Nelson and Winter, 1982; March and Olsen, 1989). These embodiments have an impact on more than one person, and are very often communicated between organizational members as the written and unwritten behavioral rules of an organization (compare Scott-Morgan, 1994). For instance, Prahalad and Bettis (1986) describe how collective beliefs create a 'dominant logic' and show how strategic decisions of diversified firms result from a variety of management logics for processing and understanding characteristic firm assets.

A second example can be found in 3M's 'respect for individual initiative', which is a key part of their collectively understood organizational identity. This idea is represented, for instance, by the so-called '15 per cent rule' where employees can spend 15 per cent of their time on projects of their own choice (see Collins and Porras, 1994, p. 82). But note that a core identity element may also be represented in human relation routines (for example, promotion) or socialization routines (for example, informal innovation circles). We know that organizational processes, routines and programs guide action and interaction in particular directions (see Starbuck, 1985). And thus we can see that an organizational identity can influence internal allocation of resources by guiding which new processes should be created or which resources and skills should be accumulated to complement the current identity. Most important to the idea of this book, identity can potentially shape routines that maintain competitive advantages in the eyes of the customers (Barney et al., 1998, p. 88).

Dutton and Penner (1993, pp. 105–6) argue that two routines are of special importance. First, routines that affect information processing will influence which strategic issues will get attention and related response. Second, communication and participation routines in organizations will guide discourses about strategic issues and actions; for instance, routines that shape communication can constrain how individuals frame strategic issues for internal discussions. At the organizational level, the often subtle impact of identity embodied in routines, processes and programs is to shape existing 'reality' for organizational members.

Despite these powerful effects, there are several reasons why identity and strategic actions and interactions may sometimes be only loosely coupled. For example, an organizational identity 'may be too weak, abstract, in flux, or outmoded to provide a clear and coherent signal for strategic choices' (Ashforth and Mael, 1996, p. 33). Or, some companies might not even have a conscious identity, because they are too young, or perhaps too incidental in the lives of most organizational members.

Strategy influences intended actions and interactions

How current market strategy influences intended strategic actions and interactions might seem evident. Strategy has been defined as the customer-oriented concept of how competitive advantages can be achieved. As Huff (2001, p. 124) concludes: 'Strategy is about action.' The creation of action plans is a core activity during strategy implementation (see Bryson, 1995; Eden and Ackerman, 1998, pp. 162–73). By this, a currently articulated strategy guides, shapes and influences intended strategic actions and inter-actions by definition. Thus, even when an organization has no conscious organizational identity, it could start out with a clear strategy (Barney et al. 1998, p. 113). Clear formulation of the competitive advantages the organization wants to achieve can guide consistent, corresponding, intended strategic actions and interactions (see Porter, 1996).

In too many cases, however, there is neither a conscious identity nor an existing articulated strategy (Barney et al., 1998, p. 114). Organizations without a strong identity will lack commitment to shared beliefs and strategy, providing no basis for *consistent* decisions and actions (Ashforth and Mael, 1996, p. 32).

But even with a strong organizational identity that guides actions and/or a clear strategy capable of guiding actions/interactions, we are only talking about *intended* action (Mintzberg, 1987, p. 11). We have only identified potential actions and interactions that are the basis for *expected* experiences of organizational members. How these actions and interactions will actually shape the organizational identity and/or the strategy (as a 'meaningful lived experience'[7] for organizational members) can only be seen *after* actions and interactions have taken place. This is a subject that requires further analysis.

3.2.2 Actions and Interactions Shape Cognition

Barney et al. (1998, p. 111) insist that 'as a theory, it is important to note that sensemaking is extremely important when you talk about identity, so identity is a product of a process of sensemaking.' At the same time, strategy is also a product of sensemaking (Gioia and Thomas, 1996, p. 383). Actions and interactions are 'events' to which organizational members give sense, and which are shaping their cognition ((B) in Figure 3.1) (Weick, 1995, p. 12). Weick (1995, pp. 17–62) characterizes seven properties of sensemaking that set this process apart from other processes such as understanding and interpretation. The sensemaking process is:

1. grounded in identity construction,
2. retrospective,

3.   enactive of sensible environments,
4.   social,
5.   ongoing,
6.   focused on and by extracted cues,
7.   driven by plausibility rather than accuracy.

All of these characteristics are important and grounded in identity construction. But in the specific context of this book, there are two notable characteristics of sensemaking that are of key interest: its retrospective and social nature.

Organizational identity and post hoc social sensemaking
The main distinguishing characteristic of the sensemaking process is that it is retrospective. Mead (1956, p. 136) states: 'We are conscious always of what we have done, never of doing it. We are always conscious of sensory processes, never of motor processes; hence we are conscious of motor processes only through sensory processes which are their resultants.' Schütz (1967, p. 52) takes the same position as Mead: 'Only the already experienced is meaningful, not that which is being experienced.'

It is important to note this aspect of sensemaking because only 'meaningful lived experiences' can infer, modify, or affirm a current organizational identity (see Martin, 2002). Thus, the creation of a current organizational identity is purely retrospective. 'Every identity, personal or ethnic or national, is founded upon memory; our egos and our societies are sustained by the circulation of recollection' (G. Taylor, 1996, p. 15). Self-focused questions of organizational members, such as 'What have we done in the past and why?' obviously refer to the past, but even the question, 'What are we actually doing and why?' (evoking the impression that we could give sense to current activities) still means that organizational members are always a little bit behind their actions or their actions are always a little bit ahead of them.

Another notable characteristic of sensemaking is that it is social. As already discussed, organizational identity is a relative and comparative concept, which means that it too is created *only* in *interaction* with others. 'How others perceive us' (image) plays an influential role on how identities are constructed (see Schlenker, 1985), as effectively illustrated by the Pygmalion studies (see section 2.2). On the organizational level, organizations' interactions with external individuals, groups or institutions, such as external stakeholders, customers, interest groups, and so on offer an arena for sensemaking. On the individual level, interactions with other members of their organization as well as with external individuals, groups or institutions provide an opportunity for sensemaking. Of course, these externals will also have – or have to be creating – a certain image of the organization. Over time, organizational members experience feedback about their organizational portrayal.

Several empirical studies have shown that these 'external' images can have a major impact on current organizational identity (see Dutton and Dukerich, 1991; Dutton et al., 1994; Gioia and Chittipeddi, 1991; Gioia and Thomas, 1996; Elsbach and Kramer, 1996; van Riel and Balmer, 1997). To illustrate this impact, we can briefly return to the study of the New York/New Jersey Port Authority (PA) where Dutton and Dukerich (1991, pp. 547–9) show that external images were an important impetus for crystallizing the PA's organizational identity. PA members became aware of the importance of image feedback, and tried to evolve their strategic actions and interactions by trial-and-error image management. In a different case involving university strategy, Gioia and Thomas (1996) also empirically found that the main driver of identity change was changing external image. 'Image often acts as a destabilizing force on identity, frequently requiring members to revisit and reconstruct their organizational sense of self' (Gioia et al., 2000, p. 67).

But organizational members also validate and negotiate organizational identity with other members of their organization (see Ashforth and Mael 1996, p. 39; Swann, 1987; Llewellyn, 2004). In short, organizational identity will only prevail after surviving a 'reality test' against external and internal points of reference, such as the image or identity claims of other organizational members. This is even true when organizations have no conscious identity or just a broad 'anti-identity'.[8] These organizations and their members also act and interact strategically, and thus they develop an organizational identity over the course of time (Barney et al., 1998, p. 113).

Strategy and post hoc social sensemaking

Both sensemaking characteristics (retrospective and social) can now be more specifically assessed with respect to strategy. The strategy research literature provides numerous examples of successful organizational strategies, such as those at McDonalds, IKEA or Wal-Mart (Fengler, 2000, p. 15). Interestingly, these examples are solely post hoc explanations: 'Everyone knows a strategy when they see one . . . We all recognize a great strategy after the fact' (Hamel, 1998, p. 10). Inversely, strategy making only creates a strategic plan by identifying potential competitive advantages (and corresponding intended actions/interactions to achieve them), but it does not realize strategy.[9] This retrospective view is consistent with Mintzberg (1990 and 1994), who suggests defining strategy as observed patterns in past decisional behavior and streams of action ('pattern of actions'). This perspective does not diminish the value of deliberate strategy making at all, but it becomes obvious that completed strategic actions and interactions will infer, modify or affirm a currently formulated strategy.

The second quality, the social character of sensemaking and its impact, can also be found in strategy research. A critical point, as already stated, is that competitive advantages are only created in the minds of the customers, which means that only customers define them. Social interactions will provide some feedback about customer images of the organization's competitive advantages, for example in stories customers tell (see Liebl and Rughase, 2002; Liebl, 2000a; Rindova and Fombrun, 1999). In earlier studies, I have shown that customers' claims of existing competitive advantages differ – very often considerably – from organizational managers' claims – what they *think* their customers value as competitive advantages (Rughase, 1999 and 2002). In accordance with Gioia and Thomas's (1996) finding that external images trigger identity changes, I found that these differences can fuel creative strategy processes, resulting in strategic reorientation (Rughase, 2002). The following chapters will outline these processes in more detail.

Up to this point, I have examined the relationship between current organizational identity and current strategy, which is mediated by actions and interactions. It has been shown that actions and interactions mediate organizational identity and strategy in multiple ways, on both the individual and the organizational level. On the one hand, current organizational identity as well as current strategy influence, guide and shape intended actions and interactions. On the other hand, completed actions and interactions are the basis for sensemaking with regard to organizational identity and strategy, inferring, modifying or affirming the two concepts. Because actions and interactions are in a continuous flow, there is no beginning and no end. Strategy and organizational identity are reciprocally interdependent on actions and interactions as displayed in Figure 3.1. There can be no understanding about organizational identity and strategy, and their relationship to one another, without ongoing contextual information about actions and interactions in the continuously unfolding past.

In essence, individuals or groups may enact and express a valued identity and/or clearly formulated strategy through actions and interactions, and these may infer, modify, or affirm an identity and/or strategy from the responses they induce (see also Ashforth and Mael, 1996, p. 33). A substantial change in either concept will affect the other concept – over the course of time.

3.2.3   Current Organizational Identity and Inertia

The discussion to this point emphasizes that organizational identity has a strong impact on an individual member's perception, behavior and motivation. Identification focuses behavior and motivation regarding identity-related issues and actions, thereby reinforcing (or perhaps destabilizing) organizational identity perceived by the individual as well as collective impressions of identity.

Identification can also support strategy. Even when there is no conscious identity, strategic actions and interactions will infer, modify or affirm an identity over time, at the organizational and individual level, because completed actions and interactions serve as sensemaking events for identity as well as for strategy (focusing behavior and motivation again). In addition, the reciprocal relationship between strategy and current organizational identity often becomes tightly coupled over time.

Sarason (1996) found out that when managers were asked to describe their perceptions of organizational identity, they often responded in terms of strategy and strategic actions and interactions. As a consequence, organizational identity itself tends to be directly reinforcing, in addition to being affected by strategy. Identity and strategy thus tend to be self-fulfilling – it can be seen as a closed system (Ashforth and Mael, 1996, pp. 49–53). It seems quite difficult to escape from such a closed system because completed strategic actions can supply a strong link from the organizational past to the future. Ghemawat (1991) found out that strategic actions create 'commitment', with a tendency for strategy to persist over time. For example, completed investments in certain kinds of factors (for example, special know-how) which infer, modify of affirm an identity can lead to a strategy 'lock-in' that facilitates future commitments to the chosen alternative resulting in the sunk cost effect (Ghemawat, 1991, pp. 17–19; Leahy, 2000, p. 356).

Due to these findings, organizational identity is often used to explain inertia during organizational change processes (see Barney et al., 1998, pp. 90–91; Pitt and Ewing, 2001, p. 138; Milliken and Lant, 1991; Hannan and Freeman, 1984; Reger et al., 1994; Fiol and Huff, 1992; Huff et al., 1992; van Rekom and van Riel, 2000). Researchers have also suggested that inertia increases over time (see Hannan and Freeman, 1984; Schwenk and Tang, 1989). Huff et al. (2000, p. 78) suggest that: 'Inertia increases if other affiliated individuals reinforce confidence in "shared" interpretations and practices.' Consequently, organizational identity as a shared organizational schema has been detected as a strong barrier against change: 'collective beliefs are perhaps the most pervasive source of inertia' (Mezias et al., 2001, p. 74).

But organizational inertia might be overemphasized by many researchers (compare Larsen and Lomi, 1999; van Rekom, 2003). Huff et al. (1992) identify an interaction between stress and inertia that can predict the evolution of change efforts over time. If stress levels continue to increase, the tendency to commit to a current strategy/identity will be reduced, making a major change effort more likely. In addition, it has been shown by Sarason (1996), Gioia and Thomas (1996), Corley (2002) and Meyer et al. (2002) that organizational identities are malleable, allowing substantial strategic change within organizations. In almost all their empirical cases, the stress level had increased in one way or another before these changes actually took place.

In connection with these considerations, only very few strategy researchers have emphasized the importance of desired (future) organizational identities. Yet, I will argue that the desired future becomes salient when significant stressors are threatening a current identity.

3.3   DESIRED ORGANIZATIONAL IDENTITY WITHIN THE CONTEXT OF STRATEGY

It is my sense that studies on organizational identity and its functions have focused almost exclusively on how current, well-substantiated self-concepts constrain information processing. But organizational members as well as collectives within organizations also have ideas, beliefs and images about their potential – about their future, about their goals, hopes and fears (see Reger et al., 1994; Gioia and Thomas, 1996; Albert and Whetten, 1985; Hultman and Gellerman, 2002; van Rekom, 2003). In other words, organizational members have an idea about a desired organizational identity in the future (compare Markus and Nurius, 1986, p. 955; see Müller and Sottong, 2000, pp. 162–3). This view can also be extended to organizations (the collective level). Ashforth and Mael (1996, p. 29) state: 'Just as a person is amenable to a variety of possible selves, so too, is an organization.'

'What do members think are the future possibilities for the organization? What do they think is ideal? Obtainable? These kinds of questions haven't been asked much in the strategy literature, but they are vital for understanding why some firms seize opportunities and other firms seem not even to notice them' (Barney et al., 1998, p. 111). Reger et al. (1994), Gioia and Thomas (1996), Pratt and Dutton (2000) and van Rekom (2003) have found empirical evidence that organizational members claim a desired conceptualization of identity. This provides an important point of departure for the new connections I am trying to make between identity and strategy.

3.3.1   Desired Identities are Realistic Visions of the Organization's Future

Desired organizational identities, made explicit by the questions, 'Who *should* we be as an organization?' and 'What *should* we stand for?', often become salient (a) when significant stressors in the organization's environment are threatening a current organizational identity (Gioia et al., 2000, pp. 65–71),[10] (b) when momentous decisions are being made (Ashforth and Mael, 1996, p. 31), or (c) when organizational members consciously work on their organizational future, for example during strategy making (Barney et al., 1998, pp. 139–55; Ashforth and Mael, 1996, p. 32). Desired identities can be seen as the cognitive manifestation of enduring goals, characteristics, aspirations, motives, fears, and threats (Markus and Nurius, 1986, p. 954; see also Leary and Kowalski, 1990; Ogilvie, 1987). A desired organizational identity actually defines a vision of the organization that is rooted in seminal beliefs and values.

It is noteworthy that desired identities are not just about selves that one would like to become, but also about selves that one is afraid of becoming (Barney et al., 1998, p. 114; Dukerich et al., 1998; Sveningsson and Alvesson, 2003, pp. 1189–90). Such an 'anti-identity' ('We aren't sure who we are and what we stand for, but we definitely don't want to be . . .') might not be as strong as a positive desired organizational identity. However, remember the case of US WEST briefly discussed in section 3.1. Sarason (1998) observes that one of the first key identity episodes of US WEST was characterized by an anti-identity. Remarkably, her observation at US WEST is that 'it was as if the collective voice exhibited a desire *not* to be a telephone company' (Sarason, 1998, p. 129). While Sarason describes the anti-identity statement as a current organizational identity at that particular time, she actually detected the first desired organizational identity of the new company.

Please note that desired organizational identities are *not* just any set of future images about the self. Desired identities emerge out of past experiences and out of the selves in the past, forming a link from the past to the future. They are an interface in the present that turns current identities into future identities. That is to say that temporality is integral to organizational identity, and fundamental to individual identity (see Mead, 1959). Desires in the present are the result of past thinking, feeling and acting, *and* also anticipations of the future. This integral view is in accord with the Japanese cyclical time concept ('makimono time')[11] of Hayashi (1990), which holds that past and future simultaneously exist in the present.[12] The present can be symbolized as a circle in which both the past and the future converge as streams from opposite directions (see Figure 3.3).

As a link between the past and the future, desired organizational identities account for another very important quality. Desired identities not only have the potential to reveal the creative and constructive nature of the self, but they also reflect the way the self is contextually determined and constrained, creating a path dependency (Markus and Nurius, 1986, p. 954;

Past

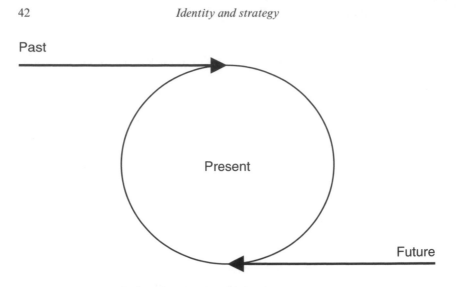

Source: Hayashi (1990) © 1990 University of Tokyo Press.

Figure 3.3   Hayashi's cyclical time concept

see also Barney et al., 1998, p. 110; Bogner and Barr, 2000, p. 213; Barney
and Stewart, 2000, p. 37; Garud and Karnoe, 2001). As Ashforth (2001,
p. 121) notes: 'The alternatives considered are strongly shaped by what is
desired . . . and strongly constrained by what is feasible (realistically available).' Seen from the individual level, desired identities refer to what a
person 'would *like to be* and thinks he or she really *can be*, at least at his or
her best' (Schlenker, 1985, p. 74). Accordingly, a desired organizational
identity remains within the bounds of realism, which makes it a practical
state that is attainable in the eyes of the claimants (compare Schlenker and
Weigold, 1989, p. 253).

In summary, a desired organizational identity defines an *attainable*
organization's vision of the future that is rooted in seminal beliefs and
values, while a current organizational identity defines the actual mission
(purpose), seminal beliefs and values of the organization (Fiol and Huff,
1992, p. 282).[13] However, because the terms 'vision' and 'mission' are given
a variety of meanings in the strategy literature (O'Brien and Meadows,
2000; Voigt, 2005), which has already created a 'land of confusion' (Raynor,
1998) this book will remain with desired and current organizational identities in order explicitly to highlight the identity roots.

It is noteworthy that the concept of current organizational identity generates a large number of theoretical and empirical issues for both organizations and strategy science at present, whereas the concept of desired

organizational identities has been given less attention. The call for additional research on future-based identities that was made by Dutton and her colleagues in 1994 (Dutton et al., 1994, p. 254), based on the encouraging findings of Reger et al. (1994) and Gioia and Thomas (1996), appears to have led only to the works of Pratt and Dutton (2000) and van Rekom (2003). However, ideas about desired organizational identities in the literature have drawn on the concept of 'possible selves' (for example, Markus and Nurius, 1986) from research on individual identity.

3.3.2   The Future Identity State within the Context of Strategy

Desired organizational identity has a natural link to future strategy. The concept of a future market strategy can be represented by the question: 'Which competitive advantages *should* our organization address in the future?' It is assumed that organizational members are likely to have ideas about the answer to this question on future competitive advantages as well as an idea of who they 'want to be'.

Both future concepts have much in common. They are influenced by the organization's (dynamic) environment, and they also guide the perception of, and sensemaking about, this environment. The ongoing emergent process between the environment and its changes and both concepts also affects the relationship between a desired organizational identity and a future market strategy. Figure 3.4 presents a framework for conceptualizing desired organizational identity within the strategy context and can be used for both the individual and the organizational level. Each link within this framework is described in more detail below.

The relationship between desired organizational identity and future market strategy (A)

As representations of potential states, desired identity and a future market strategy are very often views that have not been verified or confirmed by experience.[14] While current organizational identity and current strategy are mediated by actions and interactions, the link between desired identities and a strategy as future concepts therefore can only be imagined. However, an idea of a desired organizational identity tends to raise the strategic question: 'By which future market strategy could we express our desired identity?' Similarly, organizational members may have a future market strategy with corresponding competitive advantages in mind. This will raise the self-reflective question: 'How does this future market strategy infer, modify or affirm what we think we should stand for in the future?'

As a result, organizational identity and strategy remain closely and reciprocally related, even from a future perspective.

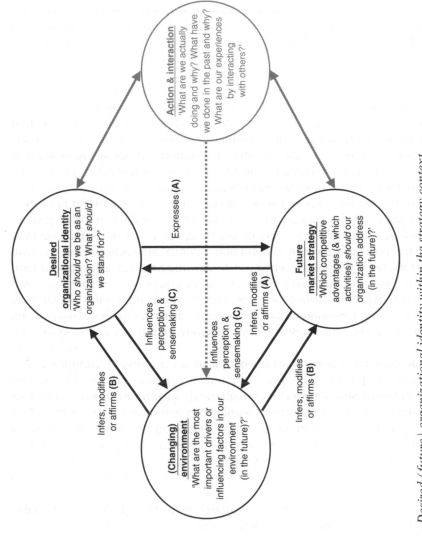

Figure 3.4 Desired (future) organizational identity within the strategy context

The organization's environment infers, modifies or affirms both future concepts (B)

The organization's environment and its changes influence both the desired organizational identity and a future market strategy concept. However, the environment cannot influence the concepts directly; it does so indirectly through organizational members. Organizational members are constantly acting and interacting in the organization's environment. They talk with customers, competitors or stakeholders, read newspapers, magazines or industry bulletins, hear relevant information on television, find relevant ideas on the internet. These actions and interactions create social experiences that form organizational members' assumptions about the environment and its changes (see Schwub-Gwinner, 1993), providing, for example, an answer to the question: 'What are the most important drivers or influencing factors in our environment (in the future)?' This link between actions/interactions and assumptions about the environment is specified in Figure 3.4 by a dotted line.

The influence of the (changing) environment on desired (future) identity is similar. Organizational members are free to generate a wide variety of desired organizational identities, yet these identities are influenced by their sociocultural context – their environment (compare Markus and Nurius, 1986, p. 954). These environmental influences can be diverse and may vary in the degree of their impact. For example, it has been shown that organizational members may adjust their desired organizational identity on their perception of an external audiences' organizational image, as well as their needs, beliefs, and expectations of the organization (Scott and Lane, 2000, p. 46).

Desired organizational identities can also be influenced by particular models and concepts in the organization's environment (for example, business models or images of 'successful' companies in other industries) that become salient to organizational members through the media and other sources (Markus and Nurius, 1986, p. 954). By conceptual combination or analogy, organizational members link these models or concepts with their existing knowledge, thus possibly leading to a newly desired organizational identity (for example, 'we should become the McDonalds of the private insurance industry'). It should also be noted that environmental influence can affect a desired organizational identity in a way that compromises its distinctiveness. In addition to potentially responding to the widely shared image of a company like McDonalds, organizational members spend a lot of their social actions and interactions within their own industry[15] and it is very likely that only a limited and industry-related set of models and concepts become salient to many participants. This limited set can have a homogenizing effect on desired organizational identities within companies of the same industry. As Markus and Nurius (1986, p. 954) state with respect to individuals: 'Many . . . possible selves are the direct result of previous social comparisons . . . What others are now, I could become.' In fact, it has been observed that important elements of organizational identities of competing firms tend to converge over time (DiMaggio and Powell, 1983; Barney and Stewart, 2000, p. 40).

The other concept, a future market strategy, is also heavily influenced by the (changing) environment. Strategy is a *customer-oriented* concept. Without considering the environment and its changes, especially the 'world of customers', a future market strategy cannot be designed. While interacting with customers, organizational members form assumptions about customers, their needs, beliefs and expectations. These environmental assumptions will infer, modify or affirm the members' choice of which competitive advantages, as seen in the eyes of the customers, the organization *should* address (Shane, 2000, p. 452). At any given time, these interactions are likely to give some organizational members a concrete idea of a future competitive advantage.

But it is also possible that organizational members will have difficulties in extracting customers' needs, beliefs and expectations from the environment. Instead, they may try to compensate for their lack of personal assumptions about the environment (and about customers in particular) by copying the successful strategies of competitors (see Huff, 1982; Andrews, 1987, p. 32). But simply copying the winning products and services of competitors will fail to create a distinctive, competitive and sustainable future market strategy. For example, the last few years have seen the airline industry in Germany following the booming 'no frills' strategy. In response to newly established 'no frills' airlines, existing airlines, such as Air Berlin, determined to become 'no frills' airlines as well. By 2005, there were eight major airlines and 15 smaller airlines competing in the same market with similar strategies. However, specialists see a market for two to three airlines at maximum (Genger and Flottau, 2002) and insolvencies resulted as the market adjusted (see N.N., 2004). This makes it clear that the environment, especially the 'world of the customers', not only infers, modifies or affirms a future market strategy, but is a necessary condition for its formation.

Desired identity and/or future market strategy influences the perception of the organization's environment (C)

Both the desired identity and future market strategy concept influence the perception of the environment, as well as how organizational members make sense of it.

I have already described how a current organizational identity guides and shapes intended actions by influencing the perception of an issue's legitimacy and importance, and suggested that identity also shapes understanding of the feasibility of resolving strategic issues. A desired organizational identity also heavily influences the perception and interpretation of environmental issues (see Gioia and Thomas, 1996, pp. 377–83). A strongly desired organizational identity is a highly motivational domain (see section 3.4). Because of this, organizational members are constantly primed to process environmental information relevant to their desired identity, resulting in higher readiness to respond to stimuli relevant to their desired states and in a greater willingness to make sense of such stimuli (see Kato and Markus, 1993, p. 75). Consequently, a desired organizational identity provides a focus for perceiving and interpreting issues in the organization's environment which defines 'what is good, real, important, possible and necessary' (Stoecker, 1995, p. 113).

A future market strategy influences the organizational members' perception of the environment in a comparable but more focused way. Having an idea about future competitive advantages will focus attention on limited aspects of the environment, especially the 'world of the customers'. In addition, the existing idea about a future market strategy is a cognitive perception filter for organizational members that gives meanings to new events and changes in the 'world of the customers'.[16]

In essence, organizational identity and strategy from the future perspective remain closely and reciprocally related. Both future concepts not only influence the members' perception of the organization's environment, but are also inferred, modified or affirmed by the organization's environment and its changes.

3.4 A DYNAMIC FRAMEWORK: DESIRED IDENTITY AS A SOURCE AND STRONG DRIVER OF MOTIVATION AND CHANGE

As we have seen, the temporal perspectives of organizational identity (present and future) are intimately connected. Merging these two temporal perspectives into a single framework creates a new and important perspective on organizational identity within strategy. Unless a current organizational identity is equivalent to a desired organizational identity, these cognitive schemas will be inconsistent with each other. 'The inconsistency between the two identities causes an *identity gap*, defined as the cognitive distance between the perception of the current and the ideal [desired] identity' (Reger et al., 1994, p. 574).[17] This identity gap can occur at the individual as well as at the organizational level.

Taking the framework into account, it is possible to reveal other discrepancies (see Figure 3.5). There also may be a discrepancy between a

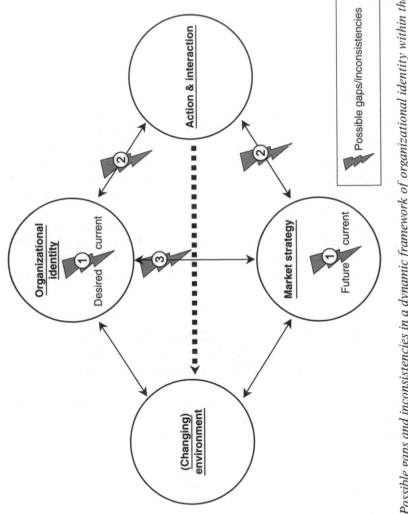

Figure 3.5   Possible gaps and inconsistencies in a dynamic framework of organizational identity within the strategy context

current and a future market strategy, defining a *strategy gap*. The identity and strategy gaps are both conceptual gaps (1) because they describe (different) cognitive schemas of the *same* concept (organizational identity or strategy), on a different time-base. In addition to these conceptual gaps, there can also be interconceptual gaps (3) if a current (future) strategy does not correspond with a desired (or current) organizational identity or vice versa. Finally, actions and interactions can be perceived as being inconsistent with a current or desired organizational identity and/or a current or future market strategy (2).

Interconceptual discrepancies and inconsistent actions/interactions on different time-bases is likely to intensify the perceived gap between a desired and a current organizational identity (see Dutton and Penner, 1993). And because of the close interrelation between strategy and organizational identity, a strategy gap can also reveal or intensify an identity gap. These perceived gaps and inconsistencies increase the stress level and provide strong motivation for organizational members to reduce the cognitive distance between a current and a desired organizational identity (see Baumeister, 1982; Tedeschi and Norman, 1985; also Reger et al., 1994, p. 574). 'It is only when . . . [organizational members] can no longer live with the consequences of their actions and they locate the causes in deeply seated, and so far unquestioned, attributes of the organization that members begin challenging its identity and trying to alter it' (Bouchikhi et al., 1998, p. 70).

Motivational function of desired identities

But which underlying process triggers organizational members to close the gap and to move towards a desired organizational identity? According to social identity theory, group behavior is guided by the quest for evaluative positive social identity, which in turn is grounded in the existence of fundamental personal motivation for (positive) self-esteem. With regard to desired organizational identity, the motivation to enhance self-esteem is primarily fueled by a process described as self-enhancement (see Banaji and Prentice, 1994; Pratt, 1998, p. 188). Self-enhancement is defined as development towards a desired self or away from a feared self (Ashforth and Mael, 1996, p. 24).[18] The force that drives this enhancement is only in part cognitive or intellectual – a much greater part is emotional and aesthetic (Cooperrider, 1990, p. 111; Polak and Boulding, 1973).[19] It is also worth noting that not only a (positively) desired self has a strong motivational function through self-enhancement, but also a feared self (compare Ogilvie, 1987; Dukerich et al., 1998). The impetus to move 'away' can be very strong in strategic change processes, as has been seen with the empirical study of US WEST by Sarason (1996).

Directive function of desired identities
In addition to its strong motivational function, a desired identity has a directive function (compare Kato and Markus, 1993, p. 76). Future organizational identity gives a specific cognitive form to the desires of organizational members, which can serve as a direction and impetus for action and development (see Markus and Nurius, 1986, p. 960; Schlenker and Weigold, 1989; Markus and Ruvolo, 1989, p. 228; Hultman and Gellerman, 2002, p. 46; for evidence see Pratt and Dutton, 2000; van Rekom, 2003).

Desired states represent the ongoing concerns and unfinished tasks of organizational members. These desired states are 'hot' domains (Kato and Markus, 1993, p. 75) because they continuously stay active in a working self-concept (see Markus and Wurf, 1987). Even more, Markus and Ruvolo (1989) hypothesize that the working self-concept is *dominated* by desired states. This means that claimants will be focused on actions instrumental to achieving the desired state, rather than on their current state (see the supporting empirical findings of van Rekom, 2003).

In short, desired organizational identities considerably regulate, and may even dominate, behavior and decision making in organizations (see Markus and Nurius, 1986, p. 966; Watkins and Mohr, 2001, p. 38).[20] Accordingly, everything that has been described for *intended* actions and interactions with current organizational identities (see section 3.2) is fully applicable to desired organizational identities. As a result, the dual-time-based framework of organizational identity within the context of strategy becomes very dynamic, allowing significant alterations of current organizational identities by desired states.

This finding highlights the importance of desired organizational identity and the significance of time-based discrepancies. Corley (2002, p. 117) states: 'Because past theorizing about the role of discrepancies in identity change has not previously considered time-based incongruities, this findings [sic] represents an opportunity to advance our understanding of why and how identity changes over time.' While recent strategy and organization science research has mainly focused on the fact that current organizational identities dynamically change due to external stressors (for example, image-identity discrepancies), it has failed to identify what provides direction and impetus for an identity change when it is externally stressed. In other words, researchers have failed to identify desired organizational identities as an important source and driver of organizational change processes.

It should be noted that the time-based dynamics of organizational identity are in accordance with findings in other fields of management theory. In their observations in the *Academy of Management's Review's* special issue about 'Time and Organizational Research', Ancona et al. (2001)

explain that the temporal lens is becoming more important and recommend that organizational researchers begin accounting for the role that temporal forces play in organizational behavior.

This book suggests that an important aspect of temporality can be found in desired organizational identities, both on the individual and on the collective level. This view of the future gives direction, motivation and impetus to organizational action and development in the strategy context. In addition, an identity gap triggers strong motivation for alterations of current organizational identities. In sum, desired organizational identity – being an attainable vision of the organization's future – is a source and strong driver of motivation and change.

NOTES

1. See also Barney (2002).
2. Originally, Freeman referred to the level of 'enterprise strategy' identified by Schendel and Hofer (1979). It identifies the relationship of the firm with society that can also be seen as the mission statement.
3. With the customer-oriented definition of strategy this book draws on, customers are the most important 'social institution'.
4. The question 'What do we stand for?' is seen as interchange with the question 'Who are we as an organization?' by organizational identity researchers. See for example Gioia et al., 2000, p. 65.
5. I consider 'shared' here as an aggregation of those individual cognitive perceptions that have sufficient similarity and connectedness to each other to guide action. Such a 'shared' organizational identity may differ in completeness and detail, and may have different but overlapping contents from individually perceived organizational identities (see Jelinek and Litterer, 1994, p. 14). As discussed earlier in Chapter 2, an individual's cognitive perception of organizational identity, therefore, may or may not match a collective identity of a group or organization.
6. See Dutton and Dukerich (1991) for complete study in detail.
7. Terminology derived from Schütz (1967).
8. An 'anti-identity' describes an identity that organizational members are afraid of becoming ('We aren't sure who we are and what we stand for, but we definitely don't want to be . . .'). See also section 3.3.
9. Nevertheless, as we have seen, strategies may influence intended strategic actions and interactions by definition.
10. Remember for instance Freeman's example of Bell Telephone (section 3.1) or significant discrepancies between a claimed organizational identity and external images (see section 2.2). Another example is mergers and acquisitions that can also significantly stress organizations and their members, especially when they are dominated during such a process (see Priddat, 2000, pp. 21–2; van Knippenberg et al., 2002).
11. A 'makimono' is a picture story or writing mounted on paper and usually rolled into a scroll.
12. Actually, Hayashi took the concept as well as the figure from Tanabe (1940).
13. Whereas an organization's mission is usually associated with the organization's purpose, why it exists (What *do* we stand for?), a vision is often associated with an image of a desired state of an organization (What *should* we stand for?) (see O'Brien and Meadows, 2000, p. 36).

14. Past identities, to the extent that they may define an organization again in the future, can also be desired organizational identities. Of course, these identities have been verified and confirmed by experiences in the past (see Markus and Nurius, 1986, p. 955).

15. For example, constantly monitoring competitors' strategic actions and moves, evaluating which valuable employees of competitors they can recruit, permanent conversations within the industry (during industry fairs or committees), and so on.

16. In strategy research, experiences with such perceptual filters that give meaning to events and changes have also been made when creating scenarios in practice (see Bood and Postma, 1997).

17. The width of the gap is also influenced by creativity. Desired identities (on the individual as well as on the organizational level) may be located along a theoretical continuum that ranges from an adaptive to a more innovative style of imagination. The main distinction between adaptive and innovative style is that while the former creates by slightly improving current identities, the latter is more likely to challenge current identities. Adopted from Kirton (1994).

18. This view is highly consistent with social identity theory (see Hogg, 2000b).

19. Markus and Ruvolo (1989) point towards a variety of interrelated cognitive, affective, and somatic effects. For details see Markus and Ruvolo (1989, p. 227).

20. This influence has also been found in consumer behavior because consumers are able to attribute certain consumption behaviors to the approach of envisioned positive possible selves (see Morgan, 1993; Munson, 1993). In addition, social movement research provides similar findings which highlight the strong motivational role of desired future states for mobilization and action (see Voigt, 2005).

4. The impact of desired identities: what docs it mean for strategy making in practice?

> Strategy is a human construction; it must in the long run be responsive to human needs. It must ultimately inspire commitment. It must stir an organization to successful striving against competition. People have to have their hearts in it. (Andrews, 1987, p. 63)

The framework developed in Chapter 3, and the likelihood of time-based discrepancies that it reveals, demonstrate the importance of desired organizational identity for strategy making. A vision of the organization's future ('who *should* we be?') and a source of strong motivation to alter current organizational identities affects the aim of strategy making in an organic way. The framework illustrates a close interdependency between desired organizational identity and a future market strategy. Consequently, the identification of desired organizational identity should be adequately considered and methodologically integrated into strategy making (see Brown and Starkey, 2000, p. 110; Bouchikhi and Kimberly, 2003; Haslam et al., 2003a).

However, before this integration can be done it is important to review the impact of desired organizational identities on strategy making in practice. This chapter will identify and formulate four new requirements for designing a practical strategy making process that are derived from the insights and conclusions of the organizational identity framework introduced in Chapter 3:

1. Developing a consensually shared desired identity as a new starting point.
2. Accepting the consensually shared desired identity as a new measure in the process of strategy making.
3. Achieving an attainable market strategy that is creative at the same time.
4. Using skilled facilitators.

4.1 A NEW STARTING POINT FOR STRATEGY MAKING: DEVELOPING A CONSENSUALLY SHARED DESIRED IDENTITY

The fact that desired organizational identities at the individual and collective level exist means that there are already mental models of 'who we *should* be' in the minds of organizational members (possibly with some ideas about future competitive advantages) to facilitate a controlled and conscious process of strategy making. Regardless of the perceived distance (discrepancy) between a desired and a current organizational identity, there is already the beginning of an answer to the question 'who do we *want* to be?' among organizational members, which then can become the focus of more formal strategy making. Not only do organizations *not* start from 'point zero' with regard to their desired identity in strategy making processes (Müller and Sottong, 2000, p. 162), but – as has been shown – these desired identities also act as reference points which will draw attention to limited aspects at each analytical step (for example, environmental or core competencies analysis) in the strategy making process.

During strategy making, it is the role of the top management (and the facilitators who work with them)[1] to reveal and challenge existing mental identity constructs and to build shared visions of the future (see Senge, 1990). 'The challenge to existing mental models and the development of new visions need to include organizational identity – a questioning of the mental models that support current views of organizational identity and the development of visions concerning the nature of the new identity the organization is working toward' (Brown and Starkey, 2000, p. 110).[2] But as outlined in Chapter 1, strategy making still draws primarily on theories of rational action. Following the rational and analytical parts of Andrews's concept, strategy researchers typically advocate a sequence of strategy making steps covering internal and external analysis that culminates in a formulated strategy which reflects an economic match that is as close to optimal as possible (see Ansoff, 1988; Schoemaker, 1992; Hanssmann, 1995; Ulwick, 1999; O'Brien and Meadows, 2000; Bea and Haas, 2001).[3]

While these strategy making processes focus solely on the building of novel future market strategies in a conscious and rational way, existing mental (identity) models in the minds of organizational members are connected to motivational domains that are left out of consideration in current models of strategy making (Müller and Sottong, 2000, p. 162; Senge, 1990, p. 213; Fengler, 2003). As Fiol and Huff (1992, p. 282) put it: 'Identities . . . tend to remain implicit and do not tend to be a part of formal planning processes.'

4.1.1 The Contest for an Organizational Future: Conflicts in Strategy Making

In contrast, Andrews (1987) included existing 'value-laden' identity-related constructs into strategy making (see Figure 2.1) that have been largely ignored by strategy researchers until today. In accordance with motivational findings about desired organizational identities reviewed in section 3.4, he states: 'We are ourselves not aware of how much desire affects our own choice of alternatives' (p. 54). However, Andrews (1987) limits the impact of underlying desired identity constructs to the top manager's *choice* of alternatives which takes place after 'the most nearly objective analysis of opportunity and resources' (p. 62). Consequently, Andrews suggests revealing these constructs *after* the analytical analysis, balancing them with the economically best match of opportunities and resources. This view is still expressed today (see Wheelen and Hunger, 2002, pp. 182–3), but the process of strategy making has become more decentralized, and it involves many more organizational members – not only top managers (Nonaka, 1988) – than it did when Andrews was writing.

When multiple organizational members are involved in strategy making, answering the questions of 'who should we be?' and 'who do we want to be?' is a quest for the soul of the organization. Since organizational members often 'hold different preferences, the quest can be seen as a contest for that soul' (Ashforth and Mael, 1996, p. 29).[4] The contest starts from the very beginning of strategy making. Since existing desired identities act as reference points, organizational members with differences of opinion will consider different aspects and/or hold different interpretations of environmental issues and resources. For example, directors of a bank who define their desired bank as becoming more of an investment bank will attend to a radically different environment than directors who define their desired bank as a universal bank that includes private customer retail services (compare Ashforth and Mael, 1996, p. 32). Another example: due to the desired self-definition of the company, the managers of a book publisher may interpret a book either as a cultural good that is on the bookshelf for many years or as a mass consumption good that is immediately thrown away after being read. During the analysis of opportunities and resources, these different foci and interpretations will almost certainly lead to emotional tension and conflict as organizational members try to pursue their individually desired organizational identity of the future (see Glynn, 2000, p. 295; Andrews, 1987, p. 57; Ackoff, 1981, pp. 94–7; Schwub-Gwinner, 1993, pp. 18–21).

In the rational and logical sequences of strategy making, organizational members – of course – know that external and internal analysis will

determine the organization's space of strategic positioning. As a consequence, organizational members will seek to influence, manipulate or dominate the process by defining issues and situations (Eden and Ackermann,
1998, p. 47). But contest defines a situation where one individual gets as
much as they can at the expense of others (Mason and Mitroff, 1981,
p. 107). In other words, it is a conflict where either one *wins or loses* at the
end. Ackermann et al. (2005, p. 19) state: 'Anticipating losing or winning
will, rightly or wrongly, set up a political dynamic and power struggle . . .
it is rare for there to be no casualties from the results of strategy making.'
Because of that, organizational members are likely to:

- try to persuade others by 'hard' scientific facts (expert knowledge) or
  numbers (see Bacharach and Lawler, 1980, p. 35);
- build coalitions to pursue or 'sell' specific strategic issues and interpretations (see Dutton et al., 1997; Dutton and Ashford, 1993;
  Bacharach and Lawler, 1980);
- use informal or functional power (see French and Raven, 1959), and
  so on.

These conflicts and their outcomes will be closely connected to existing
power positions within the organization. Depending on the willingness of
the actual power holder(s) to make use of their position, conflictual discussions can be either endless or finished quickly. Andrews (1987, p. 63) –
aware that conflict may arise – states: 'There are circumstances when the
exercise of leadership must transcend disagreement that cannot be resolved
by discussion. Subordinates, making the best of the inevitable, must accept
a follower role.' However, following this advice means that the outcome of
analytical analysis in strategy making can only vary from a superficial consensus[5] to endless debates with no consensual conclusion.[6] While the latter
would mean a failure of the strategy making process, the former buys leadership at a high cost because the strategy making process did not eradicate
conflicts within the group of organizational members.

Activities based on superficial acceptance are likely to violate beliefs or
values, be based on information that is regarded as irrelevant, or draw on a
model of reality (for example, current or desired organizational identity)
that differs from the model held as valid by some organizational members.
As a result, resistance will occur during implementation in direct propor-
tion to the degree of conflict perceived by those members (Ansoff, 1988,
p. 205). Depending on the individually perceived pressure from the strategy
making outcomes, and the extent to which they violate beliefs or values,
organizational members will create negative side effects that range from sub-
version, conspiracy, and sabotage to more unintentional counterproductive

activities (Hultman, 1998). As Scott-Morgan (1994, p. 50) says: 'People's true values do not change under duress. Even under exigencies of war, where some pretty nasty approaches have been tried, no one has ever been able to change what was really important to people through force. Instead, resistance goes underground.'

4.1.2 Valuing Desired Identities: A New Starting Point for Strategy Making

Most strategy researchers either fail to see or underestimate the impact of desired organizational identity constructs on the analytical process of internal and external analysis and its implications for resistance when one desired identity is emphasized over others (see Müller and Sottong, 2000, p. 159; Bouchikhi and Kimberly, 2003; van Knippenberg et al., 2002). These impacts cannot be managed just by trying to minimize these interferences during strategy making workshops. For example, leaders and their facilitators try to establish 'ground rules' for a strategy making process and clarify the 'roles' of the participants. They may claim that all individuals will participate equally, that agreement is reached by consensus, that all ideas are valid, and so on at the beginning of the process; sometimes even 'asking' all individuals to sign a commitment form in order to assure compliance with these 'ground rules' (see Warihay, 1992; Union of International Associations, 2005). However, it seems obvious that such efforts try to manage undesired symptoms on the surface rather than coping with the underlying problem in depth.

As a result, existing mental models of the organization's future create a hidden agenda during strategy making which *cannot* and *should not* be repressed. In accordance with Andrews (1987, pp. 57–8), existing 'value-laden' identity-related constructs need to be revealed. But in contrast to Andrews's proposal, this should happen *before* internal and external analysis takes place in strategy making and it should include not only top managers but all involved organizational members. In order to avoid conflicts and superficial consensus agreements in strategy making that are driven by (hidden) individually preferred futures, the revelation of individually desired organizational identities should be the *new starting point* for strategy making.

As already stated, during strategy making, it is the role of the top management (or facilitators who work with them) to discover and challenge existing mental (identity) models and to build shared visions of the future. Both managerial tasks are closely connected to each other because a desired organizational identity (as an existing mental model) already defines the organization's vision of the future, which is rooted in seminal beliefs and values. Due to that, the revelation of individually desired organizational identities as a starting point for strategy making becomes even more crucial because a shared organizational vision, as I am defining it, is built from these individual visions (see Senge, 1990, p. 212).

In other words, revealed individual visions (desired identities) can be used to create a shared desired organizational identity. By the collective construction of a desired self, organizational members become active producers of their own organizational development.

4.1.3   Reinforcing Reasons for a New Starting Point: Two Approaches that Deserve a Closer Look

Two important sources in the management literature (a) explicitly refer to the strong impact that anticipatory images of the future and desires have on human beings, and (b) use the creation of a consensually shared and desired organizational future in their processes. In 1981, Ackoff, one of the founders of operations research and management science in the US, developed an approach that he called 'idealized redesign', which created a turn in management science towards synthetical system thinking (Ackoff, 1981). Ackoff introduced a way of creating a holistic design for the organization's future (vision) that is based on consensually accepted desires ('ideals') that organizational members hold in the present.

The other approach – called 'appreciative inquiry'[7] – can be related to the research area of organizational development. It has grown in popularity and influence with both academics and practitioners in recent years (Fry et al., 2002; Liebl, 2001b). Appreciative inquiry develops a shared preferred organizational future based on the high moments of where the organizations and their members have been. The focus is on identifying and being 'the best you can be'. Because such a preferred future is grounded in real experience and history, organizational members know how to succeed: they repeat their success.

Both approaches deserve a closer look because (a) they apparently offer ways of closing the gap between what the organization actually is and its desired state (defined by its organizational members), and (b) they claim many benefits that result from engaging in such a process. Since it seems that the creation of a shared and desired identity (built from individually desired organizational identities) is a decisive element at the starting point of the practical design of a strategy making process, it is useful to review the reasons and core principles underlying these two approaches and to identify the benefits that are asserted for them. Therefore, a brief description of both approaches will be given, followed by an evaluation of their contribution to the new starting point in strategy making that I am proposing.

4.1.3.1 Ackoff's idealized redesign: who do we want to be right now?

Ackoff (1981) developed an interactive approach that puts the idea of the most desired organizational future of organizational members into a planning process (see also Ackoff, 1974). His 'idealized redesign' is meant to be consensually accepted by organizational members. Ackoff does not declare that idealized redesign will create an ideal, perfect or utopian organization. Rather his process identifies the most effective desired ('ideal') organization that its members can conceive. 'Idealized redesign is a way that an organization's stakeholders can prepare a vision of what they want their organization to be right now, assuming that it could be whatever they wanted' (Ackoff, 1993, p. 401).

Ackoff's idea that such a conception should be one which its designers would like to have *right now* stems from his lack of faith in forecasts ('predict and prepare') in strategy making (Ackoff, 1997, pp. 23–4). He asserts that: 'Whatever we want something to be right now includes what we expect of it in the future' (Ackoff 1993, p. 401).[8] His approach is based on the assumption that human beings want to increase their ability and wish to satisfy their own desires and those of others. Because humans are continuously ideal-seeking, the process of 'idealized redesign' merely facilitates what organizational members are already striving to develop.

Three properties are required for an 'idealized redesign' of an organization. It should be (i) technologically feasible, (ii) operationally viable, and (iii) subject to continuous improvement from within and without. Ackoff (1981, pp. 107–15) defines three steps involved in 'idealized redesign', which in practice cannot be clearly separated from each other and iteratively interact: (1) selecting a mission, (2) specifying the desired properties of the design, and (3) designing the system. By making the first step 'selecting a mission', Ackoff underscores the idea that his approach is a holistic design that covers the role of an organization as a whole, as well as its relationships with other social institutions.[9] Because organizations tend to be self-centered,[10] this step should make explicit the principal roles and functions that the organization is willing to undertake with regard to others (including customers, shareholders, suppliers, and so on).[11]

Once a focused mission has been formulated, however tentatively, the second step 'specifies desired properties of the design'. These specifications should cover all aspects of an organization's structure, operations, and relationships with stakeholders. While recognizing that no topic list will ever be suitable for all organizations, Ackoff (1981, pp. 111–12) offers a list of design opportunities that ranges from business(es), markets, marketing, and production, to personnel and finance. After preparing the list of specifications, the 'design of the system' – the third step – can begin. This process converts specifications into a design for implementation. It is a cumulative process, beginning with a rough sketch, which is gradually refined and then revised. The process continues until the design is detailed enough to enable others to carry it out as intended.

In summary, Ackoff provides an approach to organizational visioning that is based on the creation of a consensually shared and desired organizational future. Starting with a rough sketch, shared vision is employed to design a desired organizational future in full detail. Ackoff's claims for the benefits of such a process have to do with participation, aesthetic values, consensus, commitment, creativity and feasibility.

4.1.3.2   Appreciative inquiry: appreciating the past before stepping into a desired future

Appreciative inquiry is a collaborative, highly participative and holistic process that helps organizations articulate key ingredients in past successes ('life-giving forces') in order to use those as the basis for creating a positive organizational future (Watkins and Mohr, 2001; Cooperrider et al., 1999; Hammond, 1998).[12] The approach is primarily influenced by findings in the social sciences about positive image and social constructionism (Cooperrider, 1990; Cooperrider and Srivastva, 1987).[13] Watkins and Cooperrider (2000, p. 6) describe appreciative inquiry as a 'theory that rationalizes and reinforces the habit of mind that moves through the world in a generative frame, seeking and finding images of the possible rather than scenes of disaster and despair'.

Cooperrider and Srivastva (1987, pp. 160–65) propose four aspects of appreciative inquiry, suggesting that their model is simultaneously scientific/theoretical ('what is'), visionary ('what might be'), normative ('what should be') and pragmatic ('what will be'). By this, appreciative inquiry claims to be an alternative paradigm to traditional problem solving in organizations. Instead of highlighting problems to be solved, it chooses the positive aspect of 'what is' as the focus of inquiry in order to involve it into a positive future creation (Figure 4.1).

Watkins and Mohr (2001, pp. 39–51) turn these four aspects into five core generic processes as a framework for organizational change:

1.   Choose the positive as the focus of inquiry;
2.   Inquire into stories of life-giving forces;
3.   Locate themes that appear in the stories and select topics for further inquiry;
4.   Create shared images for a preferred future; and
5.   Find innovative ways to create that future.

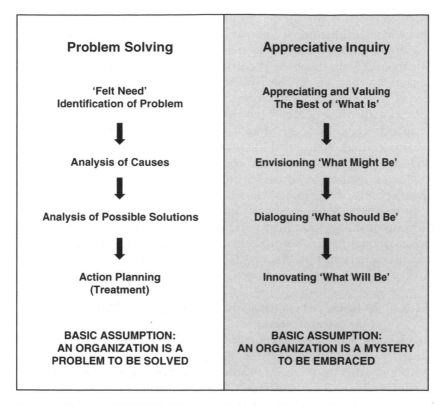

Problem Solving	Appreciative Inquiry
'Felt Need' **Identification of Problem**	**Appreciating and Valuing** **The Best of 'What Is'**
↓	↓
Analysis of Causes	**Envisioning 'What Might Be'**
↓	↓
Analysis of Possible Solutions	**Dialoguing 'What Should Be'**
↓	↓
Action Planning **(Treatment)**	**Innovating 'What Will Be'**
BASIC ASSUMPTION: **AN ORGANIZATION IS A** **PROBLEM TO BE SOLVED**	**BASIC ASSUMPTION:** **AN ORGANIZATION IS A MYSTERY** **TO BE EMBRACED**

Source: Hammond (1998) © 1996 Sue Annis Hammond. Reprinted by permission of Thin Book Publishing, Co., Bend, USA.

Figure 4.1   The traditional paradigm of problem solving in organizations and the paradigm of appreciative inquiry

The first process appreciates and values the best of 'what is' today by focusing on times of organizational excellence. The question to ask is: 'When have organizational members experienced their organization as being most alive and effective?' (Barrett and Fry, 2002, p. 6). The second process uses interviews with organizational members to research topics that have been identified in the first process. These interviews explore the 'life-giving' forces of an organization, and provide an understanding for underlying distinctive ingredients of these forces. After the interviews, the third core process looks for themes of 'life-giving' forces that appear across told stories, and then expands the dialogue within the organization about the most important forces. This process provides a link between the inquiry that has been conducted into the past and the image of the preferred future because it can

create an image of how the organization would be, if these extracted excep-
tional moments become the norm in the organization. Consequently, the
fourth core process focuses on co-creating a shared image or vision of a preferred future ('what might be') by articulating the most desired future of the
organization as a whole. This process also includes the design and description of an organizational structure ('what should be') that could make this
future a reality. The final core process is to engage organizational members
in an architectural redesign process ('what will be') that will promote continuous learning, adjustment and improvisation. For this process, Watkins
and Mohr (2001) suggest several methods, for instance, they describe the
conference method based on Axelrod (1999) that can be used to move a
shared positive image into organizational practice.

In summary, the approach of appreciative inquiry explicitly uses key
elements of the organizational past to create a consensually shared desired
organizational future. This desired vision is then used for the design of
organizational structure. Proponents of this approach claim its benefits have
to do with participation, innovation, positive focus and lack of resistance.

4.1.3.3   Reviewing and evaluating the core principles and benefits of the two approaches

Remarkably, both approaches reveal individually desired organizational
identities as a starting point for their suggested methods, even though
neither declares it as such. Ackoff and appreciative inquiry theorists
explicitly refer to the strong impact that anticipatory images of the future
and desires have on organizational members (Ackoff, 1981, pp. 34–50;
Cooperrider, 1990). They use these existing generative forces to facilitate
organizational development – that is, they employ the motivational aspects
of desired organizational identities.

Both traditions acknowledge that the desires of organizational members
are not only relevant but necessary for the creation of, and participation in,
an organizational future. Even more, both approaches make use of individually desired identity constructs to create a consensually shared desired
organizational identity (Ackoff, 1981, pp. 118–19; Watkins and Mohr,
2001, pp. 133–50).

However, both concepts have their limitations and cannot completely
replace the process of strategy making outlined in this book. For instance,
neither approach explicitly considers an exploration of the organization's environment and both miss the importance of customers. Neither
approach explores core competencies or strategic capabilities in a controlled and conscious way. Both approaches tend to focus on designing
internal structures. While Ackoff tries to enlarge the system thinking to
include relations with other social systems, he does not pay too much

attention to them during design. Appreciative inquiry explicitly limits its intention to social systems components and technical components of an organizational structure (Ackoff, 1981, pp. 107–25; Watkins and Mohr 2001, pp. 137–50). Since strategy is a customer-oriented concept, strategy making needs to focus on the purpose of an organization as a whole by understanding their most important stakeholders – their customers.

Nevertheless, reviewing the core principles and benefits of Ackoff's system thinking and appreciative inquiry provides additional insights and methodological considerations for a new starting point in strategy making. Therefore, eight of their core principles and benefits are reviewed in more detail below.

(1) *Holistic design* Both Ackoff's design thinking and appreciative inquiry use the principle of holistic design processes rather than research and optimization around the solution of partial problems. For both approaches, designing a system is architectural: architects do not analyse the requirements of someone who wants to build a house in detail, but *realize* them in an overall conceptual design (see Hanssmann, 1993, p. 135). They see interactions and interconnections of all parts of a system. If the performance of parts of a building are taken separately, the performance of the whole is not necessarily improved – it may be even destroyed. The performance of a system is based on how the parts fit, not on how they perform separately. Interestingly, this principle is in accordance with Porter's finding that a competitive advantage arises from a strategic fit across activities, not from single parts (Porter, 1996, pp. 70–75).

(2) *Linking the past with the future* Both approaches follow the principle of linking the organizational past with a desired future. While Ackoff only implicitly considers the past through desired organizational identities, appreciative inquiry explicitly uses key elements of past organizational experiences. This link is quite similar to Dutton and Penner's (1993, p. 104) finding on motivations arising from organizational identification, where members are enthused to strengthen valued parts of the current organizational identity in times of change – thus moving towards a desired organizational identity.

The link between past and future connects 'lived experiences' of success to existing mental identity constructs. Recently, besides the relatively new appreciative inquiry approach, the connection between past and future seems to have become more important in strategy making. For example, Beaver (2001, p. 3) suggests that 'strategy is focused on the future, but most good strategies pay attention to, and are well grounded in, the lessons of the past'.

Inquiry into current and past identities highlights a point that is often overlooked in strategy making and processes of change. Most strategy making processes attempt to move into a new future immediately, but forget or ignore the past. The tendency is to focus cognitive abilities on the building of novel future strategies in a conscious and rational way, whereas existing mental models in the minds of organizational members (which are connected to their motivational domains) are left out of consideration. Eden and Ackermann (1998) stand out among the few authors to avoid this trap. They suggest 'the process of strategy making is one which is grown from, or knits into, the organization as it is. It is a process which thus pays due respect to the history and inhabitants of the organization seeking to *"honour the past* while estranging from it" . . . rather than presumptively suggesting that strategic change is inevitable or determined solely by considerations of the future' (Eden and Ackermann, 1998, p. 21, emphasis in the original).

Tannenbaum and Hanna (1985) usefully identify 'ending' dynamics with identities that also play an important role in change processes. Without proper endings, organizational members have difficulty letting the past go, which can create another source of resistance to change (Tannenbaum and Hanna, 1985, p. 99). Integrating the organizational past pays attention to the needs individuals have for appreciating and affirming the past before they step into a new future (Bushe, 2002, p. 51).

(3) *Participation* Both system design and appreciative inquiry approaches are based on the principle of extensive participation. They facilitate participation because they know organizational members welcome the opportunity to share what they like and value about their work and 'their' organization, and they often welcome the chance to express what they think 'their organization should stand for'. It is often assumed that external and internal analysis in strategy making needs detailed and expert knowledge. Such an argument is often promoted by organizational members who call themselves (or someone they know quite well) an 'expert' in order to influence, manipulate or dominate outcomes of these analytical processes. This attempt makes opinions of 'non-experts' more or less irrelevant (see section 4.1.1 on 'the contest for the organizational future' above). But when it comes to business design, no one is an expert in designing a desired organization, based on what an organization ought to be. Every organizational member (or stakeholder) can make an important contribution: 'Their opinions, aspirations, dreams and preferences are relevant' as Ackoff says (1981, p. 116.).[14] For Ackoff (1981, p. 66), participation is the most important product of such a process because 'no one can plan effectively for someone else' and recent research supports this

view that participation in strategy processes is critical (see Ashmos et al., 1998; Haslam et al., 2003a; Collier et al., 2004).

(4)   *Incorporating individual values*   One benefit of participation is that it enables organizational members to incorporate their intrinsic values into the work of the organization. Due to this incorporation, Hambrick and Mason (1984) and many other strategy researchers were able to find that organizational strategies often reflect the values of top managers. But as noted in the above discussion, strategy making has become more decentralized – a reason why both the system design and appreciative inquiry approach are more broadly participative. The extensive participation is crucial because 'participants in design processes cannot help but put their ethical and aesthetic values into the design they produce' (Ackoff, 1994, p. 79; see also Voigt, 2003).

(5)   *Consensus*   Both processes aim to generate consensus among those who participate in them. The creation of consensus is of special importance because the 'elimination of conflict . . . is necessary for a continuous increase in one's ability to satisfy one's own desires and those of others; hence for development' (Ackoff, 1981, p. 94). As has been shown, the contest for the organizational future can easily create many conflicts that question the starting point of external and internal analysis. In contrast, when these two approaches are successful they are able to create a consensually desired organizational meta-identity that accommodates each of the individually desired identities.

When consensus of organizational members is targeted, creating a meta-identity from multiple individually desired identities is an appropriate response (see also section 6.2.4). Ackoff (1993, p. 406) argues that it is much easier to agree on ultimate values and desires than on the means for pursuing them: 'The more ultimate the values, the more agreement they generate.' Parallel empirical findings in social identity theory show that a concentrated and highly focused (desired) organizational identity helps reduce uncertainty, especially if they are furnished by homogeneous, consensual groups. Groups with desired organizational identities have distinct entitativity (Sherman et al., 1999), are especially cohesive (Hogg, 1992 and 1993), and offer a powerful identification to their members. These effects of building a consensual meta-identity also support organizational members' confidence in the process and create trust in working with other members.

A process that achieves consensus actually changes the perception from the individual level of identity to the collective level: from 'I' to 'we' – 'my' organization becomes 'our' organization (see Brewer and Gardner, 1996). The organizational member perceives that he/she and others in the organization share a common destiny and that the organizations' successes and failures are his/her successes or failures (Ashforth and Mael, 1989, pp. 26–32). Ackoff (1981, p. 118) states that upon having consensus, differences over means and short-range goals can easily be resolved. This value of a shared organizational future has become widely recognized in other observations on strategy theory and practice (see Bartlett and Ghoshal, 1990; Collins and Porras, 1994; O'Brien and Meadows, 2000). As Senge (1990, p. 208) summarizes: 'A shared vision is the first step in allowing people who mistrusted each other to work together. It creates a common identity.'

(6) *Commitment*   Both participation and consensus are critical foundations for commitment. If the consensual meta-identity reflects individual aspirations, the motivational force of organizational members to take efforts towards the desired state is enormous. Conversely expressed: 'If people don't have their own vision, all they can do is "sign up" for someone else's. The result is compliance, never commitment' (Senge, 1990, p. 211).

(7) *Creativity*   Ackoff and appreciative inquiry theorists claim that their processes stimulate creativity and focus it on organizational and individual development. For Ackoff, creativity is often limited by self-imposed constraints. Many of these constraints derive from concerns about implementability. As implementability is not a requirement in design, it liberates the imagination and increases the desire to invent. Then, knowing how the organizational mission and structure 'should be' eases innovation to create a structure of 'what will be'. In effect, he argues that incorrect assumptions about constraints can be reduced by this approach. It should be noticed that the approach's claim for creativity is limited to the innovative design process of organizational structure. How creative the overall strategic position of the organization is ('What should we stand for?') remains in question. I will come back to this in section 4.3.

(8) *Implementability (attainability)*   The final, but also very important benefit of system design and appreciative inquiry is that the members' conception of what can be implemented is enlarged. Following Ackoff (1981, p. 123), mobilizing (desired) ideas can remove the principal obstruction between organizational members and the future they most desire: their own minds. Appreciative inquiry theorists also claim a lack of resistance by mobilizing desired ideas (Head, 2000). This is in accordance with Dutton and Penner's (1993) observation that resolution of tasks and issues seems more feasible when they are perceived as identity-related. The idea

process makes organizational members believe that they have the skills and competencies to cope with issues that arise (compare section 3.2.2).

However, there is another factor that increases implementability. The principle of linking the organizational past and future, either implicitly through the concept of desired organizational identities or more explicitly through identifying key elements of past success, can generate 'images of realistic developmental opportunities' (Cooperrider and Srivastva, 1987, p. 161). Because these images are rooted in past experiences, there is 'founded hope' ['begründete Hoffnung'] for organizational members that their shared desired vision may become reality in the future (see Liebl, 2001b).

As has been shown, both approaches use a holistic design, try to link the past with the future, and claim extensive participation as core principles of their processes. These core principles integrate the motivational domains of individually desired organizational identities into a collective construction of a shared identity. The claimed benefits of consensus, incorporation of individual values, commitment, creativity and implementability support the view that the strong impact of desired organizational identities should not be repressed in strategy making. Instead, this impact should be consciously integrated into its processes. The benefits that are claimed for such an integrating process address the identified problems of conflict and resistance in strategy making. They provide strong support and theoretically based evidence that these problems can be avoided and that important additional benefits – such as implementability – can be achieved. Thus, the core principles of these two approaches should be objects of consideration when creating a new starting point in a practical strategy making design.

The design of a practical strategy making process that I have been developing considers the impact of individually desired organizational identities (individual visions) by using them to create a consensually shared desired organizational identity. These desired organizational identities that are already in the minds of the organizational members can serve as a wellspring for strategy making – they are a new starting point for strategy making.

4.2   A NEW MEASURE FOR STRATEGY MAKING: CHALLENGING AND EVOLVING A SHARED DESIRED IDENTITY TO REACH A VIABLE MARKET STRATEGY

Incorporating desired organizational identity constructs and their impact on strategy making should neither be seen as a simple 'tool' in order to avoid initial problems during strategy workshops (using people's motivational domains), nor should it be seen as a way to actively influence or 'manage' other people's desired constructs during strategy workshops once they have been revealed. Both views overestimate the short-term manageability and underestimate the strong impact of deep-rooted identity constructs (compare Alvesson and Willmott, 2002). In addition, Fiol and Huff (1992, p. 281) came to the conclusion that identity constructs are the most difficult to change.

The shared desired organizational identity becomes the measure in strategy making

Instead, a shared desired organizational identity provides an understanding and gives awareness of what organizational members actually 'want to do' and what they think their organization 'should do'. Because it is the 'best' picture that organizational members can conceive about their own organizational future right now, it should therefore be treated with dignity and respect during further steps in strategy making (see Haslam et al., 2003a). A useful way of thinking is that the shared desired identity becomes the *measure* for next steps in strategy making.

This is important to note because a question must remain about how useful a shared desired identity actually is from a strategic perspective – it is important to ask what the *strategic value* of a desired identity is. Due to the close interdependency of identity and strategy, the strategic value of a desired identity is delimited by the variety and robustness of possible and distinctive future market strategies it evokes. Before this point in the strategy making process a shared desired organizational identity reflects what organizational members 'want their organization to be', though sometimes in a rather vague way.

During the creation of a shared identity, underlying assumptions (for example about the environment) are only implicitly considered – but not explicitly discussed or revealed. This has been done for good reasons, as it is far easier to find consensus on ultimate desires than on means to achieve them or on assumptions that underlie them (see Ackoff, 1981, p. 118).

The major drawback – because these assumptions are not discussed – is that inconsistencies between a shared desired identity and underlying assumptions cannot be exposed. In addition, organizational members do not know which crucial and strategically relevant information they failed to consider.

Without having the opportunity to think about assumptions and other strategically relevant information in depth, the organizational members' consensually shared desired identity may have a low strategic value and may not survive even an easy and straightforward 'reality test' against external or internal points of reference. For instance, a shared desired organizational identity may be influenced by assumptions about the organization's industry environment that are the result of a homogenizing effect (compare section 3.3.2). Such a desired identity might be already threatened by the simple question: 'Does the desired identity create an image in the minds of our customers that is already "taken" by one of our competitors?'

At this point, the close link between desired organizational identity and a future market strategy can help – but take the opportunity to think about assumptions and strategically relevant information in depth. Please recall that strategy is defined as a customer-oriented concept of competitive advantages achieved by allocating resources which are available to the organization (Liebl, 1999a, p. 8). This definition reflects the essential core of strategy making – the fit between the environment and the organization. Strategy researchers agree upon the need to explore distinctive internal capabilities and external opportunities in a controlled and conscious way (see for example Eden and Ackerman, 1998, pp. 37–44). This analytical focus of strategy making will reveal and explore underlying assumptions as well as create new knowledge about distinctive internal capabilities and external opportunities. Through these important analytical steps, organizational members can create an awareness of inconsistencies, of yet unconsidered information, as well as of the identity's strategic value. Moreover, these analytical steps in strategy making may reveal a threat to a desired identity, increasing the perceived stress level for organizational members.

Revealing and exploring underlying assumptions and creating new knowledge provides a process that actually *challenges* a shared desired organizational identity and its current strategic value by using the close interrelation between organizational identity and a market strategy. This important challenge is a *test of robustness* of a shared desired organizational identity from the strategic perspective.

The benefits of the creation of a consensually shared desired identity that have been described above come into full play during this analytical process. Because organizational members are committed to their shared desired identity, they take this 'test of robustness' as a challenge for their organization – they take it as a challenge for the group, and even as a personal challenge. Because a desired organizational identity is very likely to be connected to intense positive emotions, organizational members take ownership as they face and try to cope with identity-related threats (Pratt and Dutton, 2000, pp. 121–5).

In addition to this commitment and high involvement, there is another important discovery in exploring and challenging assumptions *after* a shared desired organizational identity has been articulated. It is easier for organizational members to look 'back' and to discuss where the organization actually 'is' and the nature of the environment that surrounds it when they have a shared desired identity in mind (Ackoff, 1994, pp. 100–101).

In 1975 Mitroff and Kilmann made the observation that managers describe or recall characteristics of their current organization more easily *after* they have first described their ideal organization (Mitroff and Kilmann, 1975, p. 20). Boland (1984, p. 879) similarly found that a reconstructed imaginary future facilitates the ability to address failures and mistakes in the past and allows for more open and intense discussions over issues that normally would have been suppressed. It seems that discussing strategy and assumptions after creating a shared desired identity enhances reflexivity abilities. This is an important presupposition because the goal of the analytical processes is to challenge an existing shared desired identity (increasing the stress level) in order to evolve it, rather than actively to manipulate the construct towards a set of analytical and economical best matches.

Remember Tannenbaum and Hanna (1985) and their discussion of the 'ending' dynamics that need to take place before change occurs. The challenge and evolution of a shared desired identity that is discussed here takes these important dynamics into account. While a shared desired organizational identity typically includes a number of valued attributes of a current or of past identities (for good reasons), the evolution of a shared desired organizational identity can been seen as a system that has already let various attributes of the present go in order to move on to create new ones. Identity attributes range from peripheral issues to characteristics that affect the very core of an organization. Whereas attributes near the periphery are relatively insignificant and solitary elements, attributes near the core are basic and highly interconnected elements. Letting go of attributes near the periphery is relatively easy and does not really harm an organizational identity. While changes of peripheral attributes thus can be quite superficial, basic changes are relatively difficult to make or may even be impossible. These difficulties with basic attributes are often the reason why changes at the periphery are frequently used by companies to symbolize a change that never took place in practice. Creating a new corporate design, a new logo or name replaces a change in basic attributes, perhaps because organizational members fear the pain of a basic change (Liebl, 2001b).

However, moving from superficial changes towards more basic ones will generate more emotional pain and difficulties with organizational members. Giving up important attributes near the core of a current or desired organizational identity does not necessarily mean the 'death' of the whole organization, but increases the number of 'little dyings' of formerly valued parts. As Keleman (1976, p. 5) defines 'little dying': 'We are always losing and finding things, always breaking with the old and establishing the new. That's little dying.' Organizational members tend to respond to potential 'little dyings' more insistently than they resist more significant losses. Nevertheless, the challenge of a shared desired organizational identity creates an awareness of inconsistencies, of yet unconsidered information, as well as of the potential strategic value of these things. The strategy making process *can* and *should* provoke 'little dyings' in order to evolve the shared desired identity.

However, the challenging task is to continuously observe whether the limit and willingness to let attributes die has been reached by organizational members. This prevents transition into a new future too quickly, losing the emotional and cognitive commitment of the members, and placing implementability at risk. As a result, the scope of a strategic change is solely determined by organizational members and their willingness to hold on, let go and move on.

Such a process requirement implies a different measure of strategy making than that declared by Andrews (1987) and many other researchers in strategic management to the present day. While strategy researchers often suggest that the best match of opportunities and resources (economic strategy) only needs to be balanced with personal values and aspirations and what an organization 'should do', discussion in this chapter reveals a new process requirement. It is critical to create a shared desired identity of organizational members (which defines what people 'want to do' and what they see that their organization 'should do') and to challenge and evolve this through an analytical exploration of underlying assumptions about the organization's environment and internal capabilities. In other words, whereas many strategy researchers take the analytically and economically best (and most 'objective') match as a measure, this new requirement defines a shared desired organizational identity as a measure for strategy making. Consequently, this new measure should guide the practical strategy making process.

4.3 A NEED TO ACHIEVE CREATIVITY AND ATTAINABILITY IN STRATEGY MAKING

Starting strategy making with the creation of a shared desired organizational identity (which becomes the measure for subsequent strategy making steps) implies subjective limitations. As discussed earlier in this book, empirical findings in the field of organizational identity point toward an involuntary or unintentional restriction of creative ideas during strategy making. In spite of efforts to challenge and evolve a shared desired identity through explorations of external opportunities and internal capabilities, my experience has been that these restrictions may remain. On the other hand, only focusing on exceedingly creative or strictly logical combinations of a company's relative strengths and its environmental opportunities disconnects strategy making from institutionalized beliefs and members' shared beliefs about 'their' organization. The result is often creative ideas that are quickly seen as unrealistic.

Since the aim of strategy making is the creation of competitive and successful organizations, feasibility of change is crucial. An important point in this book is that the scope of accepted strategic change is solely determined by organizational members. But taking a shared desired identity as a measure in strategy making raises an important question: Can a strategy that emerges out of such a strategy making be realistic *and* creative?

The question of creativity is a substantial one from a strategic perspective because opportunity-seeking and opportunity-creating is becoming more important in a turbulent environment. As Ford and Gioia (1995, p. 4) note: 'Creativity is now a core necessity for success in a profoundly changing organizational world. Creativity is simply essential because organizations and environments are both changing so fundamentally.' The result in recent years is an increasing interest in creativity in strategy making (see for example, Higgins, 1996; Beaver, 2001). It seems that a creative mindset is required when founding new businesses as well as changing the rules of existing ones (see Ansoff and Sullivan, 1993; McGrath and MacMillan, 2000). It is therefore worth looking briefly at creativity research to consider how creativity and attainability might be combined in strategy making.

The ability to go beyond concrete experience to produce new ideas is one of the most salient characteristics of human beings and creativity is concerned with the generation of ideas, alternatives, and possibilities (see Mumford and Gustafson, 1988). The most common view is that creativity is not an easily scripted process (see de Bono, 1992; Perkins, 1981). There are many ways to come up with new ideas. This diversity is paralleled by a diversity of idea-generation techniques that range from informal pieces of advice to elaborate methodologies (see Smith, 1998; Higgins, 1994). Smith (1998, p. 109) who analysed 172 idea-generating techniques in regard to their 'operational mechanisms' states:

> Even when occurring within groups, creativity is essentially a mental phenomenon. A technique must prompt certain cognitive activities in users. It does so through active ingredients, devices producing desired mental changes. Active ingredients may be instructions users can mentally discharge (for example, fantasize), stimuli they can respond to (for example, visual displays), or conditions fostering idea-generation (for example, anonymity).

In summary, mental processes are the essence and engine of creative endeavor.

This key finding is in accord with findings from creative cognition research, a comparatively new field in creativity research, with origins stemming only as far back as the early 1990s. 'The creative cognition approach concentrates primarily on the cognitive processes and conceptual structures that produce creative ideas. Its complementary goals are to use empirical and theoretical advances from cognitive science to aid in understanding creativity and to use creative performance as a way of learning more about basic cognitive processes' (Ward, 2001, p. 350). Ward et al. (1997) claim that creativity is an outcome of subsets of processes (including conceptual combination and analogy) that work together to expand knowledge and conceptualization in a given domain. Creativity is an entire system within which these processes operate on cognitive structures to produce novel outcomes.

Without some meaningful link to existing knowledge and beliefs, these new ideas are unlikely to be of much use and therefore unlikely to be considered creative. Ward and his colleagues (1997, p. 19) observe: 'Because novelty is one requirement for a creative idea, most approaches to creativity focus only on novelty to the exclusion of the background knowledge that gives the novelty its meaning.' Finke (1995, p. 304) describes this link as 'structural connectedness', which is important in achieving 'creative realism'. 'Realism', in turn, refers to what people see as 'realistic'. According to Finke (1995), realistic ideas are ideas that have practical and attainable consequences.

Finke (1995) also points out that creative, realistic ideas must exhibit inspirational qualities that excite the imagination and lead to meaningful explorations. This 'imaginative divergence', as he calls it, will distinguish genuinely exciting and innovative ideas from those that appear sensible and realistic but lead nowhere (see Finke 1995, pp. 304–5). Thus, realism and divergence are both required to generate creative ideas that are likely to have a major impact on strategic issues or problems.

Figure 4.2 suggests that a creative-conservative dimension on one hand and a realistic-idealistic dimension on the other hand define four general, conceptual domains into which new ideas can be classified.

- *Conservative realism* describes ideas that focus on realistic issues or problems but are – often extremely – conventional. They are mainly generated in traditional highly structured fields (for example, engineering, law). They tend to have a high degree of structural connectedness, but a low degree of imaginative divergence.
- *Creative idealism* describes ideas that are very interesting and original but very 'fanciful'. These ideas usually show a high degree of imaginative divergence, but a very low degree of structural connectedness. As a result, they are very difficult to relate to existing ideas; the connections that are made are usually vague or inappropriate.

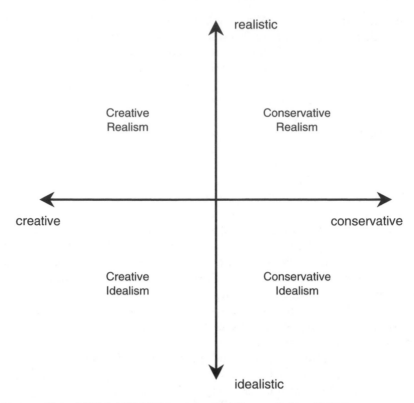

Source: Finke (1995) © 1995 MIT Press. Reprinted by permission of MIT Press, Cambridge, USA.

Figure 4.2   *Finke's four general, conceptual domains into which new ideas can be classified*

- *Conservative idealism* describes ideas that are simple extensions of common ideas that were unrealistic to begin with. These ideas are often rooted in misconceptions or irrational prejudices (for example, the misogynist assumption that women are inherently inferior to men). These ideas are low in both structural connectedness as well as imaginative divergence because they have no basis in fact or scientific support, and display little imagination.
- *Creative realism* is the category that is of primary interest for this book's agenda. It is the category of ideas that show imaginative divergence and are structurally connected to realistic issues and concepts at the same time. They tend to be inspirational and meaningful without being too fanciful or detached from existing principles.

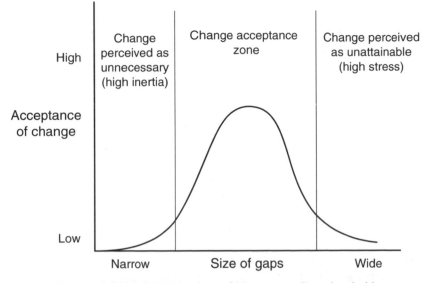

Figure 4.3   Identity gap and probability of change acceptance

These ideas are creative as well as realistic. In other words: these ideas are new but attainable in the eyes of the claimants.

The concept of 'creative realism' in creative cognition research demonstrates the powerful role of prior knowledge and past experiences in creative endeavor (see Smith, 1995; Smith et al., 1993; Ward, 1994; Ward, 1995; Ward et al., 1995). Ward et al. (1997, p. 23) state: 'creative ideas are always a mix of old and new information'. Because desired organizational identities emerge out of the selves in the past, out of 'lived experiences', these findings give strong support to the expectation that a shared desired organizational identity can be both creative and attainable. In consequence, a shared desired organizational identity should be challenged and evolved towards the category of 'creative realism'.

Let us recall the identified gap between current and desired organizational identity described in section 3.4. Referring to Reger et al. (1994, pp. 575–6), the width of an identity gap relates to the perception of attainability (realism) and acceptance of change in organizations. Figure 4.3 puts this idea into graphic form.

When a current and a desired identity are seen as equivalent or very close to each other, the narrow identity gap is a source of cognitive inertia because a change of identity is perceived as unnecessary.[15] In contrast, an identity gap that is perceived as too wide may lead to the belief that the change is unattainable (Reger et al., 1994, p. 576). Both of these problems can be avoided in 'creative realism'. A desired identity which is likely to retain structural connectedness with current or past identities and which can create visualized (imagined) potential consequences will be within the *'change acceptance zone'*.

Interestingly, with regard to the scope of strategic change that is determined by organizational members in a creative strategy making process exaggerated expectations of radical organizational changes in a very short period of time should be re-evaluated. As Weisberg (1995, p. 71) concludes: 'creative thinking moves beyond what has been done [past experience] only slowly, and when it does, it is more as a modification of the past than rejection of it'.

However, creative cognition research provides strong support for linking the organizational past with the future in order to generate creative ideas that are realistic. Thus, it reinforces the significant value of integrating the concept of desired organizational identity into strategy making from an additional scientific perspective. This research provides two important properties that are important to achieve realistic ideas with creative potential: 'structural connectedness' and 'imaginative divergence'. A shared desired organizational identity that is realistic *and* has creative potential should be encouraged in a practical strategy making process by balancing these two properties.

4.4 A NEED FOR FACILITATORS IN STRATEGY MAKING: TASK AND ROLES

The task and potential roles of facilitators is rarely mentioned in the strategy literature (for a critique that mentions that issue, see for instance Taket and White, 2000, p. 57). Within the practical strategy making process I am developing here, the task of facilitators 'is not to prepare plans for others but to encourage and facilitate . . . [organizational members'] planning effectively for themselves' (Ackoff, 1981, p. 124). The facilitator enables access to participation during the process, pays attention to group dynamics, encourages contributions, and sometimes actively intervenes. Facilitation thus is an energetic process that involves managing interactions and relationships between people, as well as structuring tasks and contributing to the effective results of such a process (see Bostrom et al., 1993).

Eden and Ackermann (1998, p. 371) pinpoint the relationship between process and content in facilitation: 'There is an intimate relationship between process management – understanding power, politics, and personalities – and content management – capturing, structuring, and analysing.'

While the facilitator has process leadership, she/he should be neutral regarding content (Schuman, 1996, p. 70). It should also be made clear that content management does not necessarily mean that the facilitator needs to be an 'industry expert', but rather needs to see each organizational member as an 'expert' whose view is essential and relevant and who should be treated with dignity and respect (Hammond, 1998, p. 48). This does not mean that facilitators just need process abilities and do not need *any* knowledge in strategic management. Facilitators need a solid understanding of strategy in order to manage process and content effectively. This makes facilitating strategy making quite different from other limited organizational problems that can be solved in group work by facilitation (see Rughase and Schindl, 2003).

The strategy making processes proposed in this book may allow strategy making to proceed more smoothly, because they aim to avoid interpersonal conflicts by creating a consensually preferred and attainable organizational future. But on the other hand, incorporating value-laden factors such as personal aspirations, desires and feelings may increase the risk of emotional and critical tension conflicts between participants (Andrews, 1987, p. 62; Mason and Mitroff, 1981, pp. 43–52). Moreover, the formerly rationally structured and analytical process in strategy making becomes more complex and challenging as it is outlined in this book and thus should be guided by skilled facilitator(s) (see Eden and Ackermann, 1998, p. 371; Bryson, 1995, p. 217).

An understanding of the facilitators' task is crucial. As described above, the scope of strategic change is solely determined by the members, thus implying that the task of facilitators is strictly limited to encouraging and promoting organizational members' strategy making efforts effectively. This is important to note because the task of a facilitator is often used synonymously with that of a consultant (Eden and Ackermann, 1998, p. 371). In practice, consultants very often explicitly refer to their 'expert knowledge' in industries, offer 'best practice' information, or provide 'best solutions' with regard to strategy making processes, despite claiming a facilitator role.

Characteristics that make the task of facilitating effective have been described by Warihay (1992). Taket and White (2000, p. 152) present an adapted version of the different characteristics that an ideal facilitator should have (see Table 4.1).[16] Reviewing the characteristics summarized in this table, the 'enabling and encouraging' task of facilitators seems

Table 4.1   Characteristics of an effective facilitator by Taket and White

I	*Respect* A sincere belief that each member of the group possesses the skills and capacities to contribute and that the group can set its own direction and make sound decisions. Underlying this respect is the belief that knowledge gained from life and work experience is as valuable to the process as is organizational status and education.	
II	*Critical awareness* Ability to differentiate between thoughts and feelings, in self and others.	
III	*Self-disclosure* Willingness to articulate thoughts and feelings about oneself, others and what is happening, and awareness to share their feelings with one intention – to help the group progress.	
IV	*Self-confidence coupled with self-disclosure* The quality of being in touch with who you are and feeling good about it, enabling the facilitator to take the risks necessary to model openness.	
V	*Questioning rather than telling* Makes no assumptions about why group members do or do not things. Instead he/she questions. So instead of saying: 'You are avoiding conflict', he/she asks a question: 'this is the third time you switched the subject when the project funding was mentioned, what might be causing the topic jumps?'	
VI	*Observant* Able to:	

      A.   watch and interpret non-verbal communication,
      B.   note (in writing) what was said, by whom and when, especially when discussions are spirited and/or emotional,
      C.   stay attuned to proxemics (where people sit in relationship to others and how they physically posture themselves).

VII	*Direct* Stating what was seen or heard without dressing it up or watering it down. Example: 'Pat, you arrived 30 minutes after the meeting started', rather than 'some of us are arriving late'.	
VIII	*Confronting rather than confrontational* Issues raised immediately (rather than later), and in non-judgemental language (rather than evaluative language, for example 'you should have', 'why didn't you', 'I would have' and so on). The ability to bring people face to face with reality. This is needed when there is a discrepancy between:	

      A.   what a group member is saying and what he/she is doing,
      B.   what a member is saying and what he/she said earlier,
      C.   what the group agrees to (for example ground rules) and their behavior,
      D.   the process the group has agreed to follow and what they are actually doing.

particularly salient to this book. However, this task also needs to be clearly understood by the client. The client is not an organization, but a (mostly powerful) person within the organization or a small group of people with very similar interests (Ackermann et al., 2005, pp. 17–20). If the client's understanding of the facilitator's task is vastly different (for example, expecting him/her to create a particular set of strategic options), facilitators should thoughtfully reconsider their engagement (see Schwarz, 1994).

Remember that conflicts are closely connected to actual power positions within organizations. Facilitators may 'force' participants of strategy workshops to adopt 'ground rules' which generate a superficially 'open' workshop atmosphere. This can protect facilitators from being utilized by the client during the workshops in a prescriptive manner they did not intend. However, it is very unlikely that any outcomes of such workshops will subsequently be realized by participants. Therefore, a clear and shared understanding of the facilitators' task between at least the client, other major powerholder(s) and the facilitators is necessary to ensure an effective strategy making process.[17]

During strategy making, the adoption of different roles by the facilitators is required. For example, facilitators should be prepared to challenge particular views/positions (especially those held by powerful individuals or groups that seem to dominate other perspectives), maximize participation, and demonstrate solidarity with participants. But as already noted, these and other facilitator roles have not been explicitly developed in strategy literature. 'For example, differences between active/intervening and less directive approaches may be seen in terms of difference in the individual style of facilitators rather than different types of facilitating roles that may be appropriate in different parts of the . . . process' (Taket and White, 2000, p. 165).

Taket and White (2000) have explored different metaphors for different facilitating roles which have been useful for them (see Table 4.2). These guises are not sharply separable and they can be intertwined in a single intervention. Taket and White (2000, p. 165) understand the role of facilitators as 'shapeshifters' as they mix and match different guises in an unfolding process. These roles, which are in most cases based on intransparency, might be used to interrupt inappropriate actions – sometimes even in a strong authoritarian manner – or to protect the group from intended/unintended manoeuvres of participants that will change the actual and agreed focus of the process. The facilitators – by definition – have the responsibility of carefully deciding what the most suitable and proper roles, methods and approaches for particular moments in the process are.[18]

It would be too rigid, inappropriate and unhelpful to expect that certain roles of facilitators could be clearly defined for particular steps in strategy

Table 4.2   Different guises for facilitation by Taket and White

Guise	Some characteristics and devices
The anarchist (subtype – the guerrilla)	Learning to live comfortably with disorder Subversion – using opponent's arguments against them Leaderlessness
The rebel (*l'homme révolté*)	Integrity 'Solidarity' Moderation Maintenance of 'relativity'
The trickster (sometimes referred to as the clown)	Use of humour Subvert notions of savior, superhuman, etc. Subvert constancy of identity Constantly deconstructs himself/herself and his/her actions Facilitate challenging people's accepted norms Reconstituting different views of themselves Breaker of taboos Ambivalence • no culture of dependency is induced • strategic/tactical device
The innocent or naive inquirer	Asks simple, basic naive questions to uncover 'taken-for-granted' assumptions and reveal new/different perspectives Innocence may be real (for example, if an external facilitator is being used) or assumed/feigned

Source: Taket and White (2000) © 2000 John Wiley & Sons Limited. Reproduced with permission.

making for the many organizations that are seeking viable strategic reorientation. It is possible, however, to say a little more about who should do the facilitator's job in practice. Eden and Ackermann (1998, p. 381) claim that a combination of one internal and one external facilitator is particularly powerful in strategy making. In my experience, however, organizational members have difficulties distinguishing between the specific task and roles of *internal* facilitators in a strategy making process and the other tasks, roles, dependencies, or opinions they hold the rest of the time in their organization; these difficulties lead me to question their neutrality when trying to facilitate strategy content. External facilitators have much less history to bias their perception, but they are much less integrated into the organization, which significantly limits their options for helpful interventions. Mostly, external facilitators are personally present in organizations or in contact with organizational members only during scheduled workshops or meetings. This limits the opportunities, for example, to intervene when important strategic issues, which may strongly affect an ongoing strategy making process, become salient and are acted upon in the daily work of managers.

Whether an internal facilitator, external facilitator or a combination of both is used in practical strategy making, it is important that a facilitator clearly understands his or her task and roles, and can use them effectively in practice (Rughase and Schindl, 2003).

In summary, a practical strategy making process calls for the use of skilled internal and/or external facilitators. 'Challenging and evolving' a shared desired organizational identity is an especially demanding task. Facilitators need to encourage creativity, and sensitively confront the group with inconsistencies within their own mental constructs, while finding the narrow path to accepted future states. What makes this task demanding is the fact that skilled facilitators will almost inevitably challenge the desires of organizational members that are closely connected to their feelings and emotions. For these and other tasks during strategy making, facilitators need to be capable of managing content and process effectively. There has long been a call for this balance but it is difficult to achieve in practice.

NOTES

1. Although it has been argued in the Introduction that top managers have now become strategic architects, designers, and coordinators of a skilful strategy process, we will see that the use of skilled facilitators is necessary to accomplish these new tasks during a strategy making process as proposed in this book. It seems obvious that top managers as 'insiders' may encounter difficulties in identifying and challenging existing mental models within their own organization. Using facilitators, however, requires a clear understanding about their task and roles during strategy making as well as a clear understanding about the role and tasks of the top management. I will come back to this important issue in more detail in section 4.4 and Chapter 7.
2. Accordingly, Glasl and Lievegoed (1996, p. 31) distinguish between the *stabilizing* and *dynamic* tasks of top management.
3. Some strategy researchers start the strategy formulation process by defining the company's mission. But either these missions are given by the most powerful stakeholder (for example, external stakeholder or CEO) or nothing is said with respect to the actual origin of these missions (see van der Heijden, 1996, p. 26; Bea and Haas, 2001, p. 48).
4. See also Pratt and Rafaeli (1997).
5. Superficial in the way that organizational members with opposite views do not see a chance to have their views considered anymore or that they are not willing to risk an open conflict with actual 'power-holders' during the strategy process.

6. I will not exclude the possibility of a 'real' consensus, although it is not very likely to happen.
7. Appreciative inquiry was mainly introduced by Cooperrider and Srivastva in 1987, based on Cooperrider's doctoral dissertation (Cooperrider and Srivastva, 1987). For detailed historical accounts see Watkins and Mohr (2001, pp. 15–21).
8. Ackoff's view is consistent with the Japanese cyclical time concept (makimono time) of Hayashi (1990) which demonstrates that past and future simultaneously exist in the present (see Figure 3.3). Ackoff actually draws on desires that are the result of past thinking, feeling and acting *and* also anticipations of the future.
9. It should be mentioned that this view is totally consistent with Freeman's view of a mission statement as an answer to the self-reflected question 'What do we stand for?' (see Freeman, 1984, pp. 90–91).
10. For instance, organizations have a tendency only to think in terms of their own growth: be number one or two in the market; doing what we do today, only on a 20 per cent higher level; and so on (see Ackoff, 1981, p. 108; also Liebl, 2001b).
11. Due to the definition of strategy used in this book, it would be necessary to clarify that role at least for the most important social entity: the customers.
12. The term 'appreciative' stems from the idea that when something increases in value it 'appreciates'. Appreciative inquiry focuses on the ingredients of past successes ('life-giving forces') that should be increased in future organizations. The word 'inquiry' refers to the process of seeking information and understanding by asking questions (see Watkins and Mohr, 2001, p. 14).
13. See for instance Watzlawick's (1997, p. 68) example of the importance of positive human imagination (as formative vital energy) for survival in German concentration camps during World War II.
14. Ackoff even took this idea to the extreme that anyone in the organization can participate in any decision that affects them. This creates a 'democratic' hierarchy that is organized in boards, assuring circularity of power (see in detail Ackoff, 1994, p. 110).
15. Because organizational members' thinking about the organization's future identity reinforces the existing 'shared' schema or belief system (see Huff et al., 2000, p. 78).
16. For facilitators' competencies see also Nelson and McFadzean (1998, p. 80).
17. Otherwise, facilitators will have problems in challenging the positions/views of actual powerholders because they lack the mandate to do so.
18. It should be recognized that facilitators influence groups through this responsibility and cannot be seen as neutral (see Hammond, 1998, p. 22). Taket and White (2000) see facilitation as an art and craft where gut feeling, hunch and intuition come into play. For them, a search for a rationalistic account of the facilitation process seems to violate the reality of practice. Because of that, the process of critical reflection (either by an individual/facilitator and/or as a group activity with some/all of the participants) becomes very important in facilitation (see Taket and White, 2000, p. 179).

5.   How to evolve a desired and attainable market strategy: designing a strategy making process

In this chapter a general design for strategy making will be proposed which meets the requirements that have been formulated in this book to generate a desired and attainable market strategy. However, this chapter also suggests that this general design is not sufficient in practice because concrete operational steps and procedures that fit the specific organization are key to successful strategy making. Thus, this chapter briefly summarizes the detailed strategy making design that is then illustrated by means of a practical case study in Chapter 6.

5.1   FIVE CORE PROCESSES: INTEGRATING ORGANIZATIONAL IDENTITY AND ITS IMPACTS INTO STRATEGY MAKING

Strategy making has been defined as a process that is a deliberate intervention to reconfirm or redesign a strategy. However, such a deliberate intervention needs at least some degree of design that supports conversations and decisions between organizational members about important elements of a market strategy, strategic issues and questions. This allows strategy making to become a continuous learning process.

Chapter 4 suggested that the design process should be organized around an investigation of organizational identity. It has been shown that the strategy making process should

- start with the revelation of individually desired organizational identities that are then used to create a shared desired organizational identity (section 4.1, p. 54);
- challenge and evolve this shared desired organizational identity through explorations into external opportunities and internal capabilities in order to test and enhance its 'robustness' and strategic value (section 4.2, p. 67);

- ensure a realistic (attainable) desired organizational future with creative potential through assessing its 'structural connectedness' and 'imaginative divergence' (section 4.3, p. 71);
- use skilled internal and/or external facilitators who are capable of managing process and content effectively (section 4.4, p. 76).

This section begins with a first rough outline of a strategy making process design that focuses on several core processes, which can structure strategic conversations and support decisions. The aim of this process design is to craft a creative market strategy that is desired and attainable in the eyes of organizational members and that will, for that reason, work in practice.

It is important to note that I am entirely aware that there are many possible ways of reaching the same goal – as many roads lead to Rome. Therefore, I do *not* claim that there is only one single right strategy making process. Nevertheless, the strategy making process that I propose here contributes to strategy theory by proposing one of these possible ways – a way that I have seen work in practice.

The basic design of my proposed strategy making contains five core processes (see Figure 5.1). The strategy making process starts with the revelation of individually desired organizational identities that are then used to create a shared desired organizational identity. This critical step is a unique core process, and when it is accomplished it changes all the subsequent steps too, even though they are named in ways that will be familiar to those who have read other accounts of strategy making.

The second core process focuses on the creation of scenarios, covering the exploration of the organization's environment. This process is followed by the third critical step of identifying customer needs that are based on and rooted in the created scenarios. The fourth core process matches a shared desired identity with these detected critical customer needs in a competitive environment. This match challenges the robustness and strategic value of a shared desired identity and tries to evolve it. The fifth core process formulates and designs a future market strategy. It detects viable strategic opportunities which are evaluated in further detail, for instance by exploring relative strengths of the organization. This core process utilizes the close interrelation between a shared desired identity and a future market strategy to formulate concrete future competitive advantages. Evaluating and formulating a concrete future market strategy that can express a shared desired identity will simultaneously infer, modify or affirm the desired identity concept created in step one, allowing an organic evolution of both identity and market strategy. Once a strategic decision has been made, the fifth core process finally includes designing consistent strategy elements.

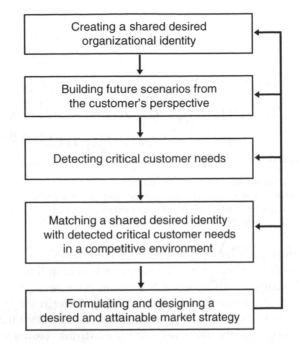

Figure 5.1   Basic design of strategy making process and its five core processes

I definitely do not mean to portray strategy making as a simple, linear process. Rather, Figure 5.1 adds some new processes to known elements in strategy making to create a workable market strategy. Feedback arrows exemplify that the process is iterative and cyclical. As Hambrick and Fredrickson (2001, p. 50) state: 'The key is not in following a sequential process, but rather in achieving a robust, reinforced consistency among the elements of strategy itself.' A robust design for the strategy making processes achieves such a consistency of strategy elements by offering systematic and logical procedures (compare Ansoff, 1988, p. 3). That is no contradiction in itself because a systematic and logical process is not automatically linear but procedurally rational for organizational members. The process of strategy making proposed in this book is designed to make sense to organizational members. The process needs to be coherent and needs to follow a series of steps where each step is understood and relates to prior and future steps (Eden and Ackermann, 1998, p. 55). The sequence of processes and number of loops may differ in practice and depend on the actual situation of the organization as well as on organizational members. Consequently, the proposed strategy making process should *not*

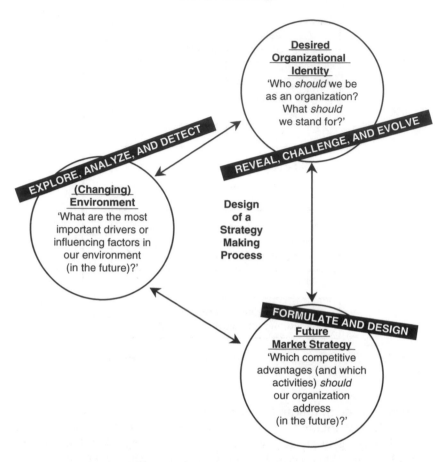

Figure 5.2   Basic design of strategy making process and its relations to elements of the framework of desired organizational identity within the strategy context

be interpreted as a simple recipe that can be applied in fixed sequential steps but as a *flexible process* that integrates necessary strategic elements and generates strategic questions in a consistent and comprehensible way.

Remembering the framework of desired organizational identity within the context of strategy (compare section 3.3), the designed strategy making process considers and treats each element of the framework in multiple and different ways to bring a viable market strategy about (see Figure 5.2).

5.2   OPERATIONAL ISSUES OF STRATEGY MAKING: ANOTHER BLIND SPOT IN STRATEGIC MANAGEMENT

When managers, strategists (or involved facilitators) become designers and coordinators of a skilful strategy making process, which involves people at many levels of an organization, they will be immediately faced with operational issues, questions and problems that lie at the very root of practical strategy making.

For example: How do we organize our strategy making process – with meetings on a frequent basis or with a special occasion (away-days/week)? Who should be involved? What strategic analysis or information will be needed at what time and how will it be practically integrated into the process? Which strategic questions should be raised, when and how? How can we assure that our efforts will lead to solid strategic decisions? How can we manage to talk freely about what we really think of our company, its resources and its future in the market rather than being politically restrained?

It is impossible to comprehend the difficulties encountered in strategy making if one ignores the reality that strategy making is actually about *operational actions* that link process and content. Strategy making consists of concrete interventions and procedures in real organizational settings, working with real organizational members. Operational issues, questions and problems are extremely important in strategic management. Problems may lie in seemingly straightforward and minor procedures that only become salient when members of the organization are faced with them in practice. For instance: How to formulate the questions to be posed in strategy making? It seems fairly simple to formulate a question for a group in a strategy making meeting if one has some idea of the kind of information that is needed. However, this does not match with my personal experiences and observations in real strategy making processes. Some questions work much better than others. Inappropriate questions can be easily misunderstood by groups, evoking information that is less valuable to the strategy making process or may even lead to no results at all. In other words: strategy making means considering very practical details in order to run effective group sessions (see for example, Hickling, 1990; Wilcox, 1994).

It becomes obvious that coping effectively with operational issues is crucial to successful strategy making in practice. However, this has been another striking blind spot in strategic management. As a matter of fact, most academic publications in the field of strategy only offer a vague and nebulous picture of strategy making processes.[1] At the same time, most practitioner publications are disconnected from theory and offer too simplistic answers to the complex process of strategy making – very often by means of recipes, checklists or step-by-step guides.

On the one hand it seems difficult and ambitious to specify a detailed design of practical strategy making processes that is also grounded in theory. On the other hand, these operational procedures and interventions are key to the creation of a strategy that is desired and attainable in the eyes of organizational members. At this point, it can be seen how closely strategy theory and practice are actually related. Whereas strategic management theory will lose relevance if it cannot contribute to operational interventions, practice requires theoretical foundation in order to understand what is the 'most skilful strategy process'. As Ackermann et al. (2005, p. 1) state with reference to Lenin: 'theory without practice is pointless, and practice without theory is mindless'.

Studying operational procedures in order to propose a detailed design led me to a research approach that was and is partly deductive (theory inspired) and partly inductive (data/experience/observation inspired). This mixed approach is fruitful in that it allows the researcher to gain creative insights from the data, experiences and observations in practical processes without neglecting or reinventing constructs and findings in management theory. Theoretical findings are being used to create operational procedures and steps, broadening their contribution into strategic management. For example, theoretical works on storytelling by Barry and Elmes (1997), Weick (1995), or Gabriel (2000) inspired me to use storytelling as a key element of practical strategy making. However, the insights gained with storytelling in practice have led to further developments in operational procedures that make them even more effective in strategy making (for instance using storytelling in a role-play recorded on video). Altogether, the approach that seems most appropriate for designing practical strategy making processes is to iteratively consider both theoretical and practical framework over time – towards a 'most skilful strategy process'.

As a strategic change facilitator, my profession allows me to constantly assess how theoretical findings can be turned into practical procedures and interventions in strategy making, gaining new experiences and observations and making further process iterations. Many parts of the process design and its operational steps and procedures proposed in Chapter 6 are the result of my experience with various practical strategy making processes at private and public organizations.

Proposing a detailed design for a strategy making process by describing it theoretically does not seem appropriate when the process was generated by such a close interrelation between theory and practice. A practical case study can give a much better impression of the whole process design by illustrating concrete steps, interventions, questions, or actions in application.

Table 5.1 Proposal for a detailed and practical design of a strategy making process

Core Processes	Parts	Steps
I. Creating a shared desired organizational identity	1. Interviews with participants 2. The first workshop	(a) Revealing individually desired organizational identities (b) Focusing on the most important (desired) attributes (c) Aggregating a shared desired organizational identity (d) Describing a shared desired identity in the form of a story
II. Building future scenarios from the customer's perspective	1. Determining the customers of a shared desired identity 2. Building future scenarios	(a) Exploring the organization's environment from the customer's perspective (b) Creating and presenting a scenario story as a 'customer' (c) Integrating results into one or more comprehensive scenario story (stories) for each customer group
III. Detecting critical customer needs		(a) Detecting critical needs of customers (b) Collecting and discussing the critical customer needs (c) Prioritizing the critical needs from the customer's perspective

Table 5.1 (*continued*)

Core Processes	Parts	Steps
IV. 'Test of robustness': matching a shared desired identity with detected critical customer needs in a competitive environment	1. Construing images of the organization and of current/potential competitors	(a) Construing an external image of the organization (b) Determining current and potential competitors (c) Construing external images and detecting influencing relative strengths of competitors
	2. Matching a shared desired identity with critical customer needs in a competitive environment	(a) Creating a strategic value matrix (b) Challenging and evolving a shared desired identity
V. Formulating and designing a desired and attainable market strategy	1. Formulating a future market strategy that expresses a shared desired identity	(a) Detecting viable strategic opportunities (b) Evaluating viable strategic opportunities (c) Formulating and determining a future market strategy
	2. Designing the substance of a desired and attainable market strategy	(a) Designing elements of a future market strategy (b) Describing a future market strategy in the form of a story

In addition, a case study describes the strategy making process in relatively high detail which makes the designed process not only more comprehensible, but also offers a deeper understanding of the purpose and intention of each particular step.

Chapter 6 therefore provides a case study based on the rough outline presented in the first section of this chapter. Keeping in mind the multidirectional interdependencies of the five core processes, Table 5.1 will be used to summarize the strategy making process described in the case study in more detail.

However, the case study and the corresponding design proposal still should be seen as a snapshot of an ongoing research process that leaves plenty of room for further development. While aware of this important reality, insights from the case study and its process design can be used to generate constructs, procedures or theoretical propositions that can serve as a basis for probing the process of strategy making in other cases. Thus, I hope this approach will contribute to the academic conversation on strategy making by providing theory-grounded concreteness that is rarely found in the literature.

NOTE

1. It should be mentioned that some strategy researchers have begun to focus on the strategy process, such as the Strategic Management Society (SMS) Interest Group on Strategy Process (for example, Chakravarthy et al., 2003). These strategy researchers have identified the most important research opportunities pointing the way towards promising new directions in research on strategy processes. However, their studies refer more to the process of research into strategy rather than focusing on practical strategy development (see N.N., 2003).

6. Designed strategy making in practice: a case study

The previous chapter proposed a first rough design of a strategy making process and called for a more detailed process design in order to cover operational actions that are key in practical strategy making. Table 5.1 has already presented the proposal of a more detailed strategy making design. The following case study will now illustrate this process design in practice, showing how it was used to craft a creative market strategy that was desired and attainable in the eyes of organizational members. Next to this illustrating purpose, it is the function of this case study to validate the feasibility of the strategy making design proposed in Chapter 5.

It should be noted that in the case study practical strategy making is understood as a *group process* being held in facilitator-guided *workshops*. Facilitation in these group workshops applied the participation principle and used widely available equipment, such as flip-charts, display walls, different paper cards (ovals, discs, and so on), colored pens, colored stickers/dots, and occasionally a video camera. As a back up, and to provide a pictorial record and reminder of the strategy making process for workshop participants, photographs were taken of the flip-charts and display walls (see Bryson, 1995, p. 95).

This particular case study refers to an important part of a private company that was, at the time, threatened by critical customer feedback as well as by other environmental (industry) developments. The name 'Retailer Services Ltd' shall be used to protect the true identity of the company that served as my research site. I have also changed the names of any other companies, products, associations or informants that appear in this study.

The description of the case study is based on my personal workshop observations (eight workshops of about eight hours each), personal records and records of a facilitator involved, reflections about observations with an involved facilitator (six meetings of about two hours each), 104 photographs of workshop flip-charts/display walls, and face-to-face interviews with workshop participants (partially tape-recorded) that were conducted before and after the workshop sessions described (about 530 minutes in total).

Obviously, a written description of this particular strategy making process can only provide a shortened portrayal of complex and dynamic workshop sessions. In addition, it would be beyond the scope of this book to include all the practical details that are in one way or another important to running effective group sessions in strategy making.

Organization of this chapter and ways to read it

Before starting with the description of the case study, I would like to comment on the organization of this chapter. Following an introduction to the company and the problems it was facing, as perceived by the company management, the case study goes through the five core processes of the strategy making design outlined in Figure 5.1. It should be made clear that the actual strategy making process did not follow such a simple and linear path. Participants went through several iterative and repeating loops within and between steps of the process. However, for the sake of clarity, the practical process will be described here in the sequence outlined in Figure 5.1. The chapter then briefly describes how the company went on to develop and to put into action their specific market strategy based on this process.

At certain points in the case study, further theoretical and practical background for the described core processes and their parts in the case study will be provided. This background reflects my research approach as described in section 5.2 and draws on relevant strategy and management literature as well as on personal practical experiences in other strategy making processes. These 'asides' help clarify important methodological and theoretical questions such as 'Why have the facilitators chosen this practical approach in particular?' or 'Which technique, theory, or thinking underlies this approach?'

This organization allows the chapter to be read in at least two ways; either skipping the background to get an uninterrupted impression of the practical case first, then reading theoretical and practical foundations and details afterwards, or reading each background note right after the corresponding part of the case study description. Whichever way is chosen depends on personal reading preferences and theoretical interest. However, both ways are viable.

6.1   COMPANY AND PROBLEM DESCRIPTION

Retailer Services Ltd was founded as a service provider and publisher for an Industry Association in the United Kingdom (UK) more than 30 years ago. The Industry Association – representing an old industry with a historic tradition – has about 5150 business members that split into roughly 1600 manufacturers, 3500 retailers, and 50 wholesale traders. Each member of the Industry Association is a mandatory member of an appropriate regional association. Regional associations are legally and organizationally independent of the national Industry Association. Nonetheless, the two are closely connected by the working principle that the Industry Association takes responsibility for national tasks, whereas regional associations take responsibility for regional tasks. Retailer Services Ltd is 100 per cent owned by the entire group of regional associations. The product range of Retailer Services Ltd includes journals, specialist literature and services for manufacturers, wholesale traders and retailers in the industry.

JOURNAL: the company's core asset

One of the largest and most important sections of Retailer Services Ltd produces a key product: an industry specialist journal named *JOURNAL*. Actually, the *JOURNAL* brand is one of the company's core assets and most people in the industry know the brand rather than the company that publishes it. It is this important section of the organization to which this case study refers. *JOURNAL* has the highest circulation of specialist journals in the industry and is the official voice of the national Industry Association. For many years, *JOURNAL* has been one of the most important sources of information in the industry.

The strategy making process began late in the year 2000. At that time, *JOURNAL* and its strategic situation can be portrayed as follows: *JOURNAL* was published twice a week in black and white with a circulation of about 8500 copies. It focused on retailers, manufacturers and their staff, as well as on anybody interested in that industry. Each member of the Industry Association got one copy of *JOURNAL* by a subscription, the cost of which was included as part of the annual membership fee. Other subscribers paid an annual subscription fee of £227. *JOURNAL* reported on topics related to three industry fields (manufacturing, wholesale, retail) with opinions, background information and analysis. It documented the speeches and contributions of politicians, association members, and academics in their field. About eight to ten out of *JOURNAL*'s 112 issues per year are published as special issues covering topics or themes of particular interest to the industry. The advertisement section mainly contained ads for new and top-selling industry products as well as job offers. The advertisement section reflected – for many readers – 'what's going on' in the industry and which products were especially promoted by manufacturers. Since the mid-1990s, *JOURNAL* had also published a free online edition.

Changes in the market challenge the current business model and threaten profits

Despite this seemingly strong market position, *JOURNAL* faced several changes in the industry that made the management of Retailer Services Ltd think about a strategic re-positioning of their company's key product. Management, editorial staff, and the advertising department were concerned about data that pointed towards a persistent short or medium-term revenue problem:[1]

- decreasing acceptance and attractiveness from/for readers (based on quantitative and qualitative customer satisfaction surveys in 2000 and 2001);
- decreasing numbers of subscriptions (down 10 per cent in 2001);
- decreasing numbers of advertisements.

Initially, the management had become aware of a decreasing acceptance and attractiveness of their publication through quantitative satisfaction surveys in 2000 and 2001 and through critical customer feedback in interviews conducted at the 2000 trade fair. In the eyes of the management, changes in reading habits and increasing quality expectations for specialist journals by customers were the main reasons for less attention to *JOURNAL*. For instance, readers expressed a wish for colored material in *JOURNAL* as well as an editorial approach that was more exciting and 'to the point'. Readers seemed to attach an old-fashioned, inflexible image to the journal that referred to the very traditional Industry Association's reputation. Because *JOURNAL* was the official voice of the Industry Association, it reported in a neutral, documentary, and balanced way about the association's activities and its members. This editorial style was negatively associated with the expression 'observations from the Royal Court' by several interviewees. A classical and restrained design seemed to support this old-fashioned and inflexible impression. As a result, readers declared that they had a need to read *JOURNAL*, but at the same time they had no real desire to do so.

Decreasing subscriptions were also due to concentration in the industry. The management of Retailer Services Ltd did not expect a change in this trend, and they also knew that the number of advertisements were decreasing because manufacturers were cutting marketing expenses and/or redirecting marketing efforts to retailers directly (for example promotion tours for special products). To make matters worse, concentration processes also resulted in a smaller number of manufacturers and wholesale traders who were potential customers for advertisements.

Altogether, these developments challenged the current business model of *JOURNAL* and created a significant threat to profits (rate of return was minus 2 per cent in 2001) that had already forced management to reduce costs. Management therefore decided to engage external facilitators to guide them through a strategy making process that should result in a strategic re-positioning and a re-launch of *JOURNAL* within 12 months. From management's perspective, the strategy should give an answer to how *JOURNAL* could deal with these significant external threats in a way that would enable the company to establish sustainable competitive advantages, ensuring a growth-oriented future.

The creation of a strategy team and the set-up of the strategy process
A strategy team was created by management to tackle redirection. The literature often suggests that a strategy team consists of key organization decision makers, important stakeholders and other key persons who are directly affected by the strategy making process, not exceeding 12 participants (Eden and Ackermann, 1998, pp. 56–60; Bryson, 1995, pp. 51–2). In this particular case, the strategy team consisted of nine organizational members: the responsible manager, four members of the editorial staff (including the chief editor), two members of the advertising department, one member of the layout department, and one member of the sales (subscription) department. This strategy team represented a mix of key decision makers, informal opinion-shapers and at least one member of each directly affected department within *JOURNAL*, but did not include any outsiders.

Very often, strategy making workshops are organized as a sequence of one- or two-day workshops that take place periodically, for instance every week (Eden and Ackermann, 1998, pp. 382–3). The *JOURNAL* strategy team decided to have one-day strategy workshops on a fortnightly basis due to the high operational workload of the editors. These one-day workshops were externally held at conference hotels in order to prevent any interruption by other organizational members and to prevent team members from returning to their offices during coffee breaks. Workshops were guided by either one or two facilitators.

6.2   FIRST CORE PROCESS: CREATING A SHARED DESIRED ORGANIZATIONAL IDENTITY

The first core process was designed to reveal individually desired organizational identities that could be used to create a shared desired identity afterwards. As emphasized in previous discussion, this core process reflects the requirement for a new starting point in strategy making. However, a workshop does not seem to be an appropriate beginning for such a new starting point, because organizational members may not be willing to immediately

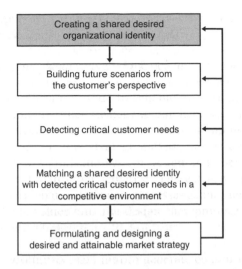

open up and to express their (value-laden) views about what the organization 'should do' and what they personally 'want to do'.[2] Instead workshop participants need to get an impression, understanding and feeling for the reason that strategy making is being initiated. They also need to meet the facilitators and learn about their task and mandate. I have therefore found that it helps facilitators to talk individually with those who will be involved in strategy making upfront, before any group sessions.

Therefore, the first core process carried out in Retailer Services Ltd consisted of two parts. The first was a series of confidential interviews with participants, and the second was an initial workshop where a first shared desired identity was created.

6.2.1 Interviews with Each Member of the *JOURNAL* Strategy Team

The two external facilitators conducted face-to-face interviews with each participant in a company conference room about two weeks prior to the first workshop. Facilitators had not met any of the participants before, with the exception of the responsible manager. Each interview took from 45 to 75 minutes.

At the beginning of each interview, facilitators explained their intention, what they hoped to achieve, and noted that the interview would be kept confidential. However, although quite a considerable time was spent on this introductory conversation, participants just did not seem to loosen up. Without exception all participants were observably nervous and stressed. Some participants were even trembling when they sat down in the conference room. The underlying reasons became clear to facilitators during the first half of each interview, when they asked the participants about their expectations for the upcoming process. In spite of the emphasis on finding a new direction for *JOURNAL*, participants expected a 'masked' cost-cutting process, at the end of which many organizational members would be laid off, according to decisions based on the expertise and advice of the consultants. In short: participants feared losing their jobs. This fear was primarily created through their mental images about consultants. According to participants, their impressions about consultants were heavily influenced by the media and stories they had heard about other consultant-guided restructuring or re-engineering processes in the industry. Consequently, external consultants were mainly seen not only as 'cost-cutters' but as 'job-killers'.

Once the problem on hand had been articulated by participants, the facilitators were able to react in a responsible and considerate manner, albeit it was nearly impossible to neutralize all such fears in the course of a short interview. Nevertheless, facilitators had the opportunity to explain their mandate and tasks once again, and to explicate their view of the goal of the upcoming strategy making process, as given by management. Participants began to relax, but were still extremely skeptical. These straightforward explanations turned out to be a good entry point for providing evidence that facilitators would take the opinions and desires of participants seriously.

Each individual was asked: 'What do *you* personally think *JOURNAL* should stand for? Which *JOURNAL* would be very attractive to *you*?' They were also asked to tell stories that might elaborate their answers, or make them more understandable to an outsider.

Despite the somewhat strained interview situation, all participants were willing and able to elaborate an individually desired organizational identity. For example, several participants wanted their section of the company to stand for *independent and substantial (reliable) journalism*. Independent journalism in their view would require considerable investigation and would treat involved association members in a fair way, due to the fact that members can be informants or advertising customers, as well as readers, all at the same time.

This positively desired future identity attribute was structurally connected with 'lived experiences'. Participants told stories in which they reported that they had no time for extensive investigation due to the enormous daily operational workload required to publish *JOURNAL* twice a week. From the participants' point of view, the operational workload limited the quality of their own editorial content to neutral and documentary articles, which they themselves even found to be unattractive to read. In addition, participants told stories in which they feared negative consequences initiated by influential association members who were adversely affected by their articles. This possibility meant they were even more likely to write in a balanced and reliable, but unexciting way. As one participant expressed it carefully:

> The reliability of the information is extremely important – the content must be correct. To tell you the truth, I highly value this principle. I used to work for a large daily newspaper. I was employed there for many years and if I didn't know it beforehand, I certainly learned it then; the reliability of the information must be in no doubt . . . especially as we are the official journal of the association, and as such scrutinized from particularly many angles.

A journal that could stand for *practical support in the daily work of retailers* is another example of an individually desired identity attribute that was articulated by many participants. This particular desired identity attribute was structurally connected to past identities of the *JOURNAL*. Participants told stories about the high relevance of *JOURNAL* in former years and how in previous decades it had influenced the industry and its daily work. Faced with the decreasing importance of *JOURNAL* in the industry today, participants desired to re-establish its impact on the daily work of association members, mainly retailers.

These are only two examples of attributes of individually desired organizational identities which were expressed by participants. Many others were articulated, almost all of them were structurally connected with past experiences.

No less important than individually desired organizational identities are barriers and problems that participants anticipate in realizing their articulated future states. The most significant barrier against achieving a desired future identity that was stated by participants was a deeply-seated lack of team-spirit among different departments. As one participant said:

> Team spirit – a theme that pursues us to the present day. The lack of a proper team-spirit! We have managed to improve it, but it's still a problem. And mainly due to the fact that the editorial staff has different ideas to those of the layout department . . .

The last sentence from this participant quite clearly points towards one of the reasons for the absence of teamwork. According to this and other participants in the upcoming workshop, the lack of team-spirit was caused by the limited and self-centered thinking of each department, as well as by missing communication between departments. An editor explained this barrier in more detail:

> There is a rift between departments – this rift characterizes the layout department on the one hand and the editorial staff on the other. Many of the layout colleagues have worked in their department for a long time – in the case of one

individual over 20 years . . . whereas the editorial staff changes far more frequently. [*short pause*] And one can observe a certain tendency in the layout
department: this is new, we don't want this! Things used to be better in the old
days and anyway, at present everything is going downhill. A factual barrier
against development and change exists.

Whereas a large part of the editorial staff perceived the layout department
as a change-blocker, the initial interviews indicated that participants from
the layout department felt excluded from decisions. Information and design
improvement efforts for *JOURNAL* were often made by the editorial staff.
Layout sensed that their abilities were not sufficiently appreciated by the
editorial staff. More broadly, it became obvious to the facilitators that there
were hidden and subliminal internal conflicts between team members and
departments which had built up over many years and which had not been
sufficiently dealt with in the past. In effect, participants thought that this
would be the highest barrier to overcome in order to achieve their individually desired organizational future.

The likelihood that the Industry Association would not agree to a strategic re-positioning that included *independent and substantial (reliable) journalism* was another barrier that was seen by several participants. In
particular, the issue of independence was a major issue. Participants felt sure
that the Industry Association would never give up its (indirect and direct)
influence on *JOURNAL*'s editorial staff and content. 'Lived experiences'
with the Industry Association thus made participants quite skeptical about
the attainability of their individually desired organizationally identity.

Finally, participants perceived their own workload as a major problem.
They felt that they were already under enormous pressure and felt burdened by numerous perceived obligations both to management and the
Industry Association. Participants anticipated problems with any additional workload that would be implemented through a strategic change
process. Towards the end of the interview, most of the participants
expressed in a restrained way that a strategic re-positioning of *JOURNAL*
was indeed necessary from their point of view. However, they made this
statement with reservations about barriers and problems that were perceived as quite substantial and very difficult to cope with, and which needed
to be eliminated first. In addition, participants mentioned that two timid
attempts at strategic change processes had already failed.

At the end of each interview, the two facilitators summarized what they
had heard and explained what the next steps would be in the course of the
workshops. Facilitators reassured participants that the information they
gathered from the interview would be kept confidential. Nearly all were surprised about the investigative kind of questions they were asked during the
interview. Even more important, the facilitators immediately began to see

that in most cases participants began to further reflect on the questions they had been asked and their desired organizational identities on their own. As one participant thoughtfully said towards the end of the interview:

> You'll have to excuse me, as there are certain questions that . . . that one has to think about. To be honest, I don't have an answer for everything, yes . . . well . . . then . . . [*short pause*] I really should think about things a bit more, about the questions you have asked me.

In summary, a commitment to a first workshop was increased in the preliminary interviews, but only to a certain degree. Due to their 'lived experiences', participants were still extremely doubtful about the whole strategy making process. Besides that, the fear of losing their jobs was still present during the whole interview with most participants. This fear became visible through repeated statements about their enormous workload and statements about the importance of their own role. Asked for final comments at the end of the interview, one participant said:

> Yes, well, one thing that is particularly important to me is . . . er . . . maybe it's superfluous for me to say it, but considering the present situation . . . er . . . becomes . . . er . . . one just can't tell anymore . . . basically what I want to say is that we all have a lot of work to do . . . which I don't find to be a bad thing. The way I see it, we've more or less reached the limit.

Obviously, it would be presumptuous to state that trust in facilitators was built up during this first interview. Another indicator that the facilitators were not trusted was shown by the fact that only three of nine participants agreed to a tape-recorded interview. On the other hand, despite personal fears, doubts or even distrust, participants also stated that they enjoyed having an opportunity to talk about their own imagination and desires with regard to the organization's future and most expressed interest in the upcoming strategy making process. By allowing stories to be told which were relevant for participants and which had originated in their own experience, the interviews attained the character of natural, intensive conversations. For most participants, this had been a new experience of involvement. Especially the fact that facilitators were really listening to what they had to say, making notes and asking questions for their own understanding, positively astonished most participants.

6.2.2 Theoretical and Practical Background for Confidential Interviews

I would like to stop at this point in the case study description to provide some theoretical and practical background with regard to interviews as a start of the strategy making process. It might be asked here: Why did facilitators start that way? Why did they ask for individually desired organizational identities (visions) and also their anticipated barriers? Which interview technique did they use to elicit this information?

From my perspective, these initial interviews with participants are an especially important first step for facilitators in enroling participants in effective strategy making efforts. Because facilitators need to create at least some commitment and trust in participants to a strategy making process and a first workshop, Ackermann et al. (2005, pp. 30–49) also propose confidential interviews to begin with. Facilitators are often confronted with workshop participants they have never seen or met before. Because the new starting point in strategy making (creating a shared desired organizational identity) is decisive for the following steps, facilitators need to gain more assurance and confidence with participants before getting insights into their thinking and feeling about the organization.

The other important purpose of such an interview, of course, is informational. The facilitators want participants to reflect individually on the organizational identity they most desire. Revealing the desired state during a (confidential) interview gives facilitators the opportunity to provide sufficient time and individual attention to the participant and his/her desired state in order to understand his/her mental model(s) in detail. Moreover, it gives facilitators the opportunity to assess the structural connectedness of the desired state to current and/or past identities which is another important purpose of the interview. This is possible because each participant – as shown from the results of the interviews in the case study – not only describes and expresses what he/she thinks the organization 'should do' and what he/she 'wants it to do', but also relates it to 'what is' today and to experiences of the past. Participants thus elaborate on *why* it should be as he/she proposes. During a workshop such an in-depth revelation would be inappropriate, mainly because of sensitively perceived personal matters that should be kept confidential, but also because of norms that restrict the amount of time that most (though not all) people are willing to spend on their own views in a group setting.

Another purpose of such an interview is to discover and discuss a participant's anticipated barriers and problems in achieving his/her desired organizational identity. These barriers expose the assumptions and concerns of implementability by a participant. They also give indications for potential and existing conflicts with certain persons/groups or about particular issues within the organization. This information is crucial for facilitation and needs special attention in order to understand certain group or individual behavior during the workshops. If necessary, this information can also be considered for procedural consequences in strategy making (as will be seen with the first workshop in the case study). And finally, the opportunity for a participant to express and discuss his/her desired organizational identity increases the level of salience and enhances further reflexivity about the construct after the interview. This phenomenon could be clearly observed in the case study. Hopefully the interview also creates interest in and commitment to the process. Finally, individual interviews give facilitators more confidence in participants, their views, opinions and desires, as well as in the 'seriousness' of the desired organizational identities they espouse at this point.

In summary, the purposes of the interviews are:

- to create some commitment and trust among participants to a first workshop;
- to reveal individually desired organizational identities and especially their structural connectedness to current and/or past identities;
- to reveal anticipated barriers against achieving the individually desired organizational identity;
- to make the concept of individually desired organizational identity salient in order to further enhance participants' reflexivity;
- to provide a foundation of personal knowledge for relationships to develop between participants and the facilitators.

The ensuing benefit is that both participants and facilitators will certainly have fewer problems in taking the steps in strategy making that are processed in later workshops.

So far, only the purposes of the interviews have been discussed. But how did facilitators get the information which has been described in the case study?

At this point, the 'narrative character' of identity provides a useful link. Section 2.1 showed that organizational identity is the product of a sense-making process which is created only in interactions with others. Because of the narrative character of identity concepts that are negotiated or communicated in interactions, Boje (1991, p. 106) states: 'In organizations, story-telling is the preferred sense-making currency of human relationships among internal and external stakeholders.' Stories are not only an important vehicle for sensemaking in general (see Gabriel, 2000, Chapter 2; Weick, 1995, pp. 127–31), but also for remembering and knowledge representation (Bartlett, 1932; Rappaport, 1993). As Schank and Abelson (1995) claim, all of the important knowledge that people acquire and retain in memory is based on stories constructed around past experiences. Consequently, stories 'provide the basis for (a) comprehending new experiences; (b) making judgements and decisions about the persons, objects, and events to which the stories refer; and (c) developing general attitudes and beliefs concerning these referents' (Adaval and Wyer, 1998, p. 208). The observation about attitudes and beliefs connects stories with the participant and his/her self-concept. Which stories are remembered is influenced by, but also influences, the self-concept of the storyteller (see Conway, 1996).[3]

Thus, a critical element in acquiring an in-depth understanding of participants' desired organizational identity concepts are the stories members tell.[4] In this form, participants can easily retrieve and elaborate knowledge associated with their desired organizational identity (see Kato and Markus, 1993; Whitty, 2002). This effect is further bolstered by the fact that desired states are a motivated domain. Because the motivational domain of desired organizational identity is also connected with the emotions and feelings of the organizational member, key 'events' that the individual associates with the desired state are likely to be remembered in more detail and clarity than others – resulting in vivid memories (see Conway, 1996). Accordingly, stories are readily available in the memory and easily accessed because of their high relevance and concern (see Kato and Markus, 1993, p. 80). In addition, the construct of desired organizational identity also has its roots in 'lived experiences' (for example identity-threatening interactions with customers or stakeholders) and past identities (remember the 'practical support in the daily work of retailers' which *JOURNAL* used to have). Consequently, stories may not only reveal desired organizational identities, but also contextual information that will assess their structural connectedness in the past. Thinking in terms of the large literature I have read in strategic management, it is interesting that this connection to the past has rarely been given much attention (for an exception, see Fletcher and Huff, 1990).

The interview method used in the *JOURNAL* case study enabled facilitators to collect important stories and to gain insights into the 'world' of organizational members that is constructed around desired organizational states. The core of this method, which is called 'storylistening'®[5] (see Liebl and Rughase, 2002; Rughase, 2002), is an open and non-standardized interview (compare with Patton, 2002) based on an *exploring* principle that is typical of ethnographic or anthropologic methods (Rughase, 2001; see also Hammersley and Atkinson, 1995; Czarniawska, 1998). Metaphorically, each organizational member is treated like a member of an unknown exotic tribe whose unfamiliar symbols, myths, individual interpretation schemes and 'worldviews' are explored by the facilitators (Liebl and Rughase, 2002, p. 37). The aim of the facilitators is to learn from and to understand an organizational member without applying personal ('cultural') measures. As Spradley (1979, p. 3) expresses it: 'Rather than *studying people*, ethnography means *learning from people*.'

Thus, using storylistening®, facilitators need to be thoughtfully inquisitive during the interview in order to discover the unexpected (Reason and Rowan, 1990). They should be well trained and experienced in passive interview techniques, such as supportive or describing questions ('Did I understand you right . . .?' or 'Could you describe to me what you mean by . . .?'), as the interviewee should ideally talk for over 95 per cent of the time. Even though the storylistening® method sounds easy to carry out there are many 'dangers' reported from using similar methods in the field (for details see Gabriel, 2000, pp. 151–2; Czarniawska, 1998, pp. 35–53). However, when heedfully practiced the method ensures that participants can tell their stories about desired organizational identity, relate knowledge and describe anticipated barriers in their own words and without restraint.

Experience has shown that the learning and understanding effect increases for facilitators when initial questions about desired organizational identity are asked as broadly as possible; for example 'What do you personally think your company should stand for in the future?' or 'How would you position this company if you would become the "peak of the hierarchy" today, having no restrictions?' (Liebl and Rughase, 2002, p. 37). On condition that participants agree, all interviews should preferably be tape-recorded, so the facilitators can focus on the participant and the development of the narrative instead of making notes. However, that might not be easy as the case study discussed in this book shows.

It was a deliberate decision to hold the interviews in a neutral environment in the company (conference room). This setting is part of the everyday environment of organizational members and does not give the impression that the facilitators hold a dominant or dependent position (which could be inferred if interviewing in temporarily free offices of the top management, in rooms on the same floor, or even in interviewees' offices). Participants are very sensitive to these unspoken signals. Although not mentioned in the *JOURNAL* case study, all participants were formally invited to take part in the interview by the facilitators (Ackermann et al., 2005, p. 42). The invitation informed participants about the purpose of the interview and who would take part. Most important, it indicated that this interview was solely at the request of facilitators and was not a demand made by top management.

The storylistening® core of the interview is embedded into beginning and finishing elements that are extremely important for the creation of a trustful and relaxed interview environment. At the beginning of the interview, the participant will usually loosen up and get into a better mood when facilitators explicitly and satisfactorily explain their task, what they hope to achieve, what they are doing with the tape-recording after the interview, how the participant's contribution will be used to support the strategy making process, and that his/her information will be kept confidential (compare Ackermann et al., 2005, p. 43).

Closing the interview, facilitators provide a 'value-added' summary of what they heard. This gives facilitators the opportunity of an immediate and direct feedback from the participant about what they have captured. Facilitators also explain the next steps in strategy making. It is noted that the first workshop will provide an opportunity for participants to further reflect on their desired organizational identity. At the end of the interview, facilitators also reassure the participant that the interview and any information that has been gained from it will be kept confidential and will not be used against the informant at any time.

Trust and the commitment of participants to a first workshop can be created – at least to some extent – by the way the interview is held and by the way facilitators present themselves and their task. The face-to-face interview offers an opportunity to demonstrate that the expertise, knowledge and desires of participants are not only relevant but necessary to the strategy making process (due to the principle of participation). In accordance with the exploratory principle of the interview, facilitators take the (in most cases real) role of innocent or naive inquirers, listening to the stories that members have to tell.

Finally I would like to mention one last practical detail with regard to initial interviews: documentation. There are several ways for facilitators to document the interview data gathered. The interviews help facilitators to gain insights and confidence in the cognitive structures of participants, making the facilitators more sensitive to certain situations raised and information received during the workshop, as well as suggesting the adaptation or addition of steps in strategy making. Because of that, the interviews do not necessarily have to be documented in a scientific manner.[6] Since this information is solely for the facilitators and their workshop preparation, it might be sufficient for them to make notes about important information from each participant while analysing the tape-recording.

In the case study, the facilitators created a mental map for each interview. When participants did not agree with tape-recording, they created the map during the interviews, but maps were created from the tape-recording in other interviews. As promised by the facilitators, the tape-recordings were deleted immediately after this analysis. In any case, the notes ensure the vivid recollection of important characteristics (stories) of the desired states, their structural connectedness and the anticipated barriers.

Let us return to the case study and see how the *JOURNAL* strategy team coped with the first strategy making workshop.

6.2.3 The First Workshop of the *JOURNAL* Strategy Team

About two weeks after the initial interviews, the first full-day strategy work-shop was held.

(a) Introduction and a first group forming exercise with the *JOURNAL* strategy team
Due to the information retrieved from the confidential interviews (espec-ially about hidden and subliminal internal conflicts between team members and departments, as well as expectations about a 'job-killer project'), the facilitators decided to begin with an exercise that would support initial group formation and clarify the reasons for the strategy making process. After a short personal introduction of the facilitators and the participants, the facilitators invited the participants to answer the following two ques-tions:

> Which reasons do *I* see for a strategic re-positioning of *JOURNAL*?
> Which problems do *I* want to solve with a strategic re-positioning of *JOURNAL*?

Because of the individual character of the questions, participants answered these questions on their own and wrote their answers down on paper cards. Guided by the facilitators, the group then discussed every card of each par-ticipant in the group before clustering them on a display wall. The group came up with a total of 38 cards. The three main reason/problem clusters that were found have already been discussed in this section: they include a decrease of acceptance and attractiveness from/for readers, a decrease in numbers of subscriptions, and a decrease in numbers of advertisements.

It became clear to participants through the first workshop exercise that their views had more in common than they initially expected. As partici-pants discussed their individual perceptions, they were surprised that many of their views were similar or even identical. Despite all the existing conflicts, individuals found out that they had something in common – they shared the same view of the company's strategic problems. In addition, they were somehow shocked by the number of things pressing on their organ-ization – issues no one in the organization had summed up before. As a direct result, participants became aware of the urgency and importance of the strategy making process. Although many participants may have retained their view that the whole strategic re-positioning process might be a masked 'job-killer project', it became obvious that there were urgent and indisputable reasons for the strategic relaunch of *JOURNAL*.

At this stage, the facilitators were able to explain their task and mandate once again and also stress the importance of the participation principle in strategy making. Facilitators then discussed with the whole group the customer-oriented strategy concept and their views on how competitive advantages are methodologically created in the market. Once conceptual questions had been addressed, the facilitators explicated their proposal of how such a strategy making process could be designed and which important *waypoints* should be crossed during this process (for example, detecting critical customer needs). Probably for the first time, participants sensed that their strategic problems might indeed be solvable. They seemed to agree that the proposed initial steps of the process were procedurally rational and agreed to proceed in that direction. More important, a first small portion of trust was created, once participants had a first experience that such a guided strategy making process would include their participation.

(b) Creating a shared desired identity of *JOURNAL*

After participants agreed to the next steps in strategy making, the facilitators immediately started with the next task. They asked each participant to work out their personally desired *external organizational image* (representing their individually desired organizational identity) by asking the question: 'What *should* a current or potential customer tell about your *JOURNAL* that would make you think: "Yes, I *love* to work here – that's what I am really *proud* of!"?' Participants worked very seriously on this question on their own and exceeded by far the given timeline of 15 minutes.

Then, each participant presented his/her desired identity to the group while the facilitators noted attributes of each participant's image on a flip-chart, cross-checking with the participant that his/her desired future image has been captured. After their presentations, participants were surprised yet again. All individually desired identities of participants were quite close to each other. For example, the presentation of one participant covered the following desired attributes from the customer's perspective:

- I am informed in a reliable and faultless way.
- *JOURNAL* has a 'human touch'.
- I am informed about topical issues.
- *JOURNAL* is of high technical standard.
- I get orientation because controversial issues are picked up and are commented on.
- *JOURNAL* really mirrors my daily work in a correct fashion.
- *JOURNAL* stands up for us in the industry.

The facilitators also found many connections between desired identities expressed during this session and what they had heard during the interviews. Without the interviews, they would not have been able to judge the 'seriousness' of the individually desired identities, or the connection of these statements to underlying structural issues.

Due to the fact that most presented identity constructs involved numerous desired attributes, the facilitators then asked participants to choose their two most important attributes in order to clarify priorities. This did not take a long time, but facilitated several later steps in the process.

After that, the facilitators invited participants to create a shared desired identity. They explained that this does not mean creating a compromise where all participants have to give up some parts of their individually desired identities. Rather, the creation of a shared desired identity tries to aggregate multiple identities that retain individual views while building links between them – it is about building a meta-identity. Therefore, facilitators asked the participants to begin with the most important attributes they had identified in their individual views and look for similarities and/or connections between their desired future states. Very quickly, participants were able to find some core attributes, representing central issues that could be found in most – if not all – individually desired identities. The passionate dialogue that then followed about the attributes also helped participants to understand each other's concepts in more depth. These intense discussions quickly created a first picture of a shared desired identity (SDI). Finally, the group came up with three core attributes as the 'heart' of their SDI:

- *JOURNAL* should provide relevant industry information faster than others (quick and topical);
- *JOURNAL* should offer practical support in daily work (implementability, orientation);
- *JOURNAL* should have a 'human touch', should be friendly and should care for the individual reader (direct contact, standing up for association members, listening to readers).

In the eyes of the participants this SDI's heart (represented by the three core attributes) was highly consistent; the core attributes were neither mutually excluding nor conflicting. Remarkably, each of the three aggregated core attributes was derived from individually desired attributes which were held by at least six of the nine workshop participants.

It should be noted, however, that these core attributes are only the strongest and most valued parts of the aggregated SDI. In the next workshop activity, participants discussed all remaining desired attributes, trying to find additional similarities and relate them to the SDI's core values, or other attributes. By increasing the level of abstraction, analysing the similarities and relationships between desired attributes, participants were quickly able to get closer to an expanded but still consensual SDI.

To accomplish the task of broadening the SDI, it was helpful for participants to draw circles with 'onion-layers' on a pinboard. They then wrote desired attributes on paper cards and positioned and repositioned these attributes on the board as their discussion progressed, placing concepts at varying distances from the 'heart' to the periphery of their SDI. The final aggregated SDI retained all individually desired attributes (see Figure 6.1). The number in parentheses represents how often this attribute was mentioned by participants. For instance, the desired attributes 'reliable and faultless information' and 'high technical standard' had been previously mentioned by participants as a crucial part of an individually desired identity. But discussions revealed that some participants did not see these two issues as core attributes that belong to the 'heart' of their SDI. Many participants viewed the attribute 'reliable and faultless information' as very close to the 'heart' of their SDI, with multiple links to other important

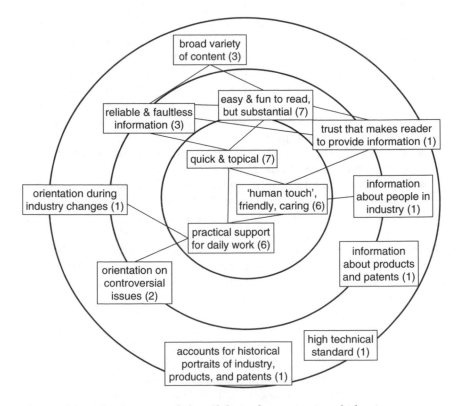

Figure 6.1 The aggregated shared desired organizational identity of JOURNAL

attributes. But the attribute 'high technical standard' was seen by more individuals as a peripheral and unrelated part of their SDI.

It is worth noting that the aggregation of individually desired identities into an SDI did not create conflict within the group at any time. The workshop task was completed when the participants were able to reach consensus on an aggregated SDI. Immediately after this conclusion, participants sensed a first gestalt of a revised *JOURNAL* coming into being, and with that, they could begin to envision their part in the organization's future.

This first gestalt became much more visible and gripping for participants when facilitators ask each participant to portray the SDI to the group in the form of a story. In their stories, participants creatively combined the three desired core attributes of their SDI and related them to other desired attributes which were also of importance to them. They used many fictitious (but realistic) examples to illustrate their pictures. For instance, one participant described a new and innovative combination of *JOURNAL* and its online edition in order to illustrate what it meant for her to be faster and more topical with industry information. Another participant exemplified several ways, such as podium discussions or new interactive sections in *JOURNAL*, to get into direct contact with readers. The SDI as a whole, its core attributes as well as its peripheral attributes, became extremely meaningful to participants through these discussions. This meaningfulness also made the SDI concrete and practicable to participants. Unfortunately, the facilitators did not have a video camera available to them during this workshop in order to record the participants' stories about their SDI.

As the stories were presented in succession, the mood of the group changed notably. Participants began to relax, use a friendly kind of humor, made more statements of agreement and began to laugh at moments where presenters described important desired future states that were obviously incoherent with the actually perceived organizational reality. For example, they laughed about visions of *JOURNAL* offering practical support and having an impact on daily work because they uniformly agreed that this was not so at the moment. Through such reactions many participants realized that, in fact, they were not on their own regarding their views and desires. Comments like 'If it will be like that, *that* would be something!' demonstrated support for a new organizational future that was also desired by other participants.

I could see the storytelling exercise bringing the group closer together. Participants began to open up and indicate a willingness to engage in the strategy making process. In addition, participants continued to experience first-hand that facilitators were guiding the workshop in a way that assured their participation. The fact that their voices were not only being heard but were also regarded as important, created another piece of trust in the strategy making process and in the facilitators. At the end of the day, participants wished to proceed with the strategy making process because they felt that there might be a lot more in their SDI than they had discovered yet. However, the first workshop ended at this point.

6.2.4   Theoretical and Practical Background for the First Workshop

I would like to interrupt the description of the case study at this point again and provide further background with regard to the second part of the first core process.

From my perspective, the first core workshop process marks an important moment in the proposed strategy making process design. It is essential that participants gain confidence that strategy workshops are not a waste of time, that their active participation is really wanted, that their opinions and expertise are crucial for success, and that they can trust facilitators to be neutral on statements about content. The first workshop is also designed to allow facilitators to clarify many topics and provide answers to questions from participants.

The case study demonstrates how facilitators accomplished these important tasks. The first workshop ensured that participants came to a shared understanding about the goal of the workshops, it was a group forming exercise that created the common view that there was a real need for such a strategy making process (compare stages of group development outlined by Tuckman, 1965). Because the goal of the strategy process became more visible, and shared among the participants, the facilitators were able to explain their proposal on how to achieve that goal with participants during the set of workshops that had been scheduled – providing understandable *waypoints* for the strategy making process. Furthermore, the facilitators were able to explain their task and mandate during this proposed process.

A key point is that the facilitators invited participants to share their expertise, knowledge and desires with the group, because this is the group that is not only designated to take part in the workshop but will also share its outcomes. Altogether, these first activities were very important for participants to gain confidence in such a strategy making process. After clarifying these preliminary topics and basic questions, it is much easier to go on with the actual strategy making process.

The workshop process – as it has been described in the case study – can be divided into four steps: (a) revealing individually desired identities, (b) focusing on the most important attributes, (c) aggregating an SDI, and (d) describing an SDI in the form of a story.

(a) Revealing individually desired organizational identities

The interviews asked for individually desired organizational identities for the purpose of initiating a personal relationship with each workshop participant and giving facilitators more confidence in and insights into participants and their organization. The revelation of individually desired organizational identities within the group was used for the critical next step: to create an agreed shared desired identity (SDI). As has been shown in section 4.1, the creation of an SDI is vital for the strategy making process for several reasons, including consensus, commitment, and implementability. However, in the case study reported here, the facilitators asked participants to work out their personally desired *external organizational image* from the customer's view. But why did they ask participants to work out an external organizational image instead of a desired organizational identity?

To reveal individually desired organizational identities in a workshop, the close interrelationship between organizational identity and image can be very useful. Remember that image as often defined in the literature is the external perception of the self; the self considered from the position of the other (section 2.2). However, identity and image cannot really be separated from each other because the perceptions of others influence identity and vice versa. This close interrelationship is the reason why desired self-states are often alternatively projected in the form of a 'desired future image' as a precursor to a desired future identity (Gioia et al., 2000, p. 68). Gioia et al. (2000, p. 67) define 'desired future image' on the collective (organization) level as a 'visionary perception the organization would like external others and internal members to have of the organization sometime in the future'. But desired future images can also be defined at the individual level, and this is an excellent place to begin when there is no real confidence in a group that they share views and opinions.

A desired future image makes explicit which principal role and function the organization should have with regard to external others. Ideally, this external image fully matches the desired self-perception of internal members. By this, a desired future image matches what individual organizational members 'want to do' and what they feel the organization 'should stand for' – it is the mirror of their desired organizational identity (Hatch and Schultz, 2002, pp. 994–6). From a market-centric perspective, customers are the most important stakeholders of the organization's purpose. Thus, a desired future image in this context is a visionary perception that the participants would like customers to have of the organization sometime in the future.

From my experience, working out a desired future image from the customer's perspective is much easier for participants than working out a desired organizational identity from their own perspective. First, it seems easier for participants to put their own deep-seated values and desires into the 'voice' of a third party, in this case customers. In earlier strategy processes with other companies, it has been my experience that participants seemed to be afraid to give colleagues and the management insight into their personal feelings and thinking.

A second reason for beginning with statements about the view that is desired from customers is that the customer's view can produce a more concrete picture of a desired state, while the more complex organizational identity desired by individuals themselves tends to remain a somewhat fuzzy concept. This fuzziness is related to the fact that there is no distinction between attributes that apply to an organization in the market (for example, we should stand for avant-garde designed furniture with good quality and fair prices) and attributes that are related to *internal* characteristics of an organization (for example, we should pay true respect to each other in the company). Both types of attributes are important, but at different stages of a strategy making process.

Desired attributes for internal characteristics become important once a market strategy has been determined; that is the time to draw attention to the question: How do we organize new tasks, roles and processes within our company in order to bring this market strategy alive? However, at this early stage of the strategy making process, the desired attributes that apply to the market are of special importance. Not only is the creation of a desired future image much easier for workshop participants to work on, it is a logical place to start in finding a workable market strategy.

After this future image is revealed through group process, the facilitators are able to briefly re-evaluate individually promoted identities. Because facilitators have already had a chance to extensively discuss individually desired organizational identities and their structural connectedness with participants during the interview, facilitators are able to identify significant differences between statements they have heard privately and espoused identities in the workshop. There were no significant differences in the case study just described. But if differences had appeared, the facilitators would have had the chance to think about other appropriate methods and approaches that are not confrontational (because the interviews were confidential) in order to reveal the authentic desired organizational identities from participants and/or to reveal the cause of differences or suppressed opinions.

(b) Focusing on the most important (desired) attributes
When organizational members describe individually desired organizational identities, they often use *attributes* in order to express the characteristics of the desired state – like people do when describing another person's identity (Schlenker, 1985, p. 68). Because an individually desired organizational

identity can easily be retrieved and elaborated by participants, these identity constructs can involve numerous desired attributes. As just described in the study, participants can often generate quite long lists of desired characteristics. It is helpful, therefore, for participants to prioritize attributes of their own desired images, and in so doing focus their own desired organizational identities.

Prioritization helps participants decide where attributes lie in the range from the periphery to the core of their desired organizational identity. Which attributes would participants certainly not give up? This step re-evaluates a desired future identity, consolidating it and making it more compelling.

(c) Aggregating a shared desired organizational identity

The third step in the workshop design is about the creation of a shared desired organizational identity (SDI). On the one hand, previous reports in the literature have shown that different desired organizational identities held by organizational members can lead to tensions and conflict (reviewed in section 4.1.1). On the other hand, the existence of multiple individual desired identities is important as a resource, and if not addressed can become an impediment to developing new market strategy. Therefore, an SDI most expresses the broadest possible range of individual views. The step that tries to gather and bundle multiple individually desired identities is very important.

The approach used in the case study is based on Ackoff's consensual approach which focuses on ultimate values and desires (rather than on the means to achieve them) in order to generate agreement. Ackoff's approach is a remarkable way for dealing with multiple identities in an effective way. In accordance with Ackoff, for example, Barney et al. (1998, pp. 156–61) conclude that finding a higher level of meaning or abstraction can be important in managing multiple identities. Creating or discovering a meta-identity that accommodates each of the individual desired identities is most appropriate when each of the identities is important and requires respect, and there is also considerable need for consensus (Pratt and Foreman, 2000a, p. 33; Barney et al., 1998, p. 160). It has been argued already that the creation of an SDI in strategy making needs consensus as well as respect for each individual desired identity.

The creation of a meta-identity in the workshop described above aggregated multiple identities (and their ultimate attributes) by attempting to retain all of the individual identity statements while building links between them. Linking different identities requires efforts to identify relationships and synergies between or among the identities. Thus, aggregation is an inquiry process with the benefit that no individual has to give up his/her personal desired organizational identity. Instead, the individual perspective becomes a valid and taken-for-granted part of a meta-identity (Senge, 1990, p. 228). Most important, by seeking synergy, aggregation decreases the potential of conflicting demands or expectations (Pratt and Foreman, 2000a, p. 32).

It is important to note that creating an SDI through aggregation is distinct from creating an SDI through integration. Integration attempts to fuse multiple identities into a separate new whole. The purest form of integration is a synthesis, whereby a single new identity emerges out of all existing desired identities. Although there is some support for synthesis in the strategy or organization theory literature (see Eden and Ackermann, 1998; Mason and Mitroff, 1981; Ford and Ford, 1994), multiple identity integration may prove to be a tough, extremely conflictual, impractical, and even impossible task during strategy making (see Pratt and Foreman, 2000a, p. 31; Mason and Mitroff, 1981, p. 108). In addition, integration is always at risk of overrating short-term manageability and undervaluing the strong impact of identity constructs. It should not be expected that organizational members will give up or change their desired organizational identities into a distinct new one within a single workshop session.

Therefore, the creation of an SDI (respectively meta-identity) through aggregation seems most appropriate for this step in a practical strategy making workshop. But this step does not mean that integration cannot and should not be reached at all over time in an organization. As Pratt and Foreman (2000a, p. 34) propose:[7]

> Meta-identities may even be a less painful means for organizations to pursue a synergistic response than integration. Rather than forcing a fusion of their multiple identities or engaging in the conflict inherent to a dialectical process of synthesis, the organization may attempt to define itself at a higher level of abstraction. Moreover, meta-identities can 'open the door' to a fully integrated response; if the organization's members strongly buy into this new meta-identity and begin to fuse their multiple identities with the subordinate identity, then the organizational identity may eventually evolve into something akin to a fully integrated identity.

The practical process I describe in this book, as illustrated in the case study, requires that facilitators help and support participants in identifying relationships and synergies between or among their individually desired organizational identities in order to create an aggregation. Remember Tannenbaum and Hanna (1985) and their view that identity attributes range from the periphery to the core of an organization. This view leads to the idea that organizational identity can also be envisioned as an onion with several layers. This image can help to aggregate the SDI, as has been done with the case study.

The case study has also shown that comparing the most important attributes of all desired identities to each other, discussing similarities, differences and possible relationships between them is a good beginning for the ongoing strategy making process. Because participants share at least some sources and the same social environment within their organization, it is very likely that there are some important attributes of different desired identities which have high similarity or are complementary to each other. Attributes that are already (to some extent) collectively 'shared' provide a wellspring for aggregation.

By considering closely related and synergetic attributes through aggregation, it is not surprising that some can become core attributes. Core attributes can be found in many, perhaps even all, individually desired identities – these are the attributes that become an important part of the SDI's 'heart'. During the workshop inquiry process, found core attributes can get more meaningful and relationships with other (core and peripheral) attributes can be defined. This process offers a new and creative way of seeing the attributes differently: it can combine existing core and peripheral attributes for a consistent identity, and is creative in the sense that previously unrecognized relationships can be brought into being (Ward et al., 1997, pp. 6–10). By this, new knowledge can be created which is based on existing (motivational) knowledge structures (Eden and Ackermann, 1998, p. 69).

The SDI created in the workshop consists of connected core attributes that are surrounded by and linked to peripheral attributes. The SDI is a concrete answer to the question: 'What *should* we stand for in the eyes of our (current or potential) customers?' Each participant is likely to agree on it because his/her individually desired organizational identity is a respected, valid and taken-for-granted part of this 'larger' SDI.

(d)   Describing a shared desired identity in the form of a story
During the fourth step of the first workshop, each participant portrayed the agreed SDI to the group in the form of a story. But what makes storytelling so important at this point?

These participants' stories of the SDI have at least three benefits:

1.   each participant reflects on and enhances his/her comprehension about the SDI;
2.   descriptions elicit 'imaginative divergence' of the SDI;
3.   descriptions create an emotional, meaningful and more dense portrait of the desired organizational future.

Because all participants were asked to portray the SDI by means of a story, each participant is encouraged to reflect on a desired identity in more depth. The narrativist stance can encourage and help participants to explore the SDI in more meaningful ways (Barry and Elmes, 1997, p. 431; also Czarniawska, 1997). As seen in the case study, participants tried to incorporate persuasive existing and not-yet existing but plausible examples into their stories in order to illustrate concrete core attributes and peripheral attributes of the identity.

Facilitators can encourage participants to look explicitly for successful past experiences within their own organization that may have taken on a different meaning through this perspective and can now be related to core attributes and other attributes in retrospection.[8] This may not only suggest structural connectedness but can also make the SDI more gripping, 'visible' and memorable to other participants as it connects to their 'lived experiences'. Although the facilitators in the case study did encourage participants to look for successful past experiences within their own organization, in this situation participants did not use any stories from the past to elaborate on their newly defined SDI. While it remains unclear why the past was not linked to the future in this case, the academic literature shows that stories are an effective aid for understanding because they are able to integrate already known aspects of a desired identity as well as conjectural ones (Weick, 1995, p. 129). It becomes evident that stories enhance reflexivity and comprehension of participants about their SDI.

Descriptions in the form of stories and the search for concrete illustrations of the SDI have a further very important effect: these activities show how the SDI promotes imaginative divergence among participants. Does the SDI encourage new explorations and discoveries, or does it seem to be headed toward a dead end? Remember that imaginative divergence is an important indicator of whether an identity (individual or collective) has creative potential (see section 4.3). On the one hand, a definition of identity should have an enlightening, dynamic quality that inspires participants' imaginations to spread out, make new connections, and raise new possibilities for the means of reaching desired ends (compare Finke, 1995). On the other hand, the desired identity should not trigger the imagination to such an extent that practitioners and academic observers lose connection with reality. Empirical evidence shows that description in the form of a story can help prevent such a disconnection (see Pavlik, 1997). However, as seen with the case study we are following in this chapter, the enlightening and dynamic quality of an SDI – enhanced through stories (see Shaw, 2000, pp. 183–4) – can be very positive because participants become intrigued by their desired identity and want to explore where it might lead.

Finally, by their nature narratives support participants' comprehension, positive emotions and imagination. Stories do not represent pure facts about an SDI, but they can enhance, enrich, and infuse a statement of identity with meaning. Stories are emotionally and symbolically charged by the participants (Gabriel, 2000, p. 135). In part this is because stories and their constructions tend to be strongly guided by the need for self-worth. Participants seek value in and justification of their activity by constructing positive stories that depict their intentions as being right and good – thus consistent with their values (Baumeister and Newman, 1994, pp. 683–6). And stories provide a comprehensive but dense portrait of the SDI. That is what makes Barry and Elmes (1997, p. 430) positive about stories in strategy making in general: 'narrativity emphasizes the simultaneous presence of multiple, interlinked realities, and is thus well positioned for capturing the diversity and complexity present in strategic discourse'.

The participants' stories – representing a comprehensive, dense, emotional, memorable, and 'visible' portrait of the consensual SDI that was developed during the first workshop – were an excellent closure for the first core process. If possible, facilitators should make use of a video camera and tape each story presentation. The presentation will thus gain a much higher importance for participants. It is also helpful if these essential and illustrative stories do not get lost; they can be very beneficial in later core processes.

In summary, the first core process and its creation of a shared desired identity (SDI) is crucial for strategy making. However, remember that this approach is a proposal and remains only one possible way to achieve an SDI in practice. One might argue that this approach focuses too much attention on single attributes of a desired identity that are somehow connected but cannot, as such, represent or sufficiently describe an organization's future identity. From a theoretical standpoint I agree. But to create an SDI one can really work with, desired attributes turned out to be valuable 'transitional objects' which allow a group to discuss in depth and to properly 'use' a shared desired identity of an organization in practical processes (see for example the fourth core process discussed below). Combined with storytelling, putting this step first, in the form just described, seems to provide an emotional and meaningful portrait to organizational members. Interestingly, there has been a recent discussion of approaches to creating an organizational identity through object-mediated processes (building 3D objects, for example, with LEGO bricks) which generate descriptions that are also grounded in rich, narrative-based and metaphoric imagery (see Roos et al., 2004; David and Roos, 2004; Doyle and Sims, 2002). Although I have, as yet, no practical experiences with these approaches, I am certain that they also help improve practical procedures in strategy making, and can be used to bring a substantial and workable description of an SDI about in the future.

Let us return to the case study and its second core process to see in which way the *JOURNAL* strategy team explored and analysed *JOURNAL*'s environment.

6.3   SECOND CORE PROCESS: BUILDING FUTURE SCENARIOS FROM THE CUSTOMER'S PERSPECTIVE

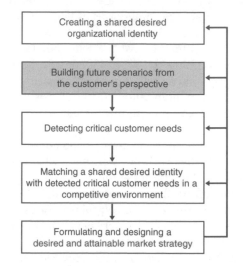

Having agreed to a shared desired identity (SDI) at a high level of abstraction in step one, this next core process in strategy making explored the underlying assumptions and perceptions about the environment of *JOURNAL*.

This core process consisted of two parts: first, the group determined which customers are targeted by *JOURNAL*'s shared desired identity. Then the group explored the organization's environment from the perspective of these customers by building comprehensive future scenarios.

6.3.1   Determining Customers of *JOURNAL*'s Shared Desired Identity

Following the initial workshop, participants expected that their shared desired identity (SDI) would be worked out in further detail. They did not think about questioning the strategic robustness or value of their SDI, and when facilitators proposed to do so first, an extensive discussion about the nature and utility of a customer-oriented market strategy concept began among participants.

However, after these strategy reflections, participants finally agreed that it *could* be useful to explore the organization's environment in order to analyse the strategic value and robustness of their SDI. But before participants were able to explore the organization's environment from the customer's perspective, they needed to determine the customers of their SDI first. When participants were asked about these customers by the facilitators ('Who would your customers be if *JOURNAL*'s shared desired identity were already in place?') in a plenary session, they easily determined two already existing customer groups: retailers and manufacturers.

From their perspective, the most important customer group was the group of retailers. More than 50 per cent of *JOURNAL*'s readers were retailers, 20 per cent were manufacturers and the others split down into diverse small industry groups. In addition, manufacturers played a major role as customers in the advertising business of *JOURNAL*. Despite this, participants gave much more importance to their readers and especially to retailers because the attractiveness of *JOURNAL* in the eyes of the readers determined the net paid circulation, which in turn influenced advertising rates.

6.3.2 Building Future Scenarios for Retailers and Manufacturers

Once these customer groups had been determined, workshop participants explored the organization's environment from each group's perspective.[9]

Facilitators created three small working groups (three members each) and asked them two linked questions: 'To which *changes* will your customer be exposed in the future and which *trends or factors* are driving these changes? What kind of *consequences or problems* may customers feel or experience due to these changes in the future?' During explorations, participants in the working groups had few problems in pinpointing the changes and corresponding trends to which their customers would be exposed in the near future. But participants had far greater difficulties finding consequences of or problems for their customers that could result from those changes. A change of perspective (putting themselves into the customer's position) offered substantial help to participants, but very often they fell back into their familiar organization's perspective. Therefore, facilitators actively supported the participants by constantly reminding them to keep the customer's perspective, which they then managed to do, most of the time. Despite these difficulties, participants gained new insights through the change of perspective, and subsequently understood much more about their customers than they had anticipated.

Other difficulties arose when facilitators asked participants (still working in small groups) to transfer their observations into a scenario story that was told from a customer's perspective. Even though participants had substantial knowledge about industry changes, trends and their customers, for all three working groups it was obviously problematic to produce a coherent and especially a practical scenario story as a 'customer' to round off their more analytical descriptions of the environment. Nevertheless, the somehow 'bumpy' presentations of the self-created customer stories increased the emotional feeling for the customer's situation.

Participants had by now intensively occupied themselves in small working groups with the world of retailers and manufacturers for quite some time, and had experienced difficulties as well as new insights in taking on this perspective. However, the integration of the groups' results went much more smoothly. For both retailers and manufacturers, the results of the three small working groups were highly correspondent and sometimes complementary to each other. Only very few seeming contradictions in trends and environmental changes appeared in the different groups' accounts. But even these were integrated into a single comprehensive scenario story after brief group discussion. The fairly smooth creation of a single scenario story for each customer group was also possible due to the fact that participants stuck fairly closely to the present customer's situation, rather than reaching further into the customer's future.

The summarized and condensed stories can be found in Box 6.1

BOX 6.1   A COMPREHENSIVE SCENARIO STORY: THE WORLD OF RETAILERS

How a retailer* experiences changes and trends in the industry:

'Foremost, I am experiencing a rapid concentration process in our industry's retailer business. Because of that, I need to specialize my business more and more, and I need to find new niches in the market in order to survive independently as a small retailer. As a large retailer who is in branch operation, I am under enormous pressure to grow – just like the medium-sized retailers are. The crowding-out competition constantly forces me to come up with innovations, new ideas and other solutions in marketing and sales. As I see it, the price-competition will also become much tougher in our industry. Because of price-competition, contracting purchases will increasingly demand me to drive a hard bargain with manufacturers. Actually, I am not prepared for that. Moreover, I need to optimize my workflows in order to cut costs when exposed to such a cutthroat competition. And finally, a bad macroeconomic situation will even worsen the whole scenario.

Despite the fact that the number of end-consumers in our particular industry is decreasing (so do sales), I need to increase my sales. This brings up the important question of the shop's location: expensive inner-city locations boost sales, but these locations increase fixed costs which are increasingly hard to meet anymore. Where should I go with my shop? Decreasing sales in our industry are also the reason why I need to have additional fast-selling and profitable products from other industries. I don't like to do that, but I am forced to do so. There should be a promotion for our industry and its products. What can I do for that?

But there are other problems as well. Our industry products have become common goods. That makes me ask myself how I can create new attractors for end-consumers to make them come to *my* shop? Because our products have become common goods, new distribution channels are appearing (such as e-business). I am losing more and more business to those new competitors. There are many substituting products in the market as well. I should enter strategic alliances within or outside of my industry to promote my products better. I really need a proper definition of how I can reach the end-consumer. For instance, I still don't know how I should use the internet.

Due to the individualization of end-consumers, their expectations get more differentiated. I need to be technologically equipped in order to fulfill their raising expectations (for example, intranet or internet). But new technologies force me to make large investments and to learn continuously. As a small retailer, I have no funds for trainings or seminars which can keep me up-to-date with these developments. As a large retailer, services for end-consumers become more important. That means qualifying my employees from time to time which again is costly. Furthermore, I have increasing difficulties in finding qualified employees, even for union wage rates. In addition, end-consumers constantly change their buying behavior. And how should I deal with a higher mobility of my customers?

In general, I am faced with new ways of sales promotion. To a greater extent, I have to deal with abstract marketing concepts and target groups. This requires new thinking for me, different calculations and sometimes new personnel. But I also need time to learn more about new products. Finally, I can't cope with the increasing number of new laws and regulations in our industry anymore. I have neither the time nor the ambition to become an expert in this particular field. Thus, I have a growing need for information and consulting.'

Note: *Workshop participants created a single scenario story which applies to all retailers of their customer base. However, when further differentiation of retailers was necessary (for example, different sizes of retailers – small, medium, large), the participants explicitly mentioned it in the story.

BOX 6.2 A COMPREHENSIVE SCENARIO STORY: THE WORLD OF MANUFACTURERS

How a manufacturer* experiences changes and trends in the industry:

'I am experiencing an extreme concentration process in our industry, which means for us, first of all, a need to lower costs (for example through merging departments such as sales and marketing) and to find new businesses in order to survive the crowding-out competition. The number of medium-sized manufacturers in our industry is decreasing, smaller ones are creating cooperatives. The range of products in our industry is much too high (originated from the need to create more sales) which in fact means that we have to survive with high-volume premium products. Standard medium-volume products can't make it through anymore. But high-volume premium products are becoming more expensive. The old principles to create a high-volume premium product don't work anymore. Because of that, we look for new markets and new distribution channels (direct sales, discounter chains, and so on). Since many inventors in our industry are independent, I also use the opportunity to trade patents of new products. This patent trade is becoming more important in our industry and is now being done between the professional patent trader and the independent inventor at a very early stage of a product development. The net value added shifts into this direction. Now, independent inventors become competitors. The selection of good patents becomes more and more a key factor in our business and marketing becomes a hot topic for us as well.

At the same time, we not only try to sell patents, but to advance into other product categories as well. Very often, we lack know-how in that field. As a small manufacturer in particular – one has to deal with many partners to get it done. That makes me search for a service provider who manages that for me. As a medium-sized manufacturer, we try to specialize ourselves in selected new product categories.

The dependency from big customers also increases in our business (from 10 per cent to 90 per cent of the sales). I get under pressure and have to accept additional conditions and higher discounts. Actually, the business conditions are already dictated to me.

Due to globalization, I experience a shift and a new creation of manufacturing sides in other countries (development of new markets with high risk potential). But what is becoming really threatening is an ever increasing price-competition. I also see a technological revolution in our industry that has taken on unexpected dimensions – especially through the internet. Actually, these developments demand a new type of manufacturer (fast, flexible, networking . . .). In addition, the old sales structures are breaking down (retailers) and new business lines are being created (such as patent trade). Profit is more important than ever because it is threatened from all sides, such as costs, advertising, fees, and so on. That is why combined costing also doesn't work anymore in manufacturing. Manufacturers like me create profit centers and stop subsidies.

Concerning end-consumers, I am finally confronted with changing buying behavior. In our industry, we are faced with a decreasing number of end-consumers. This leads me to think about new ways in which to make our existing products more attractive to a new customer base through innovative improvements.'

Note: 'Workshop participants created a single scenario story which applies to all manufacturers of their customer base. However, when further differentiation of manufacturers was necessary (for example, different sizes of manufacturers – small, medium, large), the participants explicitly mentioned it in the story.

(retailers) and Box 6.2 (manufacturers). For workshop participants, both scenario stories (from the customer's perspective) consolidated insights into the world of their customers and expressed important trends and issues to which these customers are exposed. To assist the reader, figures 6.2 and 6.3 show relationship diagrams of these future scenarios from the customer's perspective (similar to those presented by van der Heijden, 1996, pp. 190–94). Each of the figures offers a quick overview of the elements and their corresponding relations that were discovered and integrated into the scenario stories developed by workshop participants. Relationships between elements can be drawn in more detail from the scenario stories available in boxes 6.1 and 6.2.

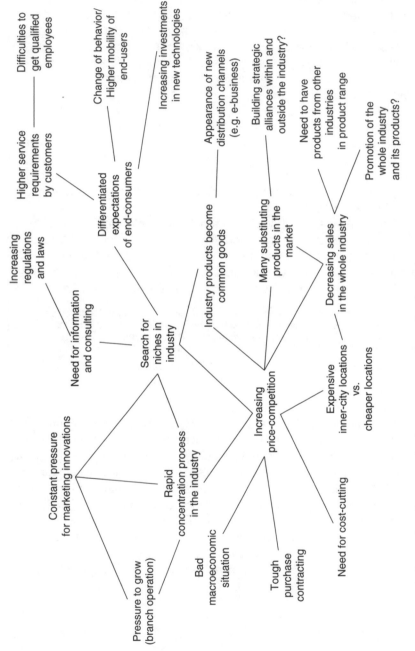

Figure 6.2   Relationship diagram of a future scenario from the retailer's perspective

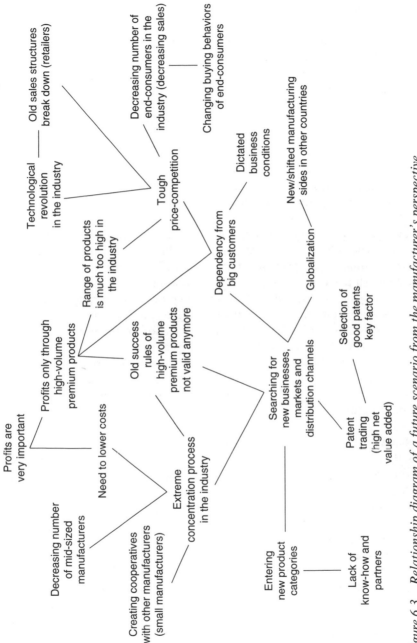

Profits are
very important

Profits only through
high-volume
premium products

Technological
revolution
in the industry

Old sales structures
break down (retailers)

Decreasing number of
end-consumers in the
industry (decreasing sales)

Changing buying behaviors
of end-consumers

Range of products
is much too high in
the industry

Tough
price-competition

Dictated
business
conditions

New/shifted manufacturing
sides in other countries

Decreasing number
of mid-sized
manufacturers

Need to lower costs

Old success
rules of
high-volume
premium products
not valid anymore

Dependency from
big customers

Globalization

Selection of
good patents
key factor

Creating cooperatives
with other manufacturers
(small manufacturers)

Extreme
concentration process
in the industry

Searching for
new businesses,
markets and
distribution channels

Patent
trading
(high net
value added)

Entering
new product
categories

Lack of
know-how and
partners

Figure 6.3   Relationship diagram of a future scenario from the manufacturer's perspective

127

6.3.3   Theoretical and Practical Background for Building Future Scenarios

At the end of this second core process I would like to stop the description of the case study once more in order to provide further background from the academic literature.

As seen in the case study, the second core process revealed the participants' assumptions and perceptions about their organization's environment, key players and future trends and issues that also implicitly influenced the shared desired identity (SDI) created in the first core process. In this next step, participants have to test the feasibility and plausibility of these assumptions and perceptions. The process created, in addition, new knowledge about *JOURNAL*'s environment and provided a new perspective on the organization's key customers.

The case description also shows that even at this relatively early stage, participants were very convinced about their SDI and took strong emotional ownership of it. This strong ownership is in accordance with the empirical findings of Pratt and Dutton (2000), who record similar instances of ownership. I am convinced that this 'bonding' is critical to further steps in the design of a practical strategy making process. Too often, strategy has become a rote procedure, following the recipe laid down in previous years. Organization members feel very little connection to the product of these exercises, with the result that strategy from year to year remains remarkably the same, even though the organization's environment can be rapidly changing (see Hamel, 1996). This book suggests an alternative to this unfortunate reality by helping organizational members make an emotional connection to strategy.

In the case study, participants were highly motivated to deal with identity-related issues, and later steps in strategy making, since the SDI consisted of their own aggregated desired organizational identities. Then, when participants realized during discussion in the second workshop that further analytical steps might actually question the strategic value and robustness of their SDI, they became highly involved in the analytical process.

Analysing the organization's environment appears well understood in strategic management and is the subject of a lot of research and practitioner writing. However, most strategy publications remain rather vague about how environmental analysis can actually be done in practice and, because of that, the literature also ignores the practical aspects of the way in which the link between the content of environmental analysis and the strategy process can be made. I would like to provide some further background that makes obvious why the facilitators have deliberately chosen the approach and corresponding interventions just described. Let us, therefore, focus on the two parts of this second core process as they have been high-lighted by the case study.

First part: determining the customers of a shared desired identity

As already outlined in section 3.1, a market strategy is logically based on an essential fit between an organization's capabilities and its environmental opportunities. Thus, the exploration of the organization's environment is a crucial task in strategy making. The management literature constantly underlines the importance of customers and their preferences to strategy making (for example, Magretta, 2002). However, when it comes to an analysis of the organization's environment, almost all books in strategic management offer only analytical tools and checklists for global societal, political-legal, or technological trends and issues (an early influential example can be found in Farmer and Richman, 1965), business industry and competitors (here the critical influence is Porter, 1980 and 1985), or business industry dynamics (where D'Aveni, 1994, has been particularly influential for textbook writers). Because focusing on abstract trends and issues or existing business industries and competitors is disconnected from the actuality of specific customers of specific companies, these approaches cannot explore, why, and especially how, customers' priorities and values may shift or change in the future.

But these changes (value migration) among customers are the most rele-vant environmental factors for an organization as they can make current business designs irrelevant and wipe out the current purpose of an organ-ization (Slywotzky, 1996). It has been shown that strategy is a customer-oriented concept; competitive advantages can only be achieved in a market. As described in section 3.1, only customers buy the products and services of the organization. As a consequence, an in-depth understanding of those parts of the customer's world that affect the business of an organization and guide the customer's behavior seems clearly to be called for. *Why* do cus-tomers buy the products and services of an organization? *Why* do customers *not* buy particular products and services? To which environmental contexts are *customers* exposed that currently or potentially affect the business of the organization now and in the future? These questions reveal that customers, their worldviews, and their contexts are the true center of interest in the environment for strategy making (Johnston and Bate, 2003, p. 154).[10]

But this customer focus in environmental analysis leads to another important question that must precede those just asked: '*Who* are the present or potential customers of the organization?' For that reason, the first part of this core process determined these customers.

It is particularly crucial to identify the customers of a future (desired) organization because customer groups can change, or additional customer groups can come into play with the SDI. For instance, a catering company that currently runs kitchens in business corporations to serve lunch to employees, might develop an SDI that also targets private customers who are living near their current business clients. For strategy making, the caterer would need to consider current and potential customers in the segment of business corporations (who need lunch service for their employees), but would also need to consider the new segment of potential private customers.

However, it is important that this step of environmental analysis is not being used by participants urgently to pursue new customer groups, but rather to consider those customers who have already been presumed by the participants during the creation of an SDI. In the case study, this issue did not occur at all – participants kept considering their existing customer groups, because these groups were also part of the SDI.

Second part: building future scenarios

The second step is to analyze the organization's environment from the customer's perspective. As already noted, customers, their worldviews and their contexts are the center of interest in an organization's environment for strategy making. But more macro sociocultural, technological, and other industry trends are also of importance for strategy making. How did the facilitators integrate these two levels of analysis?

Every organizational member constantly receives information coming from the organization's environment – for instance through interaction with stakeholders, customers, market researchers, suppliers and the media. This information is the foundation for numerous assumptions (often not recognized) that organizational members make about their organization's environment and its social entities.[11] By exploring environmental opportunities (and threats), strategy making also tries to capture environmental dynamics and changes – its trends and issues. Which means that not only members' assumptions about current entities and contexts (for example, our competitors face problems in profitability from lowering prices), but also assumptions about related future trends and issues are of special importance (for example, because of price competition some of our competitors will merge in the next few years).

Liebl (2004, p. 57) suggests that organizations are confronted with two major categories of trends in their environment: industry trends and sociocultural trends. However, an important question arises at this point: How do these trends potentially affect the business of the organization now and in the future? In accordance with Liebl, my view is that assumptions about trends and issues in the organization's environment are not important in themselves. The *implications* of trends and issues and their according importance can only be meaningfully interpreted and assessed by considering (changing) worldviews of current and potential customers (see Liebl, 2002b and 2001c).

The distinction between customers' worldviews industry trends and socio-cultural trends is important because it helps to clarify the interrelations and forces between them in order to make sense of *possible* implications for an organization's outcome or, respectively, for customers (see Figure 6.4). Analysing these interrelations and forces presents typical problems in environmental analysis. For instance, organizational members very often make premature conclusions about customers by unconsciously merging industry trends and the world of the customer: they assume 'everybody in the industry does it that way, customers obviously want it like that' (Liebl, 2001c, p. 26). It is the challenge of the second core process in strategy making to circumvent this kind of assumption.

In the workshop, the analysis of the organization's environment was deliberately designed in three steps: (a) exploring the organization's

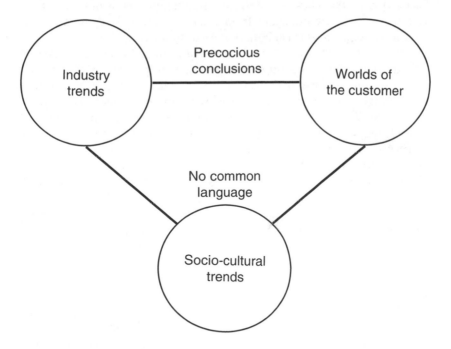

Source: Liebl (2004), © 2004. Reprinted by permission of Academy of Marketing Science, Miami, USA.

Figure 6.4   Industry and socio-cultural trends in the worlds of the customer and common problems in trend monitoring and analysis

environment from the customer's perspective, (b) creating and presenting a scenario story as a 'customer', and (c) integrating results into one or more comprehensive scenario story for each customer group.

(a)   Exploring the organization's environment from the customer's perspective   One effective way of analyzing trends and issues is through the technique of scenario building. The scenario technique tries to gather insights in the environment by identifying specific entities, their contexts, drivers, and forces affecting them, thus perhaps revealing existing structures and possible patterns of change (see van der Heijden, 1996, pp. 183–224; Eden and Ackermann, 1998, pp. 138–57; Postma and Liebl, 2005). Notably, scenarios are based on participants' assumptions and are not predictions or forecasts. As Ackoff states: 'Assumptions are about possibilities; predictions and forecasts about probabilities' (Ackoff, 1997, pp. 23–4). Thus, the focus on scenarios, drivers and contexts helps participants generally explore and evaluate *possible* outcomes for the organization (Liebl, 2001c, p. 25). This is critical: the focus on the strategy making process is not on working with the most likely outcomes from today's strategy, but finding a new market strategy that is feasible, and more desirable.

Scenarios thus offer a potential *change of perspective*. In the workshop, facilitators increased this opportunity by asking participants to develop scenarios from the customer's perspective. The customer's perspective helps participants recall and re-evaluate driving trends and consequent implications that might otherwise have been suppressed (Anderson and Pichert, 1978). It may ease assessment and translation of socio-cultural and industry trends if they are discussed from the perspective of the customer, and focus attention on creating possible, meaningful implications for them.

Therefore, facilitators asked participants in the case study to develop a scenario for each customer group that was targeted by their SDI. Facilitators asked: 'To which *changes* will your customer be exposed in the future and which *trends or factors* are driving these changes? What kind of *consequences or problems* may customers feel or experience due to these changes in the future?'

As already described, participants did not reach out into the customer's future to a great extent. From my experience, this seems more the standard than the exception. Participants tend to stay quite close to the present situation of customers and link it with more or less observable and growing trends and issues in the environment. However, the future focus remains the goal.

(b)   Creating and presenting a scenario story as a 'customer'   In the second step, the small working groups created a scenario story for each customer group. Because dealing with the future means dealing with uncertainty,

participants may have conflicting assumptions about future developments or events that cannot be brought together in a plausible way. If so, (an) alternative scenario(s) should be developed. However, as seen, the case study did not bring out any alternative scenarios that required this further step.

In the case study, one member of each working group presented the results to the whole group as if he/she were a customer. Storytelling was a particularly appropriate instrument to fuse different elements of a scenario into a coherent gestalt – a whole rather than a collection of unrelated parts. In fact, scenarios are stories: narratives that link historical and present information and interpretations with assumptions about events and developments taking place in the future. Plausibility is established when scenarios are presented in a seamless way, firmly anchored in the past, with the future emerging from the past and the present (van der Heijden, 1996, p. 213).

Presenting the results of this part of the workshop in the form of a story, as a customer, is actually a role play that underscores the consequent change of perspective that is desired in the strategy making process I designed. I have found it to be powerful in practice. Taking on the role of a customer who tells a story about his/her changing situation and concrete future consequences or problems for him/her, creates an emotional, meaningful and dense portrait of the customer's situation. Even though the customer stories in the case study were not presented perfectly (for example, presenters frequently jumped out of the role) they were still able to create an emotional and meaningful portrait.

(c)   Integrating results into one or more comprehensive scenario story (stories) for each customer group   The third step covered the integration of all the scenario stories of the different groups. As described, this process went quite smoothly in the case study. However, mutually excluding assumptions and trends are an opportunity for participants to think about the development of alternative scenarios. It should be noted that van der Heijden (1996, p. 187) points out that trying to develop more than four scenarios has proven to be organizationally impractical. The *JOURNAL* strategy team concluded this step with only one scenario story for each customer group. While they documented these stories in a written text, creating maps (like figures 6.2 and 6.3) is another valuable tool that can make knowledge explicit in practice (Huff and Jenkins, 2002).

With regard to the scenario technique as such, I am aware that there are quite a number of approaches that have been developed to analyse a future environment. It would be beyond this book to describe and evaluate each of these approaches. However, drawing from my practical experiences in strategy making, scenario building has been proven a very effective way to analyse the future environment – it is especially attractive for organizational members from a learning perspective. The narrative and visual character of the scenario building described above links content and process in strategy making in an exemplary way because plausible relations and connections between environmental entities and their drivers (content) can easily be cognitively translated into necessary strategic consequences and actions (process) by organizational members. In practice, properly linking content to process is very important for enhancing successful strategy making (Rughase, 2002), but this is not easy to do.

The exploratory and analytical second core process, as discussed up to this point, is actually the start of questioning and challenging a created SDI. As participants evolve their SDI during this and the following core processes they ask: 'Is this who we want to be?' and 'Is this who we actually can be?' These questions capture the important features of an SDI as a negotiated, interactive, reflexive strategic intent that, at its essence, amounts to strategy making in progress.

Let us return to the case study and see how the *JOURNAL* strategy team went on with their findings about the world of the customers based on the respective scenarios for manufactures and retailers.

6.4   THIRD CORE PROCESS: DETECTING CRITICAL CUSTOMER NEEDS

The third core process covered the detection of critical customer needs based on the created scenarios.

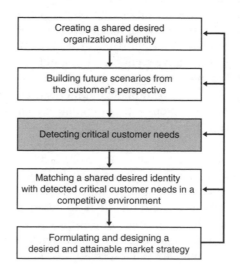

6.4.1 Detecting Critical Customer Needs for Retailers and Manufacturers

Immediately after a comprehensive scenario story for each customer group had been created by participants, the facilitators guided participants through the related detection of critical customer needs. Participants were asked 'As a customer in the dramatic scenario which had been described, what would be helpful?' Participants were asked to write down detected critical customer needs as a completion of the sentence 'It would really help me, if . . .'

Once again participants worked in small groups and were soon involved in lively discussions. However, after overcoming the initial problem of keeping the customer's perspective, each group struggled with two further problems in detecting customer needs. First, participants focused on what customers had already articulated they wanted or they began speculating about what customers might want instead of focusing on what customers would really *need and value* in the situation (scenario) they had created. As a result, some participants were arguing that customers want or do not want this or that product/service, quite independently of the scenario they had just worked out and far from critical needs that could have been drawn from that scenario.

A second problem in the workshop was that participants' detection of critical customer needs was limited by the tendency to consider their organization's capabilities at the same time. As one participant commented: 'We shouldn't write this critical customer need down because we have nothing to offer.' At this point, facilitators needed to actively support the working groups by explaining yet again the purpose and goal of this process – which was to detect critical needs resulting from the scenarios. In addition, the facilitators provided examples of critical customer needs that had already been detected by other working groups in the workshop session.

Despite these two problems, when the results of the working groups were collected and discussed in a plenary session, a substantial number of critical customer needs had been identified for each customer group. In total, the participants detected 38 different critical customer needs within the retailer customer group and 21 different critical needs within the manufacturer customer group. But which of these might be the most important customer needs in the future?

The facilitators asked participants to adopt the customer's perspective one more time and invited them to prioritize the numerous critical customer needs by 'vote'. Each participant received seven dots for voting within the retailer customer group and four dots for voting within the manufacturer customer group. Using only one dot per need, they simultaneously walked around the flipchart lists to express their opinion as a customer.

Table 6.1   Critical customer needs of retailers and manufacturers

Priority	Retailers 'It would really help me, if . . .'	Manufacturers 'It would really help me, if . . .'
1	. . . someone could help me to gain competitive advantages which will ensure a clear profile and will keep my competitors off my back. (8)	. . . someone could give me concrete advice on improving my marketing capabilities and on increasing my channels of distribution. (7)
2	. . . someone could give me ideas for additional products that are fast-selling and profitable. (6)	. . . someone can tell me more about retailers and end-consumers and their changed buying behaviors. (5)
3	. . . someone could provide me creative ideas for strategic alliances. (5)	. . . someone would give me more information about my industry and especially about my competitors and their moves in the market. (5)
4	. . . someone could advise me which technological equipment is appropriate and necessary for me. (5)	. . . someone would help me to be part of an industry community that keeps me involved with up-to-date business developments. (4)
5	. . . someone can tell me what end-consumers want, how much money they have available and how they change their habits over time. (4)	. . . someone could give me concrete advice on optimizing my cost structure. (4)
6	. . . someone can give me concrete advice on duties in human resources management. (4)	
7	. . . someone could get me more information about products and inventors. (3)	

The results in the form of a ranking for both customer groups are shown in detail in Table 6.1 (numbers in parentheses indicate the 'votes' that were given for that particular critical customer need). As it can be seen, the ranking of *really* important needs was quite consensual among participants.

6.4.2 Theoretical and Practical Background for Detecting Critical Customer Needs

At the end of this third core process I would like to provide some further background. This process is crucial in strategy making because the critical needs of customers determine future strategic opportunities for an organization. In fact, critical customer needs *are* strategic opportunities for organizations when organizations are in any way capable of providing a solution (products/services). Therefore, strategy innovations must be based on these critical needs, because strategy innovation must be about how critical customer needs can be creatively resolved – creating a unique value for the customer (respectively creating a competitive advantage) by effectively responding to the strategic opportunity.

In the case study, the facilitators supported participants during the detection process by guiding them through three steps: (a) detecting critical customer needs in small groups, (b) discussing and collecting critical needs across groups and (c) prioritizing the critical needs from the customer's perspective. While these practical process steps are self-explanatory, I would like to provide some further background on the substantial content question here: What actually are critical needs?

As I define it, critical needs are unarticulated customer desires, rooted in their 'world', which would have high value to them – if addressed. For example, before 1979, good stereophonic music had to come from hi-fi systems with large components, placed on a shelf or board at home. Music lovers were satisfied with these systems as there were no alternatives available. However, at the same time people increasingly enjoyed mobility – such as travelling internationally or engaging in outdoor sporting activities (for example jogging). Good music and mobility were both of value to people, but were in conflict at that time (except in cars). As these desires were perceived as being separate from each other, the chances that someone would make a connection between them were extremely low and it is even less likely that they would have come up with a request for a solution. But because people are not able to consciously express a need, it does not mean that the need does not exist. Because music and mobility are of value to customers, one can *imagine* (well-founded in the 'world' of the customers) that there actually *is* a desire for a portable stereo (Johnston and Bate, 2003).

As we all know today, Sony detected this latent critical customer need and creatively solved it with the Sony Walkman.[12] Because simply 'listening to the voice of the customer' does not help when customers do not know what they need (Lester and Piore, 2004), it is no surprise in retrospect that Sony's market research predicted that CEO Akio Morita would fail with the Sony Walkman that he supported. Nevertheless, Akio Morita went ahead with it. Although there are many versions of the origins of the Sony Walkman (du Gay et al., 1997, pp. 42–4), most include the idea that 'the founder' clearly imagined the existence of a critical need that was supported by his personal observations in the 'world' of customers as well as by his own experiences.

For instance, Morita himself recalled that one day Sony's co-founder Masaru Ibuka came into his office carrying one of Sony's portable tape recorders and wearing a pair of standard sized headphones. Ibuka wanted to have some music entertainment when he was out, while not disturbing third parties – but he complained that the tape recorder was just too heavy. Already having the first idea for the solution to this need, Morita then made further supporting observations of friends and family (see Morita, 1986). Regardless of how Sony actually detected this critical customer need, they did, and their success with the Sony Walkman is legendary. Sony has now sold more than 335 million Walkmans worldwide. They not only shaped the lifestyle of the 1980s (du Gay et al., 1997), but paved the way for other companies to offer technological improvements to further address this now obvious need (for example, MP3 players, iPod[13]). However, this is only because Sony detected and creatively resolved a latent need more than 25 years ago.

The obvious conclusion for strategy making is that organizations have to provide something that customers would like to have (based on a critical need), even though they never knew that they were looking for it. In retrospect the customer should say that it was something he/she always wanted (Liebl, 2000a, p. 125).

There is another aspect of critical needs that should be noted here. Because critical needs are pre-existing in the world of customers they can be detected and potentially be used by *any* organization. These critical needs can become strategic opportunities for any organization that is capable of providing resolution via a product or a service. The critical need for a portable stereo was, of course, also a strategic opportunity for Siemens or Philips at that time. However, Sony detected the critical need first. Companies can be said to compete on the basis of their level of speed and ability to detect critical customer needs.

Because scenarios describe customers' worldviews and their contexts, these scenario stories are a wellspring for detecting critical customer needs and succeeding in this competitive situation. The created scenarios make the 'world' of the customer particularly vivid and 'visible' in the minds of participants. They provide rich imagery for this crucial detecting process. It is important to note, however, that participants do not discover opportunities by searching for them directly, but by recognizing the value of new information that they happen to receive through other means (see Shane,

2000, p. 451). Through the change from being a provider to taking the perspective of a customer, participants may discover consequences for or problems of customers that they had never thought of before, or that they had thought about in a very different way. In consequence, the change of perspective can be seen as an effective technique for *creative* idea generation (see Adams, 2001; de Bono, 1992). As Smith (1998, p. 121) states: 'Empathic identification helps one recognize interests of other stakeholders, promoting idea generation.'

Taking a different perspective has been criticized for lacking a theoretical foundation (Butler and Kline 1999, p. 326), but there is support for it in the memory literature (for example, Fisher and Geiselman, 1988; Anderson and Pichert, 1978) as well as in the business literature (for example, Boland and Tenkasi, 1995).

This third core process asks participants to detect as many critical needs of customers as possible. Thus, it is primarily a creative detection process which ignores whether the uncovered critical needs could become a source of strategic opportunities for a specific organization or not. This was an issue in the case study. The process was driven by a single question: What would help customers in a situation described in the scenario? Two problems with the recognition of critical customer needs – which are very common in my experience – have been described. First, participants were often confused about what customers want and what they *need*. Because organizational members get a lot of information about customers from customer satisfaction surveys, market research and possibly personal interaction, they often think they know what customers actually need. But in most cases, this information only covers what customers want. What customers want refers to the customer's known and expected domain – based primarily on what customers have experienced in the past (Liebl, 1999b). This information may provide some incremental product or service improvements, but it does not help detect strategic opportunities that have the potential to provide innovative or creative new customer functions. As described in the Sony example, the unarticulated desires of customers, which will be important to them if met, have the potential to do so.

The key task for facilitators, as in the case study, is to provide illustrative examples that help participants understand the difference between wants and critical needs, as well as the high strategic value of identifying these critical needs. As seen in Table 6.1, participants were finally able to find a number of critical needs that were, at that time, latent rather than already expressed issues among retailers and manufacturers.

The second problem that the facilitators encountered in step three was that the workshop participants' recognition of the value of detected critical customer needs was very often expressed in terms of how the company might make *use* of detected needs ('we could offer our customers a new product like . . .'). In other words, participants immediately offered a solution instead of detecting and explicitly articulating an underlying critical need. It is my observation that this phenomenon is caused by a tendency among organizational members to think in terms of products and services. Even when identifying critical customer needs, solutions tend to be closely connected to their existing knowledge about their own organization and its capabilities (Shane, 2000, pp. 451–2). In effect, the solutions are mostly limited to what participants perceive *their own* organization 'can do' today (obvious strategic opportunities). However, this cognitive anchor limits creativity and the number of critical needs identified.

It is important not to be misunderstood: creative ideas about new products and services are very important during strategy making. However, they are not the goal of this particular step in the strategy making process I am describing. Ideas about new products and services will come into play at later core processes. Nevertheless, the expression of ideas for solutions at this point sometimes can help participants to discover underlying critical needs of customers.

In summary, the third core process is extremely important because the detection of critical needs can be seen as *the* genuine entrepreneurial task in strategy making. The outcome of this process heavily influences the future strategic position of an organization in a targeted market. As I see it, it is important in strategy making that the strategy team creates scenarios and detects critical needs in the 'worlds' of customers themselves instead of having them detected and presented by others, such as consultants, research institutes or internal teams. As seen with the example of Sony and its CEO Akio Morita, understanding the world of customers and corresponding critical needs in depth and linking this knowledge to one's own beliefs and insights is a necessary condition for personally pursuing a strategic opportunity in practice (see also Shane, 2000).

Let us return to the case study and see how *JOURNAL*'s strategy team went on with their detected critical needs in practice.

6.5   FOURTH CORE PROCESS: MATCHING A SHARED DESIRED IDENTITY WITH DETECTED CRITICAL CUSTOMER NEEDS IN A COMPETITIVE ENVIRONMENT

The second and third core processes encouraged and helped *JOURNAL*'s strategy team to reveal and explore their underlying assumptions about the environment and to detect critical customer needs among retailers and

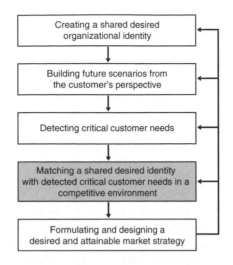

manufacturers. The fourth core process turns from exploring and analysing underlying assumptions to questioning and challenging the group's shared desired identity (SDI).

In the first part of this core process workshop participants construed images of *JOURNAL* and of current/potential competitors, and then assessed the relative strengths of competitors. In the second part of the process they matched the SDI with critical customer needs in a competitive environment for both customer groups, retailers and manufacturers.

6.5.1 Construing an Image of *JOURNAL* and Images of Current/Potential Competitors

When participants had finished the exploration of their organization's environment and the detection of critical customer needs, they declared that they had a much better understanding and a clearer picture of their industry and their customers than they had before. Participants were satisfied with their results up to this point. At the same time, they had also become slightly worried because they were no longer sure whether they could actually deal with these demanding critical customers needs in such a dramatically changing industry – the pressure, which all had felt at the first meeting, now seemed even higher.

However, when faced with various new customer needs many participants naturally asked themselves some critical questions: 'Where does our *JOURNAL* stand right now in the eyes of our customers?' At the same time, participants also wanted to know: 'And where do our competitors stand at the moment?' The following proposal of the facilitators to construe an external image of *JOURNAL* and of their competitors relieved some of the pressure.

(a) Construing an external image of *JOURNAL*
Participants were able to draw customer feedback from a number of sources in order to construe an external image of *JOURNAL*. Being a specialist journal in a particular industry and also being closely connected to the Industry Association, workshop members already had contacts with many people in the industry and with association members. These people were not only informants for the editorial staff or customers for the advertising department, but also regular readers of *JOURNAL*. These contacts constantly brought the perceived external image of *JOURNAL* to organizational members. In addition, management had quite recently conducted face-to-face, qualitative interviews with a number of key customers during the industry's most important trade fair in 2000. Thanks to these multiple feedback sources, participants were able to construe an external image of *JOURNAL* that had a good chance of being very close to the current customers' perception. In a opening session, the explicit construction of this image was guided by the question: 'Looking back on your personal experiences with customers – what feedback and images have been expressed to you about your organization and its performance?' The facilitators noted shared and agreed attributes of the construed external image on a flip-chart.

Participants perceived that readers viewed *JOURNAL* as a medium which:

- is always present and at hand (two issues per week);
- has the most advertisements that can be used as a source of industry information ('what's going on?');
- is the market leader (circulation, distribution and market penetration);
- is reliable and reports in a credible way;
- reports about industrial politics;
- needs to be read (although there may be no desire to do so);
- contains important facts.

After further discussing these elements of the current *JOURNAL*'s external image, participants finally condensed the image into three main components:

(i)   market leader with high market penetration;
(ii) provides reliable and credible facts that are a must for everyone in the industry;

(iii) contains advertisements that are an important source of industry information.

The current external image that they had created seemed to give participants some certainty about their starting position, although they were still worried about whether they could deal with the critical customer needs they had detected. At any rate, it seemed that the participants had at least reassured themselves about their good strategic position at present.

(b) Determining competitors
After construing the external image, which re-established the self-assurance of the group to a certain extent, participants were in a much better state of mind to deal with competitors. When participants began determining competitors in the plenary (in response to the questions: 'Are there competitors who have chosen the same customer group(s) as your organization?' and 'Can you identify at least one detected critical customer need for the future that they are likely to address – regardless how they do it, and irrespective of which technology they use?'), they immediately named current and well known competitors. These well known competitors were two specialist journals which focused on the same customer groups in the industry.

However, participants were quite surprised when they started thinking about potential competitors. Depending on the detected critical customer need, they recognized that *JOURNAL* in the future could also be in competition with different kinds of consultants or market research institutes. In all, participants determined the following competitors:

- specialist journal *MONTHLY*;
- specialist journal *WEEKLY*;
- business consultants;
- market research institutes;
- IT consultants;
- marketing consultants.

(c) Construing external images and detecting influencing relative strengths of competitors
Despite the fact that participants had recognized new potential competitors, their main focus remained on the two direct competitors *MONTHLY* and *WEEKLY*. According to participants, these two journals were perceived as direct alternatives to *JOURNAL* by their customers, and, consequently, participants viewed them as the most dangerous strategic competitors needing further attention. Information about both competitors was received through the same sources and channels that have already

been mentioned. To construe the images and to detect influencing relative strengths two working questions were used: 'How do I/we think customers perceive competitors *MONTHLY* and *WEEKLY*?' and 'What can competitors *MONTHLY* and *WEEKLY* do particularly well (compared to us and other competitors) that is difficult to imitate and that influences the current customer's impression about competitors *MONTHLY* and *WEEKLY*?' In a plenary discussion guided by the facilitators, participants worked out the following images and influencing relative strengths of *MONTHLY* and *WEEKLY* that were noted on flip-charts:

1. *MONTHLY*
    MONTHLY is a national specialist journal which was founded over 20 years ago. It is published on a monthly basis in full color with a circulation of about 3000 copies. Subscribers pay an annual subscription fee of £112. *MONTHLY* also provides free online information.
        Participants perceived that customers viewed *MONTHLY* as a medium which:

    ● is practice-oriented;
    ● covers topical issues and is fast with information by using the internet;
    ● talks about people in the industry in a friendly and uncomplicated style;
    ● is critical about the Industry Association and about manufacturers.

Participants identified the founder and managing director of the journal as an important relative strength that influences this image of *MONTHLY*. Through his personal abilities, the managing director had created a unique network in the industry over the last 20 years. This personal network has influenced *MONTHLY* to become practice-oriented and to 'gossip' in a friendly way about people in the industry. Another relative strength was *MONTHLY*'s extensive practical experience and knowledge of processing topical online information that had been built up over many years. Because of this knowledge, the journal had been internally organized in a very specific way in order to get the topical information published online quickly. However, *MONTHLY*'s fast and topical online information often involved sacrifices regarding accuracy and plausibility from the viewpoint of workshop participants.

2. *WEEKLY*
    WEEKLY is also a national specialist journal. It is published on a weekly basis in full color with a circulation of about 2500 copies.

Subscribers pay an annual subscription fee of £210. *WEEKLY* also provides free, although very limited, online information.

Participants perceived that customers viewed *WEEKLY* as a medium which:

- is fast and topical with its print edition;
- is cheeky, perky and critically investigative of scandals;
- is clear and easy to read ('information at a glance');
- has very important (self-investigated) industry market data.

The participants identified one relative strength of *WEEKLY* that seemed fairly important: *WEEKLY* had unique knowledge from their own market research in the industry. This enabled *WEEKLY* to provide important market data that no one else could offer. A related relative strength of *WEEKLY* was their cooperation with several premium end-consumer magazines. These magazines frequently published selected market data from *WEEKLY* that was relevant for end-consumers. Further relative strengths of *WEEKLY* were not identified by the participants.

Other competitors, such as consultants or market researchers, were seen as being less relevant by the participants. In addition, participants thought that they were incapable of creating construed external images or of identifying influencing relative strengths for these competitors. Participants consensually agreed to pay more attention to these competitors at a later stage, when further steps in strategy making would reveal a necessity for doing so.

6.5.2 Theoretical and Practical Background for Construing Images

Before continuing with the second part of this fourth core process, I would like to stop and give some further background. Several questions might be raised here: Why does the recognition and concept of *images* become important at this point? When determining competitors, why do the facilitators use such a multifaceted working question? Why do facilitators not ask participants to initiate a comprehensive competitor analysis?

First of all, it has become evident in running this kind of workshop that missing information about both the organization and its competitors needs to be discovered and analysed by participants before their SDI can be matched with critical customer needs in a competitive environment. While critical customer needs have already been detected, a determination of competitors and information about a competitive environment has not been uncovered. Clearly, the workshops already have a good deal of information, but it must be specified, and agreed upon. Therefore, this first part of core process three specified *JOURNAL*'s image as well as current/potential competitors' images. This exercise included the identification of competitors' relative strengths. But why images and relative strengths?

Strategy making is about gaining sustainable competitive advantages. It has been argued before that the competitive advantages of an organization are only created in the minds of customers. These competitive advantages determine the strategic position of a company. But which positions do customers actually make available for *JOURNAL* or competitors in the market? This is where the concept of organizational *image* becomes important as it helps to locate organizations in a competitive environment.

An organizational image is a perception and/or judgement of the organization's actions, products (brands), services or achievements by external audiences, corresponding to the question: 'How is an organization perceived by others?' These images – perceived by customers – are crucial for workshop participants to consider because the customer's perception determines whether or not the organization's shared desired identity (SDI) will, in fact, be able to create competitive advantages and corresponding unique strategic positions in the market. In addition, the sustainability of future strategic positions depends on potential strategic moves and shifts of competitors. By discovering the existing relative strengths of competitors one might be able to make assumptions about such future moves and shifts.

As described in the case study, the first part of the fourth core process was divided into three steps: (a) construing an external image of the organization, (b) determining current and potential competitors, and (c) construing images and detecting influencing relative strengths of competitors.

(a)   Construing an external image of the organization
The first step elicited how participants perceived the customer's image of 'their' *JOURNAL*. As already outlined, images are perceptions and judgements of external audiences. Because the customer's perception will determine the viability of sustainable competitive advantages, the primary task is to gain access to their perceptions and to incorporate these in a proper form into the strategy making process.

There are many sources for organizational members to access customers' feedback about their own organizational performance, products or services; for example through market research studies, customer satisfaction surveys, complaint management information or personal interaction. However, all this feedback information is filtered and interpreted by organizational members who generate or modify mental models of their organization's image from it (see Barr et al., 1992, pp. 16–19; or Hatch and

Schultz, 2002, p. 995). These beliefs about an organizational image are an answer to the other-reflective question: 'How do I/we think customers perceive us?' Dutton et al. (1994, pp. 248–9) define this mental model as a *construed external image*.

A construed external image of the organization helps to locate a current position in a competitive environment from the customer's perspective. But participants 'sometimes have a distorted impression of what others believe, either believing their organization is perceived in a more positive or a more negative light than outsiders see it' (Dutton et al., 1994, p. 249; see also Corley, 2002, pp. 119–20). Next to these positive or negative impression differences, customers might value other factors of the product/service or might even use it for different functions than participants think (Rughase, 2002, p. 55; Liebl, 2002a, p. 126). In the workshop these differences need to be minimized by (a) appropriate information about customer perceptions and (b) by processes that help to interpret and incorporate the information into strategy making. Being aware of these two requirements is important in strategy making.

From my practical experience, formal analyses – as discussed in the field of strategy analysis – are often used here as they seem to provide 'objective' information – not only about an image of an organization member's own organization but also about customers, competitors or markets. These analyses often rely on quantitative methodologies to elicit (statistically) reliable facts, such as assigned attributes/characteristics to the organization, actual reasons for buying, or market share. But dealing with images of one's own organization or any competitor means only dealing with customer perceptions. The extent to which solely quantitative approaches are suitable for transmitting customer perceptions which are valuable for a practical strategy making process can be questioned. First, most quantitative approaches pre-define questions for customers in order to be able to analyse results statistically. Although customers might be able to answer all the questions, these questions represent what the *researchers* think is important (Liebl and Rughase, 2002). This means that it remains unclear how survey questions match the customers' world and which important customers' perceptions are excluded. Second, most information on perceptions is context-dependent. Specific experiences or incidents will have shaped or created a customer's perception. Given that it would be important to know more about these influences in order to understand information from customers, quantitative research methodology is inadequate.

From my perspective, qualitative research methods or combinations of qualitative and quantitative research methods may be more appropriate in acquiring information about complex customer perceptions. Again, the

storylistening® method with its exploratory principle – as described in
section 6.2.2 – is a feasible approach. If the facilitators had had more time
in the case study that I have been describing they would probably have taken
this approach.

Fortunately, however, gaining information from external analyses is
not the only way to acquire appropriate information about customer perceptions and judgements. As shown in the case study, facilitators may also
use the available information and existing experiences of organizational
members. When there are several qualitative sources of customer feedback
available (such as the qualitative interviews made at the trade meeting and
multiple other customer feedback channels used in the case study), organizational members may come up with a realistic understanding of perceptions which can adequately reflect outsider images of their organization. In
addition, the personal experiences of participants were important in giving
available information even more meaning.

(b)   Determining current and potential competitors

A construed external image of their own organization is not sufficient in
itself. Being in a competitive environment, the determination of current
and potential competitors as well as their images are extremely important
in order to evaluate the organization's current place and potential future
opportunities for strategic positioning in a market. Therefore, the determination of current and/or potential competitors is a necessary condition for
strategy making. As we have seen in the case study, the facilitators asked
participants a multi-faceted question to discover this: 'Are there competitors who have chosen the same customer group(s) as your organization?
Can you identify at least one detected critical customer need for the future
that they are likely to address – regardless how they do it, and irrespective
of which technology they use?' Let me offer you some theoretical background on this deliberately constructed question.

As practical experience and empirical studies have shown, participants
often consider competitors from a very limited perspective; for instance,
they only think about competitors who they refer to in their own business
definition, or only consider competitors who are in the same geographical
area (Reger and Huff, 1993; Porac et al., 1989). This is the 'focusing effect'
discussed in Chapter 1 and section 3.3. In response to its subjective constraints on competitor detection, there are a number of tools and methods
in strategic management which have been developed to assess a business
definition. However, these tools suffer from certain deficits. They often look
only at one industry, for example, or only describe current states; most of
them lack a customer-oriented perspective (for a critique see Sulzmaier,
2001, pp. 27–8).

As an exception to these limited tools, Abell (1980) introduced a customer-based business definition along the dimensions of (a) customer groups, (b) customer functions, and (c) alternative technologies. According to Abell, the competitive arena of a market can be defined as the intersection of selected customer groups who are served certain functions by substitutional technologies (see Figure 6.5; for full details see Abell, 1980, pp. 191–214).

Because Abell's definition of a competitive arena is customer-based, it easily connects to prior processes and steps in the strategy making process I am proposing. During the second core process, customer groups were determined by the participants. And customer functions (concerning customers' problems to be solved) can be seen as synonymous with critical customer needs which were detected during the third core process by workshop

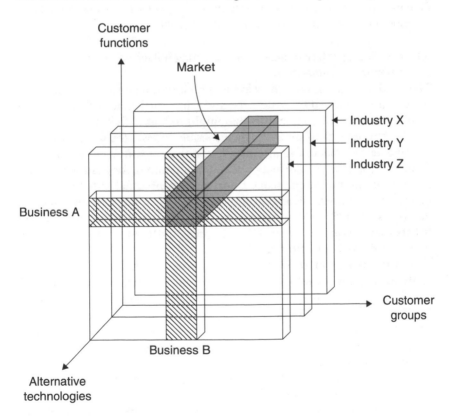

Source: Abell (1980), © 1980. Reprinted by permission of Pearson Education, Inc., Upper Saddle River, USA.

Figure 6.5   Abell's definition of a market

participants. I am less concerned about Abell's emphasis on technologies, which may have been a good indicator for (manufacturing) industries in the 1980s, as today's industries serve critical customer needs using more sophisticated business models. By expanding substitution technologies to *all* alternative ways in which a particular critical customer need can be solved, Abell's 1980 definition can be easily adapted to today's requirements. With this small adjustment, the multi-faceted question used to determine competitors in the case study considered all three dimensions of Abell's customer-based market definition.

The case study shows that this working question was able significantly to overcome subjective constraints in competitor detection. Next to current and known competitors who are targeting the same customer group(s) and who are also very likely to address at least one detected critical need, participants became aware of new potential competitors (for the importance of potential competitors see Porter, 1980, pp. 49–50).

(c)   Construing external images and detecting influencing relative strengths of competitors

The third step also covers the ways in which participants think that competitors are perceived by customers, and what participants believe are the relative strengths of competitors that might influence that perception.

As with the organization's image described above, the concept of construed external images can also be applied to competitors. Organizational members also receive information about competitors, for example through industry communication, market surveys, or personal interaction with members of competitive organizations or their customers. Again, all information is filtered and interpreted by organizational members, creating beliefs that answer the other-reflected question: 'How do I/we think customers perceive competitor XY?'

As with images of their own organization, information from external analyses or available information and the existing experiences of participants can be used to create construed external images of competitors. However, the same limitations of solely quantitative research methods – which have already been discussed – need to be considered as these images of competitors are also perceptions and judgements of customers. As described in the case study, the facilitators again used multiple available information sources and the existing experiences of participants in an attempt to overcome this potential problem.

Next, the relative strengths of competitors were identified by the participants in the case study. But what are relative strengths? As I define it, relative strengths are distinctive internal capabilities. They are what the competitor 'can do' particularly well compared to their own organization and to other competitors – they are what is difficult to imitate (Aaker, 1989; Hamel and Prahalad, 1994; Wernerfelt, 1984). The construed external images of competitors that have just been created can help workshop participants identify these relative strengths.

Again, it should be remembered that the relative strengths of an organization can create future competitive advantages if they can be transformed into products and services that are perceived and valued by the customers (Liebl, 2002b). Construed external images can also be used to identify those relative strengths of competitors that influence current customer perceptions. These relative strengths of competitors are not only important for understanding the internal basis of the competitive advantages of competitors, but also for making assumptions about competitors' future responses and possible strategic shifts (Porter, 1980, pp. 63–71).

With regard to relative strengths, I would like to comment on another tool of strategy analysis: competitor analysis. Even though competitor analysis creates the impression of being able to provide necessary information (especially about internal capabilities), information gathering remains an extremely difficult task in practice (Bea and Haas, 2001, p. 104). In my experience, it might be sufficient to consider those relative strengths of competitors that are apparent and already known by participants for many strategy making processes. If further information about competitors is wanted later, participants can consider the information's usefulness and the practicality of gathering that information (for further details about competitor analysis see Porter, 1980).

After reflecting on these aspects of the first part of the fourth core process in strategy making, let us return to the case study and see how the *JOURNAL* strategy team coped with the actual challenge of assessing their shared desired identity.

6.5.3 Matching a Shared Desired Identity with Critical Customer Needs in a Competitive Environment

Once participants had assessed their competitors, the facilitators invited them to recall the shared desired identity (SDI) that had been developed in the first workshop, eight weeks previously. With this in mind, the facilitators asked participants to study the photographs of flip-charts and display walls from the first workshop (as videotaping had not been possible). After about 15 minutes, two participants voluntarily presented the SDI in form of a story to the other group members.

When the SDI was freshly in the minds of participants again, the facilitators asked which customer group should be considered first in order to test the robustness and strategic value of the SDI. Because participants believed retailers to be the most important customer group, they decided to begin there.

The facilitators then proposed that the group create a strategic value matrix (see Figure 6.6) by matching the three core attributes of the SDI (quick and topical, practical support for daily work, and 'human touch' – as described in section 6.2.3) with the detected critical customer needs of retailers (as shown in Table 6.1). Whereas the core attributes of the SDI are all seen as being equally important, critical customer needs were prioritized from the customer's perspective. This strategic value matrix was intended to help participants to answer the question: 'Does a shared desired identity align with important critical customer needs?' Each box of the matrix reveals a desired attribute's *relevance* for a particular critical customer need. If an attribute is not relevant for a critical need, this particular box can be crossed out.

In a plenary session, facilitators proposed that participants should evaluate the relevance of their desired core attributes for each critical customer need. For such an evaluation of relevance, facilitators asked the participants: 'How and with which products/services may your organization and *JOURNAL* resolve the critical customer need, considering the desired core attribute?' Very quickly, it became clear to participants that their SDI had a high strategic value. Only three boxes of the strategic value matrix were crossed out because participants had come to the conclusion that their desired 'human touch' of *JOURNAL* was not relevant for some critical customer needs (see Figure 6.6). Inspired by this result, participants went directly on to incorporating the competitive environment (*MONTHLY* and *WEEKLY*) into the strategic value matrix – guided by two questions: (1) 'Are important critical needs already addressed by *MONTHLY/WEEKLY* with an equivalent, identical or closely connected attribute of our shared desired identity?' (2) 'Can *MONTHLY/WEEKLY* potentially address critical customer needs with an equivalent, identical or closely connected attribute of our shared desired identity?'

Participants broadly discussed each competitor in the plenum, before stickers, which represented the competitors (*MONTHLY* squares; *WEEKLY*, triangles), were placed on the matrix. The external images and identified relative strengths of competitors were of significant help to participants in accomplishing this task. For example, the practice-orientation of *MONTHLY* could be clearly made out in the matrix (see Figure 6.7).

Participants then evaluated the performance of each competitor in resolving an addressed critical customer need by labelling the stickers with high (h), low (l), or middling (m). Even though the facilitators proposed several times that they should also consider potential future shifts and moves of competitors (second question above), they primarily stuck to the

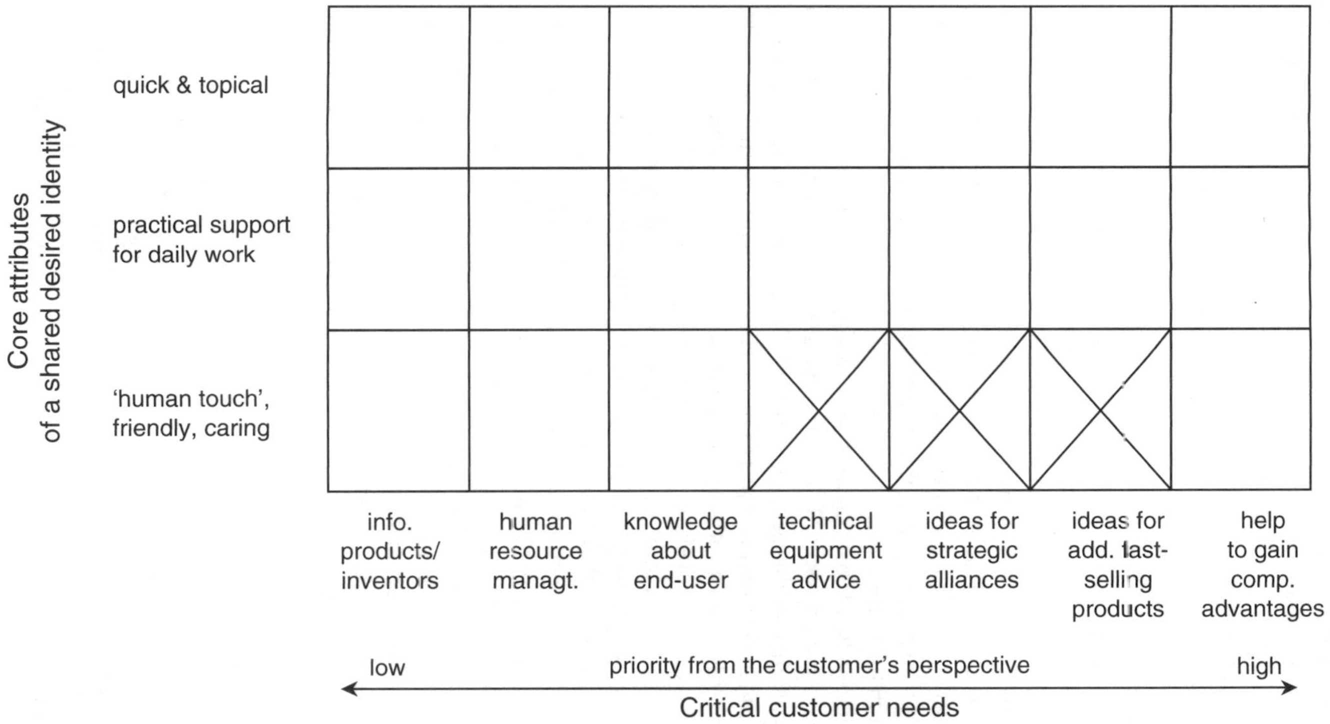
Core attributes
of a shared desired identity
quick & topical
practical support
for daily work
'human touch',
friendly, caring
info.
products/
inventors
human
resource
managt.
knowledge
about
end-user
technical
equipment
advice
ideas for
strategic
alliances
ideas for
add. last-
selling
products
help
to gain
comp.
advantages
low
priority from the customer's perspective
high
Critical customer needs

Figure 6.6 Basic strategic value matrix of JOURNAL

current positions of competitors. In the final step, participants placed circle stickers on the strategic value matrix in order to see which critical customer needs were currently addressed by *JOURNAL* (see Figure 6.7).

Once all these very active procedures and discussions had ended, participants began to settle down. They looked at their strategic value matrix for a few minutes without saying a word. Then, the whole situation turned into an awkward silence and finally participants became deeply consternated. After a while, the facilitators carefully asked participants about their first impressions. Participants were able to connect their consternation with two facts. First of all, *JOURNAL* was not as future-oriented as participants had personally believed up to that point. The current *JOURNAL* was only strong on a critical need which had the lowest priority for customers. Furthermore, it became obvious to the group that both competitors were acting with a strategic intent that had already led to an innovative strategic position in the market.

On the one hand, participants were disappointed in themselves. As one participant commented: 'These crooks have recognized developments in the market that we haven't seen so far!' On the other hand, participants were trying to defend themselves. One participant said: 'Somehow, I always suspected this!' And another participant said: 'I made that point more than three years ago, but nothing has ever happened.'

After these first emotional expressions of overall disappointment, the group slowly began to reflect on their strategic situation. The extensive and dynamic discussion that followed showed that participants now felt challenged by their competitors. Participants claimed that certain areas of the strategic value matrix should 'belong' to them. For instance, participants expressed the view that 'topicality' was what they would like to claim for *JOURNAL* – especially for the most important need of the retailers – to help them gain competitive advantages. Remarkably, the agreement evolved out of a passionate discussion over placing an additional circle sticker on the strategic value matrix. The sticker was placed in the box 'quick & topical'/ 'help to gain competitive advantages' in order to highlight their (desired) claim. Participants realistically evaluated their performance in the box as being extremely low (even non-existent). But it seemed very important for them to demonstrate their future-oriented ambitions (see Figure 6.7).

In contrast, the desired attribute 'human touch' was rarely mentioned during the whole discussion. The third desired attribute 'practical support for daily work' was highly relevant when discussing the strategic situation. But it was also an attribute that participants deemed strongly taken by *MONTHLY*. In addition, it became clear during the discussion that participants now felt that they were somewhat further away from the true retailers' practice than this competitor.

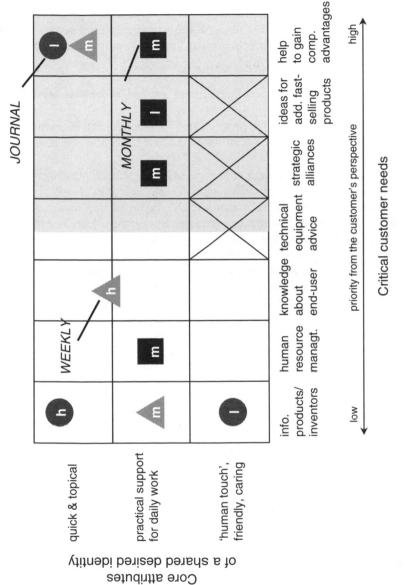

Figure 6.7   *Strategic value matrix of JOURNAL (retailers) in a competitive environment*

155

In summary, participants began to evolve their SDI during these lively discussions. They felt challenged by the confrontational situation and were motivated to 'prove' their forward-looking ambitions. As a direct result of this, the group did not want to create a strategic value matrix for the manu- facturer customer group at this stage of the strategy making process, but instead preferred to go on with their most important customer group and to develop strategic opportunities.

6.5.4 Theoretical and Practical Background for the Challenging Match

At the end of the fourth core process and its second part in particular I would like to interrupt the description of the case study and provide some further background.

This second part of the fourth core process takes a central position in the proposed design of a strategy making process because it explicitly reflects a shared desired organizational identity (SDI), being the new measure that has previously been formulated as a requirement (section 4.2). The fourth core process ends by matching an SDI with detected critical customer needs in a competitive environment in order to test and challenge its robustness and its strategic value. While critical customer needs test and challenge the robustness and strategic value of an SDI from the perspective of its rele- vance in the market, competitors test and challenge an SDI from the per- spective of its ability to gain sustainable competitive advantages and corresponding unique strategic positions. Thus, this step in the strategy making process really considers what participants 'want to do' and what they think their organization 'should do' as a measure for strategy making.

The second part of the fourth core process – as described in the case study – can be divided into two steps: (a) creating a strategic value matrix, and (b) challenging and evolving the shared desired identity.

(a) Creating a strategic value matrix
As we have seen, creating a strategic value matrix helped the case study group relate their SDI to detected critical customer needs. If an organiza- tion has several customer groups, such a matrix needs to be created for each customer group. The strategic value matrix represents a space of critical needs for a particular customer group that could be in alliance with an SDI to some certain degree. The right half of the matrix is of primary interest, because the priority of critical customer needs decreases from right to left (see basic structure in Figure 6.8).

But how did the facilitators come up with this particular strategic value matrix? The proposed strategic value matrix is a result of experiences gained in several practical strategy making processes. This experience indicated

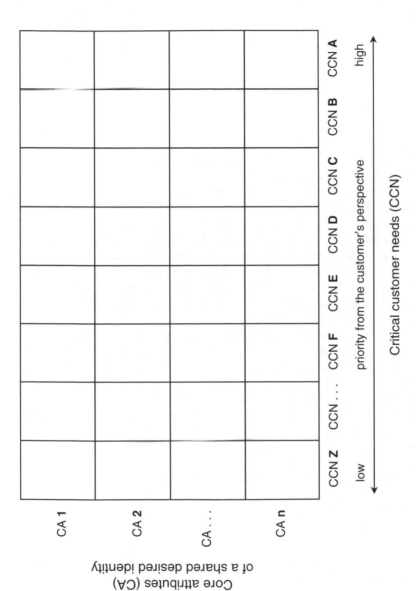

Figure 6.8   Basic strategic value matrix

that an SDI can become very complex, in part because it is an aggregated construct. As seen in section 6.2.3, an SDI consists of various attributes, ranging from the 'heart' to the periphery, attributes are also likely to have multiple connections to each other. In my earlier practical strategy making processes, I developed approaches to take into account this complexity while matching an SDI with critical customer needs in a competitive environment, but they were not very successful. In most cases, it turned out that the complexity of their own SDI was demanding enough for participants and discussions somehow became fuzzy, confusing and even misleading (despite strong facilitators' interventions), which made it difficult to actually challenge the construct. More structural guidance was needed to make the procedure more rational for participants. The strategic value matrix was created for this particular purpose.

However, I am aware that this matrix has its deficits. First of all, the strategic value matrix only considers attributes of the SDI's 'heart'. This selection of attributes reflects the core of the SDI, representing the most desired and valued characteristics by all participants. Although it is the most important part of an SDI, it remains only a part. Second, the selected attributes seem independent from each other. It has been argued before that core attributes are highly interconnected and have also multiple links to other attributes near the core or even at the periphery. However, the matrix cannot represent those linkages.

Despite these limitations, the strategic value matrix has proven to be very helpful and effective in challenging the initial views of an ideal future identity. The reduced selection of attributes and their seeming independence may appear radical to theorists in terms of simplifying an identity, but it made the complex construct manageable in practice. There might be other – much better – ways to solve the complexity problem of this part of the strategy making process. However, in terms of practicability the strategic value matrix was the best solution I came up with.

(b)   Challenging and evolving a shared desired identity
The second step mindfully challenged and evolved the shared desired identity (SDI). This challenge may reveal that an SDI is insufficient or even inappropriate with regard to detected critical customer needs and/or differentiation against current/potential competitors. The case study has shown the emotional outcomes that are likely when participants gain new insights into the market relevance and strategic potential of their own desired state.

However, the description of confronting participants with their own discovered strategic 'realities' in the case study, shows that they accepted that the logic of the process, and then the confrontation itself constituted a challenge. But there are two important aspects that promoted a successful challenge of the SDI: (1) structural guidance by the strategic value matrix, and (2) deliberately promoting the SDI's evolution by facilitators.

(1) The strategic value matrix and its design reveal the robustness and the strategic value of an SDI in a relentless way. Participants are asked to evaluate the relevance of desired attributes of the SDI with regard to detected critical customer needs – box by box. Through this visual representation, it becomes clear to participants how their SDI aligns with important critical customer needs by the number of boxes which are crossed out. Though this can be disappointing, it is very unlikely that the strategic value of an SDI is excessively low or even nonexistent. Because an SDI is inferred, modified or affirmed by participants' perceptions and experiences within the organization's environment (see section 3.3.2 – Figure 3.4), an SDI is linked one way or another with critical customer needs.

In addition, the strategic value matrix introduces current and potential competitors. Again, each box is checked for whether there is or could be a competitor. This not only illustrates the desired state within the competitive environment but at the same time shows how an SDI may be influenced by other (successful) competitors in the industry.

(2) Next to this structural guidance of the strategic value matrix, the facilitators deliberately promote the SDI's evolution in a careful and respectful way. They use the information about the competitive environment and market relevance that has been revealed by the strategic value matrix. At the same time, the facilitators constantly remind participants about the consequences of each entry for the organization's future and also emphasize that a clear strategy decision will be needed. This is important, because agreed findings about strategic issues (for example, critical customer needs, competitors' images, and so on) are relatively risk-free and harmless for participants as long as they cannot (or choose not to) connect them to any fundamental consequences that will affect the individually desired organizational identity that is now aggregated into an SDI.

These two aspects of the second part of the fourth core process ensure that the challenge to an SDI takes place. At this point it becomes obvious that extremely skilled facilitators are needed in the proposed design of a practical strategy making process (as discussed in section 4.4). Facilitators sensitively confront participants with their own results and encourage them to think creatively about possible but still desired alterations to their desired identity – always ensuring cognitive and emotional commitment. This demanding challenge is the first test of how willing participants are to hold on, to let go or to move on with regard to their SDI. As seen in the case study, participants immediately noticed the first 'little dyings' of desired attributes coming into sight ('human touch'), but it was too early to move into concrete alterations to the current SDI. Nevertheless, a reconsideration and evolution of the SDI had already begun in the minds of the participants.

Let's return to the case study to see which strategic opportunities in the retailers' market the *JOURNAL* strategy team developed and what strategy they finally formulated.

6.6 FIFTH CORE PROCESS: FORMULATING AND DESIGNING A DESIRED AND ATTAINABLE MARKET STRATEGY

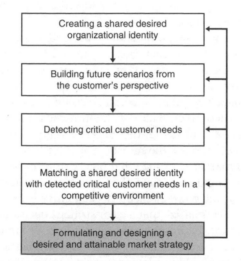

The fifth and final core process consisted of two parts. During the first part the *JOURNAL* strategy team formulated a future market strategy that expressed their shared desired identity after they had detected and evaluated their strategic opportunities. During the second part the strategy team roughly designed the substance of their future market strategy.

6.6.1 Formulating a Future Market Strategy that Expresses a Shared Desired Identity

(a) Detecting viable strategic opportunities
The dynamic discussion about the strategic value matrix of retailers created a workshop atmosphere that was emotional, ambitious, and encouraging.

Because of this atmosphere, the invitation of facilitators to move towards finding viable strategic opportunities was not received in a particularly rational manner. Instead the group continued to discuss their disappointments, expectations, evaluations and desires for a future strategic positioning in a very emotional way. This vigorous discussion constantly led the group's attention towards those critical customer needs where competitors particularly threatened their SDI.

The critical customer need 'help to gain competitive advantages' proved to be an especially 'hot area' for participants. It really seemed to spoil their SDI. Despite the fact that there were already two other competitors in this segment, they persistently declared this critical customer need as a viable strategic opportunity. During the discussion, the facilitators took on a mainly observational role, watching the proceedings, and sometimes intervening when participants were about to lose track completely. The facilitators used the discussion as an opportunity to gain additional insights into individual value judgements about desired attributes and their meanings to participants. For instance, the facilitators observed that the desired attribute 'quick & topical' became more important to participants than the other two attributes.

After participants had had enough time to let off steam about strategic positions and possible solutions, the whole situation slowly relaxed. It now became possible for the facilitators to guide the detection of viable strategic opportunities in a more analytical manner. The participants primarily focused on the right half of the strategic value matrix. In the end, they detected 'technical equipment advice' and 'ideas for additional fast-selling products' as viable strategic opportunities because the group sensed that their SDI had a quite high relevance to resolving these critical needs. Moreover, only one of these critical needs was already being addressed by a low performing competitor (compare Figure 6.7).

The critical need 'ideas for strategic alliances' was not perceived as a viable strategic opportunity because workshop participants did not see a high relevance for their SDI, but participants were highly attracted by the opportunity in 'help to gain competitive advantages'; they also wanted further to evaluate their other detected opportunities. From their point of view, an evaluation guaranteed that no other opportunities were simply ignored, and they wanted to be sure that their ability to make a deliberate choice would be strengthened by additional information.

(b) Evaluating viable strategic opportunities
Consequently, participants assessed each of the three opportunities ('technical equipment advice', 'ideas for additional fast-selling products' and 'help to gain competitive advantages') revealed by the matrix in core

process four in further detail. The facilitators created three small groups and each group focused on one strategic opportunity. The evaluation was guided by the following four questions:

(i) Which resources and competencies should an organization ideally have to make the best use of this particular strategic opportunity?
(ii) Which resources and competencies does your organization already have and to what extent?
(iii) Does a future market strategy (which would focus on this particular strategic opportunity) create competitive advantages?
(iv) Does a future market strategy (which would focus on this particular strategic opportunity) seem feasible from the viewpoint of the customers as well as from your viewpoint?

Each group presented their results afterwards to the other groups, discussing and improving the outcomes with them. The facilitators noted the conclusions on a flip-chart, cross-checking with the whole group that evaluations have been captured accurately. The group's conclusions to each question (i–iv) and for each viable strategic opportunity can be briefly summarized in this way.

1. Giving advice for technical equipment
   (i) Participants found the following necessary competencies and resources:
      - precise and up-to-date knowledge about workflows of retailers and manufacturers;
      - excellent and up-to-date knowledge about current developments in the areas: products, services, logistics, manufacturing, and administration (retailer and manufacturer) as well as about corresponding soft- and hardware solutions;
      - reliable contacts and easy access to companies which offer and implement such soft-and hardware solutions;
      - high understanding and long-term experience about/with IT projects.
   (ii) Participants agreed that they had knowledge about workflows of retailers and manufacturers to some extent. But the organization lacked all the other necessary competencies and resources.
   (iii) Participants estimated that it would be very difficult to create competitive advantages with this strategic opportunity. It would be tough to differentiate from other IT and technical journals in the market. In addition, they considered their strategic position as extremely weak against IT consultants.

(iv) Participants anticipated that customers, as well as organizational members (plus the Industry Association), would perceive such a new strategic position of *JOURNAL* as barely credible. From the participants' point of view, customers would more probably link such a position to IT consultants.

2. Providing ideas for additional fast-selling products
    (i) Participants found the following necessary competencies and resources:
        ● excellent knowledge about trends in relevant end-consumer industries and about changing end-consumer interests;
        ● good ability to keep track of these trends and changes;
        ● excellent and up-to-date know-how in marketing;
        ● perfect ability to transfer the marketing know-how to retailers and manufacturers in a practice-oriented way (for example, direct marketing, and so on).
    (ii) Participants perceived that they had limited knowledge about trends in relevant end-consumer industries. They did ascribe the ability to keep track of these trends to themselves. But the organization lacked marketing know-how and the ability to transfer this know-how.
    (iii) Participants anticipated that this strategic opportunity could create strong and sustainable competitive advantages. After all, this critical need was important for the customers and there was no real supply of information to meet this particular need in the market. *MONTHLY* only performed on a very low level and other current/potential competitors were not detected in this area at all.
    (iv) Whereas participants expected that such a new strategic position of *JOURNAL* would be feasible from the view of the customers, they anticipated that the Industry Association would definitely not support such a position. By helping to promote products from other industries, *JOURNAL* would undermine the Industry Association's efforts to keep up the importance of the whole industry.

3. Helping to gain competitive advantages
    (i) Participants found the following necessary competencies and resources:
        ● excellent and trusting high-level (for example, managing directors') contacts with retailers and manufacturers (for example to get information about current and future strategic activities);

- excellent knowledge and understanding about the world of the customers (retailers and manufacturers);
- very broad and functional industry network;
- good strategic and organizational development competencies;
- reliable contacts (network) and easy access to persons who are experts in strategy and organizational development.

(ii)   Participants believed that they had most of the necessary competencies and resources at their disposal, except strategic and organizational development competencies and reliable contacts to persons who are experts in these fields.

(iii)   Participants expected that this strategic opportunity might create sustainable competitive advantages, although differentiation from competitors would be not an easy task for *JOURNAL*. Furthermore, many customers were not yet fully aware of this critical need.

(iv)   Despite the fact that many customers were not yet fully aware of this critical need, participants expected that such a strategic position would be readily accepted by customers. Also, participants estimated that the Industry Association would strongly support such a position because *JOURNAL* would reinforce the association's efforts to defend the industry.

After this detailed assessment participants began to concentrate on strategic opportunities and to discuss how attainable they actually were. During this discussion, it quickly became clear to the group that the opportunity 'giving advice for technical equipment' would not lead to any competitive advantages in the market. Nevertheless, participants stated that the topic itself was important to customers and should play a future role in the content of *JOURNAL*. The opportunity 'providing ideas for additional fast-selling products' seemed by far to be more attractive to participants. Even though they lacked some competencies, the group was sure that they could cope with the challenge. There were many good reasons for responding to this strategic opportunity, but the political concerns by the Industry Association made participants very skeptical about its attainability. Again, participants stated that this topic was very important for customers and should be considered in the future *JOURNAL* content.

Finally, participants turned their attention towards the opportunity 'helping to gain competitive advantages'. Although participants had detected this opportunity as a hot and highly desired domain before, they were very aware of the related differentiation difficulties in making an effective response. However, participants believed that they had many of the necessary competencies and resources, which were also quite distinctive in the industry (for example, they had a broad, functional industry network; and excellent and trustworthy high-level contacts in the industry through the Industry Association). This would give them a good starting point for establishing a strategic position. Missing competencies might be addressed by extending the existing network towards experts in the fields of strategy and organizational development. Participants were certain that such an extension would not take too much time and effort because of their existing networking capabilities. In addition, participants concluded that a focus on this strategic opportunity would be extremely credible in the eyes of the customers, as it fitted the Industry Association's aim to defend the competitiveness of the whole industry. Although well aware of the fact that differentiation was still a weak flank, all participants were confident that they would find a creative solution to address that issue. In summary, this strategic opportunity was perceived as highly attainable and desired by all participants.

Encouraged by such an attractive strategic opportunity, participants went on with their assessment. When the group reviewed the critical customer need 'help to gain competitive advantages', they made a central discovery which they obviously had overseen so far. As soon as it comes down to the success of retailers' own (already threatened) businesses, they urgently need substantial information that is reliable and faultless. This important demand perfectly connected to the current external image of *JOURNAL*. As mentioned previously, from the customer's perspective *JOURNAL* provided reliable and credible facts. Even more, 'faultless & reliable information' as well as 'substantial' journalism were two closely connected desired attributes near the core of the SDI which also had multiple links to the SDI's 'heart' (see Figure 6.1 on page 110).

When the participants' attention had been drawn to these two desired attributes, they recognized that both competitors lacked a style of journalism that was connected with 'reliable and faultless information' and 'substance'. Even though *WEEKLY* was fast and topical on issues which could also be linked to the critical customer need ('help to gain competitive advantages'), their journalism was reduced to basic information which was mainly praised for being easy to read. Moreover, participants declared that the cheeky and perky style of *WEEKLY* did not support the impression of 'reliable and faultless' or 'substantial' journalism for customers. On the other hand, *MONTHLY* was practice-oriented on issues, which could contribute to the same critical customer need for information. But *MONTHLY* lacked substantial journalism as well. According to the workshop participants' experiences, *MONTHLY* preferred to publish practical relevant information immediately (though perhaps not totally accurately) rather than later. Finally, after careful consideration, workshop participants concluded that neither of their competitors systematically addressed this particular critical customer need.

Because of these newly gained insights, a new strategic opportunity became concrete and gripping to participants. They already began to imagine the consequences of responding to it in their daily work. For instance, participants assumed that such a commitment to substantial journalism would call for the need to carefully select, evaluate, and weigh information for its support for customers' competitiveness.

As the workshop drew to a close, a somewhat modified SDI for *JOURNAL* took on a concrete gestalt to participants through the evaluation of this particular strategic opportunity. During the whole evaluation process, participants worked very hard and were highly concentrated. According to participants, they gained many important insights and experienced deep emotions through evaluating and weighing up the organization's different viable opportunities. Moreover, the facilitators did not observe any persistent cognitive or emotional resistance by any participants during the whole evaluation process.

(c)   Formulating and determining a future market strategy

At this point, participants became very confident about *JOURNAL*'s future competitive advantage in the market. When the facilitators finally asked which benefits *JOURNAL* was going to offer their retailer readers ('Which concrete *benefits* are you going to offer your customers?'), participants tried to summarize their thoughts, ideas and desires. They came up with one condensed sentence that expressed a desired future market strategy for *JOURNAL* from their point of view:

> *JOURNAL* helps retailers to get forward-looking competitive advantages in their business by reporting topical issues in a professionally substantial way.

The participants were very content with their result. However, they also realized that this future market strategy had been created solely for their most important customer group – retailers. What about the manufacturers, who are also a quite important group of customers? After a brief discussion, participants consensually decided to assess the customer group of manufacturers in order to verify influences on a retailer-focused future market strategy.

At this point, participants began to study the comprehensive scenario story of manufacturers (see page 124) and related critical customer needs (see Table 6.1 on page 136) in detail. While discussing the detected critical needs of manufacturers, however, participants discovered a close connection to retailers' needs. For instance, both groups were seeking solutions to avoid cutthroat competition, both groups needed knowledge about end-consumers, and both groups were looking for ways to increase sales. As a final point, the group concluded that the future market strategy which had been formulated for retailers was also highly relevant for manufacturers. However, they also found out that they would need to consider customized content for each customer group because topical issues and possible competitive advantages were quite different for both groups. After these important findings, participants decided that it would not be necessary to create a strategic value matrix for manufacturers. Instead, they immediately started to seek a new definition of their desired future market strategy. In conclusion, they formulated the market statement:

> *JOURNAL* helps customers to get forward-looking competitive advantages in their businesses by reporting topical issues in a professionally substantial way. The future foci of *JOURNAL* will be on possible differentiators, strategic alliances, market observation, new ways/tools to increase sales, and know-how about end-consumers/customers. These foci need to be customized for retailers and manufacturers.

At the end of this process, participants were convinced that this future market strategy expressed what they really wanted *JOURNAL* to be. They had come to a positive strategic decision that had been reached in consensus.

6.6.2   Theoretical and Practical Background for Formulating a Market Strategy

I would like to stop at the end of the first part of the fifth core process and provide some further background with regard to this complex and important step in strategy making. A number of questions may come up during this part of the strategy making process. For example: What are viable strategic opportunities? Why was the evaluation of the strategic opportunities guided by these particular four questions? And what makes a strategic decision so distinctive in a strategy making process?

This first part of the fifth and final core process prepared and requested participants to formulate a future market strategy that best expressed their shared desired identity (SDI) and seemed attainable for them.

As described in the case study, the first part of this process consisted of three steps: (a) detecting viable strategic opportunities, (b) evaluating viable strategic opportunities, and (c) formulating and determining a future market strategy. Each step has an interesting background.

(a)   Detecting viable strategic opportunities

The first step covers the detection of viable strategic opportunities for a customer group – namely retailers in the case study. But what are viable strategic opportunities? And how can participants detect them?

The term strategic opportunity has already been used in section 6.4.2. It was argued that a critical customer need can become a strategic opportunity when an organization is capable of providing something (products/services) to resolve the particular customer need. Such a strategic opportunity is *viable* when (a) the shared desired identity (SDI) and its corresponding core attributes are relevant to resolving that customer need and (b) the resolution of the need can create future competitive advantages, which means that the specific customer need is not already (or potentially) addressed by relatively strong competitors. As a result, viable strategic opportunities are possible ways of expressing an SDI in a market by using them to create future competitive advantages. Each viable strategic opportunity is a potential basis for a possible future market strategy of an organization.

Although it has not been explicitly mentioned in the case study, participants did use the strategic value matrix to detect viable strategic opportunities in this way. By matching their SDI with critical customer needs, it becomes evident to participants which customer needs may turn into *viable strategic opportunities* for the organization. Thus, the strategic value matrix (see Figure 6.7) not only challenges an SDI, but also offers important information for the formulation of a future market strategy. The right half of the strategic value matrix is of primary interest as these critical needs are more important to customers and because of that are likely to provide the best opportunities for the organization to create competitive advantages in the eyes of customers.

During this step, it is important for facilitators to pay close attention to the cognitive and emotional resistance of individual participants. A strategic choice may exclude customer needs that were underlying assumptions for individually desired organizational identities. If there is notable participant resistance, or strong disagreement among participants about a strategic opportunity's viability, it may be preferable to declare the need in contention as a viable opportunity and take it into further evaluation. Working on an organizational concept as fundamental as strategy, facilitators need to prevent participants from hastily turning down possibly viable strategic opportunities without adequate consideration. Participants too are likely to be very conscious of the importance of what they are doing, as they were in the case study, and unwilling to ignore or miss any strategic opportunity.

The detection of viable strategic opportunities still implicitly evolves an SDI. On the one hand, participants see which new and attractive strategic opportunities emerge out of critical customer needs that fit their SDI. On the other hand, participants see that each attribute of an SDI fits different strategic opportunities to a different extent. This inevitable reality makes participants think about their SDI in more depth, reconsidering single attributes.

(b)   Evaluating viable strategic opportunities

The second step of the fifth core process evaluates viable strategic opportunities in order to prepare participants to make necessary strategic choices. This was described in the case study as a brief conclusion, but was actually more difficult for participants, because each viable strategic opportunity was able to express their SDI in the market to a certain extent. It was therefore difficult for participants to focus on their future strategic activities. As Andrews (1987, pp. 78–9) put it: 'Some of the most difficult choices confronting a company are those that must be made among several alternatives that appear equally attractive and desirable.' But participants have to focus, to limit their strategic options, because the organization's resources are limited and therefore need to be concentrated on a very small number of deliberately chosen, highly attractive strategic opportunities.

Participants are asked to evaluate each viable strategic opportunity by considering three major criteria: relative strength, differentiation and feasibility. In the case study, these three aspects were represented by the four guiding evaluation questions. But why these particular aspects and their corresponding questions?

(1)   First, relative strengths are very important to accomplish sustainable and defendable competitive advantages   They are probably the most important consideration during this evaluation because they will determine to what extent an organization can make use of a viable strategic opportunity (Fengler, 2000). Which available competencies and resources are distinct and difficult to imitate for competitors? On the one hand, the relative strengths of an organization can create future competitive advantages if they can be transformed into products and services that are perceived and valued by the customers. On the other hand, available internal capabilities constrain the set of competitive advantages that can be chosen because competitive advantages from the viewpoint of a customer must be realistic, must rely on plausible resources and competencies. Further, distinctive competencies and resources can only be brought into effect if a company is aware of them and if this perception is shared by organizational members (see Liebl, 2002b). Thus, identifying distinctive resources and competencies of the organization and interpreting them properly is important during strategy making (Fengler, 2000, pp. 36–46).

Many strategists identify distinctive resources and competencies by analysing strengths and weaknesses within the SWOT framework. But how can one decide whether a resource is a strength or a weakness? From my practical experience, resources and competencies can only be meaningfully assessed with respect to a concrete viable strategic opportunity, because their strategic significance is solely established by a reference point (Fengler, 2000, p. 71). For example, a German retail bank detected the critical customer need for 'appropriate and flexible accumulation of financial resources for retirement'. While the bank's capability to have a 'high influence on cooperating financial institutions, such as life insurances or mortgage banks' could be seen as strategically significant (because it could be used to make cooperating partners create special products/services for the bank's customers), another internal capability, for example 'dense ATM network in Germany', could be seen as strategically insignificant or irrelevant for this particular need. This little example demonstrates that formerly perceived weaknesses may turn into relative strengths in the light of new strategic opportunities and vice versa (see Ansoff, 1980; Ansoff, 1984; Liebl, 1999c).

However, identifying distinctive resources and competencies of an organization remains a difficult task. The process tends to be haphazard and political because each participant wants to ensure that the activities managed by him/her are seen as distinctive internal capabilities of the organization (Hamel and Prahalad, 1994, p. 247). This is understandable. Anticipation of winning or losing from the strategy making process will influence organizational participants to value some skills and resources more than others (Eden and Ackermann, 1998, p. 47). As a result, no other procedure is seen by participants as a better opportunity for self-aggrandisement in strategy making than the identification of relative strengths, and identification attempts normally produce lengthy lists of competencies and resources (Liebl, 2000b, p. 120), where a much smaller list of relative strengths can be found. Similarly, participants tend to associate relative strengths with the products and services in which they are embedded. Finally, participants are problematic evaluators because they tend to confuse relative strengths associated with their perceived value, and benefit the customer is likely to perceive (Hamel and Prahalad, 1994, pp. 245–9).

Due to these demonstrated difficulties, the evaluation described in the case study took a different approach, which was strongly influenced by Fengler (2000). With the first evaluation question, facilitators drew the participants' attention away from their own organization and towards the viable strategic opportunity ('Which resources and competencies should an organization ideally have to make the best use of this particular strategic opportunity?'). Instead of battling about existing resources and competencies, this question triggers another aspect that has much less potential for conflict: wishful thinking about needed resources and competencies to use a strategic opportunity – having no budget constraints.

After having created such a wish-list of resources and competencies for a specific strategic opportunity, it is much easier to relate them to the internal capabilities of the organization by using a single evaluation question: 'Which resources and competencies does your organization already have and to what extent?' This single question includes three important perspectives on internal capabilities which have been briefly addressed above: (1) Can internal capabilities (which were seen as relative strengths in the past) be broadened or adapted to these new requirements? (Hamel and Prahalad, 1994, pp. 252–3); (2) Are there internal capabilities (which were seen as weaknesses in the past) that now become relative strengths in the light of new strategic opportunities? (see Ansoff, 1980 and 1984; Liebl, 2000b); (3) To what extent are internal capabilities sufficient? And which internal capabilities are *missing* that would need to be viewed as a central *weakness* for the organization when choosing this particular strategic opportunity? (Fengler, 2000, p. 77).

Finally, participants need to evaluate their own internal capabilities compared to competitors. Are their resources and competencies distinctive? Can their capabilities be imitated by competitors in a short period of time? Only those resources and competencies that are unique to a certain degree and difficult to imitate by competitors are relative strengths which can be expected to create sustainable competitive advantages in the future. Only as a result of answering this question does it become obvious to participants whether a future market strategy (that focuses on a particular strategic opportunity) is based on existing relative strengths or not. Furthermore, the results of this question indicate which relevant capabilities are actually missing.

(2)   The second aspect of evaluating viable strategic opportunities is differentiation   Competitive strategy is about being different and the aim of strategy is to enable an organization to gain sustainable competitive advantages (see Porter, 1996). Consequently, participants need to answer the question: 'Does a future market strategy (that would focus on this particular strategic opportunity) create competitive advantages?' Only competitors within the strategic value matrix were considered in order to review a competitive environment for an SDI. In the case study, other detected competitors, such as business consultants, IT consultants or market research institutes, were not considered in the strategic value matrix. But can the organization also compete with other organizations that address the same critical customer need in a very different way or with a different

technology? In addition, participants need to consider these competitors' future responses and strategy shifts with regard to the discussed strategic opportunity.

This very important differentiation question needs to be widely discussed and explored by participants because it determines whether an organization will be able to 'win a market' in a competitive environment created by a strategic opportunity or not.

(3)   The third aspect of evaluating strategic opportunities is feasibility   In the case study, this evaluation was represented by the question: 'Does a future market strategy (that would focus on this particular strategic opportunity) seem feasible from the viewpoint of the customers as well as from your viewpoint?' This question tries to relate an existing image of the organization to a desired new one, for both customers and participants. While participants evaluate the attainability of change from their perspective (remember the 'change acceptance zone' with the identity gap that was discussed in section 4.3), they evaluate the credibility and trustworthiness of their desired image from the customer's perspective. This question ensures that a desired identity does not lose connection with reality. This third evaluative discussion assures attainability from both ends: the realization of a strategy within the organization and the creation of competitive advantages in the eyes of the customers.

Evaluation of strategic opportunities by assessing these three aspects in detail is of vital importance in a design of a practical strategy making process. But as seen in the case study, the real evaluation actually starts after having completed the detailed assessment of each strategic opportunity. A broad discussion was initiated around questions such as: 'Which strategic opportunity can be used to a high extent because of existing relative strengths?' 'Which strategic opportunity will provide maximum differentiation?' 'Which strategic opportunity covers an extremely important need of our customers?' 'Which strategic opportunity is feasible for customers and organizational members?' Which strategic opportunity best expresses our SDI in the way we "want to be"?' The broad discussions lead to intuitive discriminations of strategic opportunities. In the case study, for example, participants already knew their organization was not likely to respond to the opportunity 'giving advice for technical equipment'.

The whole iterative evaluation process deliberately uses the close relationship of an SDI and a future market strategy. An SDI defines an organization's future identity which is rooted in seminal beliefs and values, a future market strategy refers to future competitive advantages and corresponding activities to achieve that SDI. The relationship between both future concepts has already been discussed in section 3.3.2 (see Figure 3.6). During the intense evaluation process, participants constantly ask themselves: 'Is this who we want to be?' Due to discrimination between opportunities, some core attributes of an SDI may become more important than others. This helps participants to further infer, modify or affirm their SDI, while working on a concrete future market strategy at the same time. A desired organizational identity, capturing the questions 'Who should we be as an organization?' and 'What should we stand for', attains more gestalt and strategic concreteness for participants, as they can think of real competitive advantages for the future.

That this interrelation worked out in practice, has been seen in the case study. Participants gained an improved sense and impression of what their organization can do for customers' needs in a competitive environment in a way that is aligned with and expresses their SDI. Discriminating strategic opportunities as well as gaining an understanding of an SDI that has come to have more of a gestalt over time, has created a limited space of desirable and attainable strategies.

(c)   Formulating and Determining a Future Market Strategy

The third step describes the formulation and determination of a future market strategy, but it is inseparable from the second step, and indeed emerges from it. However, this step is crucial in a strategy making process and I would like to focus on two aspects of it that may explain why I see it important enough to create a separate step. First, it is important to highlight the difference between systematic and logically sound procedures in strategy making and a strategic decision; and second, I would like to underline the role of facilitators during the making of this vital decision.

Up to this point, the strategy making process has offered a series of systematic and logically sound procedures: revealing individually desired organizational identities, exploring and analysing the organizational environment and organizational capabilities, discovering competitors and detecting critical customer needs and strategic opportunities. In a procedurally rational way, the facilitators ensure that each step is understood by participants and that each step relates to prior and future steps. Nonetheless, all these systematic and logically sound procedures only help participants to make a strategic decision, they do not determine it.

As was the case in the practical case study, participants often become aware that more than one strategy is possible to express their SDI and that there is no single right strategy. Once the limited space of desired and attainable strategies has turned into a visible and gripping set of options in the minds of the participants, it is the next systematic and logical step for participants to formulate and determine the future market strategy that is most desired and seems most attainable. But in contrast to other steps, facilitators do not offer any further guidance by providing new perspectives, matrices or measures to help participants with their decision. During formulation and determination of a future market strategy, participants are on their own.

It is extremely important that facilitators take their role seriously at this point. They must not push participants or give any advice that leads toward a certain direction. It is the role of facilitators to encourage and facilitate the participants' strategy making process effectively for themselves, but not to decide *for them.*

A strategic decision is one that needs to be consensually reached by participants after all the explored and analysed factors have been considered and the implications of each assessed. Andrews (1987, pp. 78–9) describes the process of a strategic decision as follows:

> Whenever choice is compounded of rational analysis that can have more than one outcome, of aspiration and desire that can run the range of human ambition, and a sense of responsibility that changes the appeal of alternatives, it cannot be reduced to quantitative approaches or to the exactness management science can apply to narrower questions. Managers contemplating strategic decisions must be willing to make them without decision rules, with confidence in their own judgement, which will have been seasoned by repeated analyses of similar questions . . . The final decision, which should be made as deliberately as possible after a detailed consideration of the issues . . . is an act of will and desire as much as of intellect.

Due to the methodological integration and evolution of what people 'want to do' and what they think their organization 'should do' in the proposed strategy making design, it is very likely that there is a will as well as a desire to make a strategic decision. In the evaluation process just described, the limited space of desired and attainable strategies unfolds in a way that maximizes creative and imaginative power about solid and concrete future competitive advantages. A final working question ('Which concrete *benefits* are you going to offer your customers?') further supports the formulation of future competitive advantages which describe which customer functions are addressed in which way.

Consequently, as seen in the case study, at this particular stage of the process participants are able to find a creative balance between highly attractive strategic opportunities in the market, the organization's distinct resources/competencies and their own desired organizational identity. They are in a situation to do so because their efforts to analyse the organization and its environment have resulted in newly generated knowledge and an evolved self-assurance about their SDI that merge into a solid picture of what the organization should do for their customers in the future. Through that, participants are able to creatively link or choose strategic opportunities which generate a consistent and sound strategy for their customer groups. They are able to formulate this desired and attainable strategy by describing future benefits to customers which are also their targeted future competitive advantages. Making a consensual strategic decision on such a future market strategy offers a high chance of realization because it reflects what participants think they 'want to be' (desires) and what they think is attainable, regardless of whether it is in more abstract terms the best economic match or not.

However, formulating and determining a future market strategy at a high abstract level is not sufficient as an outcome in strategy making. Let us return to the case study and see how the *JOURNAL* strategy team designed the substance of their future market strategy.

6.6.3 Designing the Substance of a Desired and Attainable Market Strategy

After the important market strategy decision was made by workshop participants, the facilitators proposed that they should further design the substance of a customer-oriented strategy which defines *how* their deliberately chosen competitive advantage could be achieved.

The whole designing process was guided by five elementary questions:

(1) What types of products and services should the organization provide and what special characteristics should these have?
(2) In which geographic areas should the products and services be sold, how, by whom, and with how much emphasis for each of our customer groups?
(3) How should the organization fill the gaps between strategically necessary and currently existing resources and competencies?
(4) Which products and services that have an extremely high impact on customer benefits can be introduced, adapted or broadened within six months?
(5) Which costs are we going to face, and what pricing policy should we set for which products and services?

Participants addressed each important element in intensive group work sessions. Three small groups were created by the facilitators and each group had to present their results to the other groups. Then, for each element, the facilitators merged the outcomes of discussion with the participants by letting them look for similar, identical, or closely connected key features of the strategy being designed. Each time, a forceful discussion about the interactions between different key features and their combination, relevance or contribution to the achievement of the future competitive advantage started among the participants. It is worth noting that no substantial conflicts arose during these concentrated group processes. The deliberately chosen market strategy seemed to discipline participants to work hard on how to make their vision happen. Participants never lost touch with their formulated future competitive advantages (future market strategy). As the design of all elements took shape, key features were invariably changed and extended to create an agreed whole with features that were desired and seen as attainable by participants. As a result, the *JOURNAL* strategy team was able to make a first broad and consensual decision on each element. These final decisions on each element are briefly described in the following way.

(1)   What types of products and services should the organization provide and what special characteristics should these have?   Participants decided that their targeted competitive advantage could be gained through a set of three different products: the printed *JOURNAL*, the online *JOURNAL*, and *JOURNAL* e-mail newsletters. The printed *JOURNAL* should now be published only once a week, but in full color. The color was supposed to increase the reading pleasure and to increase the design options for the layout department. The editorial style should be exciting, pragmatic, and easy to read (for example, short sentences). *JOURNAL*'s content should mainly provide deep and substantial information, including commentaries (meaning selected, evaluated, and weighed information) about selected topical issues. A new structure of sections would represent the new foci of *JOURNAL*. The printed *JOURNAL* should be complemented by the online *JOURNAL* which would mainly provide daily updated topical issues. The online *JOURNAL* should underscore a fast delivery of topical issues. The online editorial style should be concise and news-like. Finally, *JOURNAL* e-mail newsletters would provide hot relevant news and pure information for pre-selected main foci.

(2)   In which geographic areas should the products and services be sold, how, by whom, and with how much emphasis for each of our customer groups? Because *JOURNAL* covers a national industry, participants reconfirmed remaining a national journal that focuses on existing customer groups.

(3)   How should the organization fill the gaps between strategically necessary and currently existing resources and competencies?   Participants decided to build up missing strategic resources and competencies through

internal development within the next year. However, they also decided to get external support in order to realize a new (and strategy-corresponding) layout and design. In addition, the online *JOURNAL* and *JOURNAL* e-mail newsletter system would also be technically realized by external service providers.

(4) Which products and services that have an extremely high impact on customer benefits can be introduced, adapted or broadened within six months? Although not previously mentioned, the team actually had a time target from the beginning of the whole strategy making process, and by the end of the workshop participants were able to confirm that they would keep to it. The relaunch/start of all three products was planned for 1 January 2002. Other milestones for *JOURNAL* were determined to be October 2001 for a first 'dummy' of the new *JOURNAL* and December 2001 for the 'zero issue' of *JOURNAL*.

(5) Which costs are we going to face, and what pricing policy should we set for which products and services? The economic logic of *JOURNAL* would still be based on a subscription fee. The subscription fee would cover the printed *JOURNAL* and the online *JOURNAL*. *JOURNAL* e-mail newsletters would be additionally charged, but the price had to be determined. Although the number of printed issues for *JOURNAL* would decrease by 50 per cent per year, the subscription fee would remain the same (£227). Moreover, new advertising customers could be attracted by a full color option. Despite the fact that advertising rates would be raised by 30 per cent (full color), these advertising rates would still be less than those of competitors, which have smaller circulations. Workshop participants calculated that even in the worst economic case (50 per cent decrease in advertising sales), the profitability of *JOURNAL* could be held, due to significantly lowered production costs.

At the end of the whole strategy making process, the facilitators invited each participant to present the future market strategy to the group in the form of a story. Every participant presented a story. Remarkably, many participants told very passionate stories that deeply moved the other participants. In addition, most participants not only described the future market strategy and its elements, but also illustrated consequences for them personally and actions they would take in order to make the new strategy visible and concrete to the group. In accordance with the storytelling experiences of the first workshop, participants were relaxed, used a friendly kind of humor, and were laughing a lot. The way participants presented themselves and their stories, it became obvious that participants not only perceived the strategy as attainable but also as strongly desirable. In all, these stories gave the signal to participants actually to launch the strategy they had worked to create.

6.6.4 Theoretical and Practical Background for Designing the Strategy's Substance

I would like to provide some concluding background with regard to the last part of the strategy making process just described. While the first part ended with the formulation of a future market strategy, the second part designs its substance.

Following the case study, the second part of the fifth and final core process can be divided into two steps: (a) designing elements of a future market strategy, and (b) describing a future market strategy in the form of a story.

(a) Designing elements of a future market strategy
As described in the case study, this step immediately directs participants into the design of a customer-oriented strategy. Up to this point the future market strategy is only a deliberately chosen future competitive advantage. But strategy is a customer-oriented concept of *how* competitive advantages can be achieved. Participants must innovate a set of products and services that will deliver a unique mix of value to their customers, and design a business model that ensures its profitability.

This part of the strategy making process explicitly refers to and makes use of the holistic design principle discussed in section 4.1.3.3. While Ackoff (1981) and researchers in appreciative inquiry (see Watkins and Mohr, 2001) use a similar approach to design a whole organization – including its structure, operations, and its relationships to stakeholders – the process here focuses only on the substance of a future market strategy. But why did the facilitators use these particular five working questions to guide the design of the market strategy's substance?

The five questions reflect the five major elements of a market strategy defined by Hambrick and Fredrickson (2001), which was introduced in section 3.1:

(1) How will we win in the marketplace?
(2) Where will we be active and with how much emphasis?
(3) How will we get there?
(4) What will be our speed and sequence of moves?
(5) How will we obtain our returns?

Providing these five elements of strategy immediately raises other questions, such as: What is the meaning of these elements? And how are questions which were used in the case study linked to these elements? With regard to these questions I would like to provide some further details on each element of strategy raised by Hambrick and Fredrickson:

(1) One of the most important elements of a strategy is differentiation: 'How will we win in the marketplace?' This element of strategy must define how deliberately chosen competitive advantages can be gained through an innovative set of products and services. Competitive advantages arise from both conscious choice of products and services and how they are 'performed' (Porter, 1996, p. 62). Consequently, this element is reflected within the question: 'What types of products and services should the organization provide, and what special characteristics (for example, aesthetics, content, and so on) should these have?'

(2) When a set of products and services is determined, Hambrick and Fredrickson's second element is the question: 'Where will we be active and with how much emphasis?' For instance, in an organization with several customer groups or several geographical markets, some groups or markets might be identified as more important, while others are considered as less crucial. Due to the limitation of organizational resources, a prioritization of these arenas is a fundamental element of a future market strategy. Therefore, this element is behind the question: 'In which geographic areas should the products and services be sold, how, by whom, and with how much emphasis, for each of our customer groups?'

(3) After deciding on products and services as well as on arenas, participants need to concentrate on the question: 'How will we get there?' This question mainly focuses on currently *missing* resources and competencies of the organization that are necessary to create future competitive advantages with chosen products and services in preferred arenas. In the strategy making process I have been describing, participants use the lists of strategically relevant resources and competencies that have been created during the first part of the fifth core process. For instance, once they decided to extend the service range of their organization, participants had to raise the question of whether they should accomplish that by internal development of competencies, or by other options such as joint ventures or acquisitions. This element of strategy is reflected in the question: 'How should the organization fill the gaps between strategically necessary and current existing resources and competencies?'

(4) Decisions based on the first three elements of the future market strategy subsequently led to a fourth element that needs to be designed:

'What will be our speed and sequence of moves?' The realization of a future market strategy is not done at the same time on all fronts – it requires a purposeful sequence of initiatives (see Bryson, 1995). For instance, an organization may decide to begin with their national market before spreading to other markets because of their limited resources. According to Hambrick and Fredrickson (2001) a decision on sequences is driven by multiple factors, such as resources, urgency, achievement of credibility, or early profits. Participants need to define and balance these factors for their own organization. An initial question can support a first decision for sequences by focusing attention on impact: 'Which products and services that have an extremely high impact on customer benefits can be introduced, adapted or broadened within six months?'

(5) The final strategy element that needs to be designed focuses on the question: 'How will we obtain our returns?' This element defines the economic logic of a future market strategy. Participants should imagine how customers will monetarily value their products and services, how their cost structure will develop under consideration of the other strategy elements, and if they are able to gain reasonable profits. Even though the real outcome of a strategy can only be evaluated in retrospect, it is useful to anticipate it. Serious discussion now helps bring out the financial feasibility and corresponding financial risks of a future market strategy. This element is reflected in the question: 'Which costs are we going to face and what pricing policy should we set for which products and services?'

Each of these five elements of strategy is important and needs appropriate time and attention by participants. Participants should work on each element until they are able to make a first broad and consensual decision on it, as described in the case study. In doing so, it becomes apparent to participants that strategy turns into a *system of decisions* where every single decision takes into consideration the overall design of future market strategy. That means that a strategy as a whole has properties that none of its elements do, and its elements acquire properties by being part of the strategy that they would not have when considered separately (Ackoff, 1981, p. 122). Consequently, the aim of this step in strategy design is to achieve a robust, reinforced consistency among the elements which promotes an overall future market strategy as well as future competitive advantages (Hambrick and Fredrickson, 2001, p. 50).

Participants need at least the first rough answers to these five elementary questions before starting with new activities, including the design process that focuses on internal operations, organizational structures, and so on.

However, covering these internal design processes would exceed the aim of this book, and they are described elsewhere in detail (see for example Ackoff, 1981, pp. 126–68).

At the end of this step in the fifth and last core process of strategy making, participants will have determined a set of rough but consistent elements that should support each other and create an overall future market strategy. During the design of the five elements of a future market strategy, participants constantly measure the consequences of their strategic decisions by asking themselves: 'Is this who we want to be?' It is the close relationship between a future market strategy and an SDI that simultaneously ensures an iterative evolution of both concepts, reflecting what participants 'want to do' and what they think their organization 'should do'. The result is a desired and attainable future market strategy.

(b) Describing a future market strategy in the form of a story
As a final workshop step in the fifth core process, each participant portrayed the future market strategy they had designed and its elements in the form of a story.

The description of a strategic concept in the form of a story had already been used during the first core process (see section 6.2.4). This step is identical in form and rationale. Accordingly, the participants' stories account for almost the same benefits:

- each participant will reflect on and enhance his/her comprehension about a future market strategy and its elements;
- the descriptions will create an emotional, meaningful and dense portrait of the future market strategy;
- descriptions will reveal elements which are still vague in the future market strategy.

The powerful advantages of storytelling with regard to obtaining these reflections on a strategic concept have already been discussed. The dense portraits from stories by participants are an excellent closure of the fifth core process. It makes a future market strategy more gripping, visible and memorable to participants. Again, the facilitators may make use of a video camera and tape each story presentation of the participants in order to keep these important illustrative portraits for future use.

At the end of the proposed design of a practical strategy making process, participants have created and determined a desired and attainable market strategy as well as its first substantial elements – a strategy that is very likely to come alive in practice.

6.6.5   Linking Deliberate Strategy Making to Continuous Learning

It should be recalled that strategy is conceived as a continuous learning process, where strategy making is a conscious intervention into this cycle. The designed strategy making process that takes place only in workshop meetings ends here because at this point, the boundaries between a conscious intervention and a re-entered (practical) learning process begin to blur. As participants begin to take the first actions on their strategic decisions, they will simultaneously continue the design process that now focuses on internal operations, organizational structures, and so on. For any further design tasks, the five strategy elements can be considered as the center for creating a comprehensive and integrated activity system as outlined by Porter (1996).

These blurring boundaries between thinking/designing and action are necessary for effective strategy making. As Andrews (1987, p. 81) puts it:

> An idea is not complete or even completely understood until it is put into action. A unique corporate strategy is only rhetoric until it is embodied in organization activities that are guided by the strategy but in turn continually reshape it.

The strategy making process must therefore connect to the continuous flow of strategic actions and interactions as has been described with the dynamic framework found in section 3.2.

6.7   A BRIEF EPILOGUE: HOW *JOURNAL* WENT ON WITH ITS FUTURE MARKET STRATEGY

The entire strategy making process, described up to this point, took about five months and required one day for face-to-face interviews with participants and eight full-day workshop sessions. After having a first rough and consistent strategy for *JOURNAL*, the team then continued to work out the five elements in further detail, and designed internal operations (for example, core workflows) and other supporting activities. At the same time, the participants began to realize their first decisions and put new internal processes into practice. The facilitators still encouraged and supported participants in their efforts. Finally, the strategic repositioning of the printed *JOURNAL*, the modified online *JOURNAL* and the new *JOURNAL* e-mail newsletters started on time on 1 January 2002.

Most of the strategy details described in this book were realized as originally designed. It is also worth noting how the desired attributes of an aggregated SDI were combined in practice. Although *JOURNAL*'s focus is to help customers get forward-looking competitive advantages in their businesses by reporting topical issues in a professionally substantial way, other desired attributes (such as 'human touch' or 'support for practical work') were creatively integrated into the concept in a remarkable way. When reporting about people in the business ('human touch'), editors try to connect these reports to *JOURNAL*'s main focus. For example, an article in the new *JOURNAL* provided a portrait of the managing director of a manufacturing firm and how he successfully manages his product range.

Reader surveys in 2002 revealed that *JOURNAL* hit the right topics in an appropriate way and that the 'new' *JOURNAL* reached more readers per copy than before (as subscribers give their copies to employees, friends, and so on). The reduced frequency, to one issue per week, seemed to be a relief to many readers burdened with heavy workloads and increasingly perceived lack of time. The new design and color layout was also well received. Right after the first issue of the 'new' *JOURNAL* had been published, a reviewer in the business concluded on 7 January 2002: 'Altogether, *JOURNAL* makes a great impression: Now, it has become a true journal.'

Looking back, the team and the whole organization accomplished a remarkable change in *JOURNAL*. The surveys and other feedback gave the strategy making team as well as all other organizational members confidence about being on the right track. Importantly, this feeling was finally confirmed by solid numbers. *JOURNAL* was able to stop the dramatically decreasing number of subscriptions (down 10 per cent in 2001) in 2002. By 2003, the number of subscriptions increased by 5 per cent. At the same time, sales of *JOURNAL* (subscriptions and advertisements) increased by 15 per cent in 2002 and by an additional 7 per cent in 2003. Most significant, the negative rate of return of the year 2001 (−2 per cent) turned into a positive rate of 5 per cent in 2002 and to 9 per cent in the year 2003. Finally, *JOURNAL* had found a viable and profitable market strategy that expressed what organizational members really 'wanted to do'.

NOTES

1. These issues were formulated during the first workshop (see section 6.2.3) by the participants and by the management.
2. Very often, this relates to organizational members' (negative) past experiences with members of the top management and/or consultants/facilitators in former strategy processes or to existing prejudices about consultants and/or top management (see for instance Meier, 1999).
3. Which is in accordance with the close link of organizational identity and identification that has been discussed in section 2.1
4. Reviewing existing operational measures of organizational identity was not helpful at this point. None of the approaches do consequently consider the idiomatic peculiarity

of organizational members nor do they reveal organizational identity with sufficient cognitive structural complexity (see van Rekom and van Riel, 2000).

5. Storylistening is a registered community trademark (EU) of Schindl Rughase Partners. The storylistening method has been called Sensor in earlier publications (see Rughase, 2002).

6. It should also be mentioned that some strategy researchers (for example Eden and Ackermann, 1998) use the method of cognitive mapping for interviews in order to capture the cognitive structure in a diagrammatic format. This precise and detailed method could also be employed here. But while Eden and Ackermann (1998) use created cognitive maps during the following workshops, the extremely time-consuming work needed to create these maps might be inappropriate for the purpose described here (see Eden and Ackermann, 1998, pp. 94–101).

7. For empirical evidence see Young (2001).

8. In accordance with appreciative inquiry, key elements of organizational past experiences are linked with a shared desired identity. But while appreciative inquiry takes key elements of the past as the origin of a desired identity, the approach that is proposed here employs them in a supportive way for the desired identity. See section 4.1.3.2.

9. Whereas participants started this exploration for the group of retailers at exactly this point in the strategy making process, the exploration for manufacturers was done at a much later stage. However, for reasons of simplicity the latter exploration will also be outlined in this section.

10. This customer-centered analysis does not mean that customer-unrelated trends and issues that can also affect the organization in the future are not important at all in strategy making (for example political regulations). But while the customer-centered analysis is central to *determining* the purpose (strategic position) of an organization in a market through detecting strategic opportunities (section 6.4), customer-unrelated trends and issues can be used later to *validate* the feasibility of such opportunities.

11. As seen, this assumption making is also heavily influenced by current and desired organizational identity. See sections 3.2 and 3.3.

12. Sony and Walkman are registered trademarks of Sony Corporation.

13. iPod is a registered trademark of Apple Computer, Inc.

7. The impact of identity: lessons learned

This chapter briefly reviews the *JOURNAL* case study and its feasibility, and highlights selected lessons learned. It then describes other practical experiences concerning the impact of desired organizational identities and the proposed strategy making process design, in particular in larger organizations.

7.1 THE CASE STUDY: REVIEW AND LESSONS LEARNED

From my perspective, the *JOURNAL* case study clearly verifies the feasibility of the designed strategy making process proposed in Chapter 5. Two of the most critical elements of a strategy making design turned out to be practicable: the new starting point and the change of measure.

With regard to the new starting point in strategy making, the case study shows that participants were willing and able to express their individually desired organizational identities. More important still, they were able to reach a consensual agreement on an aggregated shared desired identity (SDI) by *avoiding paralyzing conflicts*. This is important because the revelation of desired identities and the consensual creation of an SDI was possible even though (a) there were major hidden and subliminal internal conflicts between team members and departments, (b) there was limited and self-centered thinking in departments, and (c) participants were extremely suspicious of their management and of external facilitators. These initial organizational conditions are more the rule than the exception. I do not mean that the new starting point completely eliminated conflicts, fears or even distrust. But the participation principle and first positive experiences of sharing desires and creating a common desired identity created an initial spark of trust in working with the other participants, enough to avoid resistance. Despite the fact that participants remained hypersensitive and somehow skeptical about the whole process in the first few steps, they worked together in a productive and creative way. Eventually, the workshop experience built new trust and commitment over the course of time.

Another critical element of the proposed strategy making process design is the *change of measurement*. The case study demonstrates that an SDI can be used as a new measure in strategy making. After having created an SDI, participants began to feel a strong sense of ownership, which made the SDI the referent point for the strategy making process in an organic way. It was procedurally rational to them to work with their somehow promising idea of *JOURNAL*. Furthermore, the case study shows that the SDI can be *evolved* by challenging its strategic robustness and value. The strategic value matrix proved to be a valuable tool for challenging the SDI in a structured way. In this particular case, threatening competitors increased the stress level for participants, which resulted in an exposure of desired attributes that were of special importance to customers as well as to themselves (quick & topical).

The case study also illustrates interesting 'ending' dynamics as participants began to let formerly highly valued core parts (for example, 'human touch') drift towards the periphery. Participants were able to integrate 'new' core parts (reliable & faultless journalism/easy & fun to read, but substantial) into their SDI.[1] As they did so their SDI evolved and they designed a market strategy to express it that was clearly linked to current and past identities. The importance of these links was pointed out by the chief editor: in the first issue of *JOURNAL* in 2002, he concluded his editorial with the sentence: '*JOURNAL* changes to remain faithful to itself – for you.' The proposed design paved the way for integrating what participants 'want to do' and what they see their organization 'should do' in an organic and procedurally rational way.

In addition to validating the feasibility of designed strategy making, the case study also provided significant practical experiences. Many points of learning have already been described in the case study itself, including for example, how initial ideas for personal interviews were insufficient to create reasonable commitment for a first workshop, how important story-telling was for creating excellent group dynamics, and so on. Some other, less obvious but also key experiences for a process design, might also be mentioned in conclusion.

First, the case study has shown the central role of actual power holders with regard to the participation principle. The participation was a crucial – if not the most important – process principle to achieve a desired and attainable market strategy. The participants' trust – and with that their commitment – was slowly but steadily created when facilitators *and* the actual power holders constantly reassured participants through verbal statements *and* behavior that their participation was not only relevant but necessary. The actual power holders needed to honestly apply 'transformative' leadership, which is collective. There 'is a symbiotic relationship between leaders and followers, and what makes it collective is the subtle interplay between the followers' needs and wants and the leader's capacity to understand . . . these collective aspirations' (Bennis and Nanus, 1986, p. 217; see also Frost and Egri, 1990).

During strategy making, the responsible manager of Retailer Services Ltd, and the chief editor of *JOURNAL* (the actual power holders) seriously supported the participation principle, trying to empower organizational members to find and fulfill a new strategic position for *JOURNAL*. Due to their behavior during the workshops and beyond them, the trust and commitment of the other participants increased over time. Nevertheless, because the actual power holders felt insecure in the area of transformative leadership at the beginning of the process in one way or another, the facilitators had to actively and individually coach them. The facilitators helped these leaders to understand their supporting role and encouraged them to deal with it. Through this, the facilitators helped to keep up the power holders' continuous support for the true participation of all participants. Even though such an understanding can be enhanced by facilitators to a certain extent, it becomes a vital presupposition for strategy making that it is the sole responsibility of actual power holders. It can be clearly stated that without the actual power holders' understanding of transformative leadership, and their support for the true participation of all participants, the designed strategy making process would have failed.

Second, the case study also underlines the necessity of skilled and neutral facilitators in practice. As already mentioned, conflicts between organizational members and departments are quite common in organizational life. Ackoff (1981, p. 94) claims that the elimination of conflict is necessary for organizational development. However, that is much easier said than done. The fact that participants were willing to get involved in the *JOURNAL* strategy making process (despite strong conflicts) indicated a first fragile belief in a new chance of solving their conflicts. These beliefs were closely connected with (expressed) expectations about the facilitators and their professionalism, trustworthiness, and credibility. In other words: the facilitators were especially expected to be *neutral* regarding conflict positions (content). Willingness to meet these expectations was constantly verified in a hypersensitive and skeptical way by participants. That means that facilitators who are perceived as dependent on actual power holders or particular conflicting parties would have had an even higher trust barrier to overcome than neutrally perceived ones. This barrier also excludes the option that group members become facilitators (even though participants occasionally say 'one of us needs to do the guiding job!'). In short, skilled and neutral facilitators of change processes are particularly important in conditions of potential conflict and tension, and these conditions almost always exist.

Third, the case study demonstrates the practical meaning of creativity in strategy making. As already discussed, creativity is about generating new ideas, alternatives, and possibilities. When the *JOURNAL* strategy team detected and evaluated 'helping to gain competitive advantages' as a viable strategic opportunity they were challenged by the already existing solutions of competitors in that field. However, workshop participants were confident about finding an additional creative solution. And they did. Due to their understanding of the customer's world and needs, they came up with a particular editorial style (which they thought of as reliable and substantial journalism) to meet the particular need they had identified better than competitors. One might say that this is not creative at all. However, the creativity of a solution depends on the perception and judgement of the market (in this case retailers and manufacturers as readers in a specific industry). It does not matter whether a similar idea already exists in other contexts or not, the solution *JOURNAL* came up with did not exist in their particular market and, therefore, they generated a *new* alternative. What they did might not be seen as a breathtaking novelty, but it is a new alternative that is in accord with what people need and *JOURNAL*'s shared desired identity. It helped *JOURNAL* increase sales, subscriptions and profits against trends experienced by the publishing industry. In fact, transferring objects and concepts from established contexts into new ones can be described as a character of new and creative ideas or innovations (see Groys, 1992; Liebl, 2001c; see also practical examples in Lester and Piore, 2004). This view and the case supports Weisberg's (1995) opinion that creative ideas that are realistic may be more a modification of the past rather than 'spectacular' innovations. It provides a good example of 'creative realism' (see Figure 4.2 on page 74) in strategy making that was made possible through a process of intense evaluation of strategic opportunities.

7.2   OTHER EXPERIENCES IN PRACTICAL STRATEGY MAKING PROCESSES

Since the *JOURNAL* case study in the year 2001, I have had several opportunities for further experiences with the strategy making process design proposed. Many of these experiences supported findings already described in this book. However, there is a particular practical experience, which I would like to share: strategy making and the impact of desired identities in larger companies.

Strategy Making and the Impact of Desired Identities in Larger Companies

When talking about strategy and strategy making many people immediately think about large companies such as IKEA, The Body Shop, Charles Schwab, Wal-Mart, Dell Computer, Microsoft and the like. Because they are extensively covered in the public (business) media as well as in academic publications, which preferably use them as case studies, their names and financial successes are highly recognized and their unique strategies seem to be well known. On the other hand, the company described in this book's case study is rather small. The part of the company that covers *JOURNAL* employs about 25 people in total and the strategy team, which consisted of nine key persons, represented almost 40 per cent of the workforce. The *JOURNAL* case study has shown that the strategy making process worked for a small company. But what about companies like those mentioned above that have more than 10000 employees? Will the proposed design of a strategy making process work with such large companies as well?

First of all, it should be noted that focusing only on the CEO's range of responsibility is too limited when it comes to strategy making in large companies. Of course, it seems of special interest how CEOs such as Jeff Immelt (GE), Richard Branson (Virgin), or Dieter Zetsche (Daimler-Chrysler) strategically manage large companies and conglomerates of 10 000 employees and more. In reality, however, we know that these CEOs cannot manage all their business operations personally and in detail. Large organizations consist of numerous operational organizations, divisions, departments and work-groups. In fact, many managers or leaders of these numerous smaller organizational entities are often faced with similar strategic issues and problems. Thus, strategy and strategy making is as important for them and their part of the organization as it is for their CEO. For these many managers or leaders, the larger company and its aims and intentions are only of interest to the extent that it is a powerful stakeholder, which influences the strategic future of their organizational entity (see Ackermann et al., 2005, p. 14). *JOURNAL* is actually a good example of such an entity as it is a small part of a medium-sized company (Retailer Services Ltd) which belongs to a number of larger organizations (regional industry associations). In short: strategy and strategy making in larger organizations is often applied on much smaller scales than is reflected in contemporary literature on strategic management.

Nevertheless, organizational entities of larger companies and individual companies which are seeking a desired and attainable market strategy can be quite large. And there are a number of questions that arise when thinking about the proposed design of a strategy making process in larger organizations: How can desired organizational identities of many involved people be revealed? How can a shared desired identity be aggregated? Or how can the participation principle be applied in general?

To illustrate how the design of strategy making as proposed in this book has been applied to a larger company, I would like to briefly present another practical case.

Two owners of a German manufacturing firm were seeking a new market strategy for their company, mainly to reposition their brand in the global market. Their company serves the European and US market (business-to-business) and produces in Eastern Europe and China. The company has about 1100 employees and the international top management team consists of 14 managers (including the two owners).

As a first step, the whole top management team engaged in a strategy making process as presented in this book (five core processes). At a certain point of the facilitator-guided process, the top management team had formulated a future competitive advantage and roughly designed basic strategy elements. Up to this point, the process took eight full-day workshops over a period of three months. Although the members of the team personally felt that their market strategy was creative, innovative, highly attainable, and reflected what they really 'wanted to do', they interrupted the strategy making process at this particular stage. They did so, because they were asking themselves how they could get the market strategy into practice by involving their employees. Essentially, the top management team was simply looking for an effective way to get their employees as excited about the market strategy as they actually were to accelerate the progress of the process of change.

It is my experience that in many larger organizations the top management would now begin to 'communicate' and 'sell' the designed market strategy to their employees via storytelling, spectacular strategy events, presentations, brochures, project layouts, leadership training and the like. The top management team of this particular company, however, became aware of the fact that individually desired identities can have a massive impact on strategy making. This awareness was mainly created by their own experiences during the development of the first rough market strategy. Having realized that the desired identities of their employees could have a strong impact on successful strategic change, the top management team wanted to assure serious and broad participation. Especially, they required participation in the final design of the market strategy of those employees who would be responsible for managing strategic changes in organizational practice (including middle-management, lower-management and informal leaders). But how could this be accomplished?

The facilitators and the top management team found a way for participation that is diametrically opposed to 'communicative' and 'convincing' approaches. Instead of presenting the top management team's market strategy to their employees and discussing it afterwards, the top management asked their middle and lower management (including some informal leaders) to develop their own desired and attainable market strategies. They wanted their managing employees to undertake the same kind of facilitator-guided strategy making process than they did, only in a more condensed way (two full-day workshops). The top management team explicitly pointed out that these developed strategies will be received as strategy proposals on a par with their own result.

Altogether, 70 managing employees of the company became actively involved at this stage of the strategy making process. Five strategy groups were created, each consisting of 12 to 19 people of different hierarchy levels which more or less reflected functional departments of the organization (marketing, sales, production, R&D, administration). This functional group formation was chosen because operationally working together on a daily basis supports certain perceptions on strategic issues, creates a common language and forms related desires among employees which can be helpful in a condensed, two-day strategy making process. It is important to note that none of the groups got any information about the top management's market strategy, because it would have influenced their own process.

In spite of the time constraint, the roughly designed market strategies of the five groups were remarkably good with regard to quality and detail. At the end of each workshop, the facilitators presented the top management's market strategy to participants. After these presentations, the participants were always astonished at the similarity to their own market strategy. However, none of the developed strategies was completely identical to the top management's strategy or to the others. Despite broad overlapping contents, each market strategy had important differences and nuances. Very interestingly, each of the five strategies included a seemingly important element, which was rooted in the company's history and was not considered by top management.

Each team presented their market strategy proposal to the top management team. Differences between both strategy concepts were discussed and the top management team as well as the managing employees were able to reach a better understanding of the underlying assumptions and conclusions of one another's concepts. The top management was impressed by the passion of the employees and by the quality of their work. During each session, the top management team learned something new and important from their employees.

After these presentations and discussions, the top management team integrated the results, and continued strategy making together with group representatives in separate meetings. During these meetings the market strategy and its elements evolved step by step towards an organizational future that had many inventors, and which was in alignment with most desired identities of the individuals involved. For example, the important element that was mentioned above was integrated into the market strategy. Finally, the top management team and the managing employees agreed on a commonly designed market strategy.

Once the strategic decision was made by the top management team, the managing employees themselves started to further design internal operations and organizational structures as well as to put them directly into action. It is worth noting that the managing employees also used the participation principle to organize their design tasks and to diversify responsibility for 'implementation' (see the 'grassroots' approach of Voigt, 2003). Depending on the task, they created cross-functional and cross-hierarchical teams which consisted of employees who were directly affected by the substantial changes of internal organizational operations and structures. These teams reported to their responsible middle-manager (if not a member of the team) and top manager on a frequent basis, reassuring corporate strategy coherence and discussing the implications of their activities. As a result, almost the whole organization was engaged in the strategic change process – evolving the company's market strategy at many organizational levels by designing and implementing simultaneously.

When top management and managing employees of the company were asked which outcomes of the overall strategy making design were of special importance to them, they offered three conclusions:

- top management and especially employees openly claimed that the designed market strategy is 'their' strategy, which was created by themselves – demonstrating strong commitment;
- top management and employees created a common language about strategy issues and about the content of the market strategy that eased their daily communication and decision making;
- top management and employees never talked about 'strategy implementation', because (after the general strategic decision was made by top management) strategy making meetings were focused on practical designs and concrete decisions about these designs which were then put immediately into action by the same people who created them.

The way the facilitators and top management worked in the case just described decentralized strategy making in a larger organization. While they have chosen a counter-current process (top-down-bottom-up) that ensured employees' participation, it is important to note that this is not a democratic approach. This distinction is crucial: although the employees' capacity to think creatively about strategy is widely used here to make contributions and to use the impact of desired identities in strategy making, top management remains solely responsible for making the decision on resources (see Tannenbaum and Schmidt, 1958). As Hamel (1996, p. 77) puts it: 'Senior managers may not have a monopoly on imagination, but they do have a board-sanctioned monopoly on the allocation of resources.'

The most obvious benefit of the approach is that it enhances the decision-making ability of top management (see Rughase and Schindl, 2003, pp. 162–3). When employees create market strategies similar to that of top management, top management receives confirmation that managers at operating levels of the organization share their views on strategic issues and their desired organizational identity. When employees, however, create vastly different market strategies, these differences are of special importance for top management. For example, they may have overseen important aspects in strategy making or misjudged operational feasibility. Moreover, the top management team gets a clear understanding of the employees' desired organizational identity. Top management may disagree with it, but it will certainly enhance the quality of their decision making.

The brief practical case shows that the design of a strategy making process presented in this book can also be applied to larger organizations. However, the practical coordination of the whole process is more complex and demanding for the facilitators as well as for top management. But it is also possible to give many people in larger organizations the chance to (a) participate, (b) espouse their individual 'visions' (desired organizational identities) and (c) get involved in designing and acting upon the company's strategic future.

NOTE

1. New in the sense, that this part of the existing organizational identity has changed its practical meaning due to new insights (detected critical customer needs).

8. Conclusions

This book has had one main goal: to propose a practical design for a strategy making process that can help organizations evolve creative market strategies that are desired and attainable in the eyes of organizational members.

To reach that goal, the concept of organizational identity was linked to strategy, because a growing body of empirical evidence points towards significant impacts of identity on organizations and the results that organizations do and do not achieve. Reconsidering strategy making with regard to these findings has led to important insights about new requirements for strategy making. Identity provides a new starting point for designing the strategy making process and is used as a standard for measuring process outcomes. Finally, a facilitator-guided strategy making process has been designed which methodologically integrates the concept of desired organizational identity and its significant impacts. As the *JOURNAL* case has shown in practice, this process can help organizations to evolve desired and attainable strategies that also have creative potential.

Trying to integrate the aspirations, feelings, beliefs or values of organizational members into a strategy making process raises the fundamental question of how to weigh and balance value-laden factors with rational and analytical factors. Remember Abell (1980, p. 18) who put the weighing and balancing of Andrews's four factors at the very heart of strategy making. In the end, this fundamental balance is located along a theoretical continuum between two extremes. One extreme is represented by the rational mind-set that considers the optimal economic strategy as best for the company's future, and therefore proposes that it should be pursued. The other extreme is represented by a human-centered mind-set that believes the aspirations, feelings, beliefs or values of organizational members determine strategy, regardless of its economic value. Obviously both extremes have considerable problems. As Andrews (1987, p. 63) expresses the dilemma:

> You should . . . not warp your recommended strategy to the detriment of your company's future in order to adjust it to the personal values you hold or observe. On the other hand, you should not expect to be able to impose without risk and without expectation of eventual vindication and agreement, an unwelcome pattern of purposes and policies on the people in charge of the corporation or responsible for achieving results.

By largely ignoring value-laden factors, many of today's strategy makers avoid the difficult question of weighing and balancing, tending toward the rational mind-set's extreme. In contrast, this book recognized the other end of the continuum, reflecting motivational findings from the academic stream of organizational identity. However, this book has tried to creatively balance and weigh the rational and the emotional by designing a process that creates a collectively shared desired identity, which is then challenged and evolved by rational and analytical factors towards an attainable and profitable market strategy. Through this deliberate combination, the book ensures that such a new organizational market strategy will be robust *and* of economic value.

Even though this design of strategy making means that an organization might not pursue the best market strategy from an economic perspective alone, it develops a strategic orientation that is desired and attainable in the eyes of organizational members and, therefore, has a high chance of realization. As a result, conscious strategy making is reconnected to the emergent view of strategy which is embedded in a continuous learning process.

In the past, strategy researchers have also overemphasized the rational and almost disregarded initial definitions of strategy making which Ackoff among others felt 'should consist of the design of a desirable future and the invention of ways to bring it about' (Ackoff, 1981, p. 245). This book contributes to strategy theory and practice by offering one feasible way to discover such a future.

Bibliography

Aaker, D. (1989), 'Managing assets and skills: the key to a sustainable competitive advantage', *California Management Review*, **31** (2), 91–106.

Abell, D.F. (1980), *Defining the Business: The Starting Point of Strategic Planning*, Englewood Cliffs, NJ: Prentice Hall.

Ackermann, F., C. Eden and I. Brown (2005), *The Practice of Making Strategy: A Step-by-Step Guide*, London: Sage.

Ackoff, R.L. (1974), *Redesigning the Future: A Systems Approach to Societal Problems*, New York: Wiley.

Ackoff, R.L. (1981), *Creating the Corporate Future: Plan or Be Planned For*, New York: Wiley.

Ackoff, R.L. (1993), 'Idealized design: creative corporate visioning', *OMEGA International Journal of Management Science*, **21** (4), 401–10.

Ackoff, R.L. (1994), *The Democratic Corporation*, New York: Oxford University Press.

Ackoff, R.L. (1997), 'Strategies, systems, and organizations: an interview with Russell L. Ackoff', *Strategy and Leadership*, **25** (2), 22–7.

Adams, J.L. (2001), *Conceptual Blockbusting: A Guide to Better Ideas*, 4th edition, Cambridge, MA: Perseus.

Adaval, R. and R.S. Wyer (1998), 'The role of narratives in consumer information processing', *Journal of Consumer Psychology*, **7** (3), 207–45.

Albert, S. (1998), 'The definition and metadefinition of identity', in D.A. Whetten and P.C. Godfrey (eds), *Identity in Organizations – Building Theory through Conversations*, Thousand Oaks, CA: Sage, pp. 1–13.

Albert, S. and D. Whetten (1985), 'Organizational identity', in L.L. Cummings and B.M. Staw (eds), *Research in Organizational Behavior*, **7**, Greenwich, CT: JAI Press, pp. 263–95.

Albert, S., B.E. Ashforth and J.E. Dutton (2000), 'Organizational identity and identification: charting new waters and building new bridges', *Academy of Management Review*, **25** (1), 13–17.

Alvesson, M. (1990), 'Organization: from substance to image?', *Organization Studies*, **11** (3), 373–94.

Alvesson, M. and H. Willmott (2002), 'Identity regulation as organizational control: producing the appropriate individual', *Journal of Management Studies*, **39** (5), 619–44.

Ancona, D.G., P.S. Goodman, B.S. Lawrence and M.L. Tushman (2001), 'Time: a new research lens', *Academy of Management Review*, **26** (4), 645–63.

Anderson, R.C. and J.W. Pichert (1978), 'Recall of previously unrecallable information following a shift in perspective', *Journal of Verbal Learning and Verbal Behavior*, **17**, 1–12.

Andrews, K.R. (1987 [1971]), *The Concept of Corporate Strategy*, 3rd edition, Homewood, IL: Irwin.

Ansoff, H.I. (1965), *Corporate Strategy*, New York: McGraw-Hill.

Ansoff, H.I. (1980), 'Strategic issue management', *Strategic Management Journal*, **1** (2), 131–48.

Ansoff, H.I. (1984), *Implanting Strategic Management*, Englewood Cliffs, NJ: Prentice Hall.

Ansoff, H.I. (1988), *The New Corporate Strategy*, New York: Wiley.

Ansoff, H.I. (1991), 'Critique of Henry Mintzberg's "The design school: reconsidering the basic premises of strategic management"', *Strategic Management Journal*, **12** (6), 449–61.

Ansoff, H.I. and P.A. Sullivan (1993), 'Optimizing profitability in turbulent environments: a formula for strategic success', *Long Range Planning*, **26** (5), 11–23.

Ashforth, B.E. (2001), *Role Transitions in Organizational Life: An Identity-based Perspective*, Mahwah, NJ: Lawrence Erlbaum.

Ashforth, B.E. and F.A. Mael (1989), 'Social identity theory and the organization', *Academy of Management Review*, **14** (1), 20–39.

Ashforth, B.E. and F.A. Mael (1996), 'Organizational identity and strategy as a context for the individual', in J.A.C. Baum and J.E. Dutton (eds), *Advances in Strategic Management*, **13**, Greenwich, CT: JAI Press, pp. 19–64.

Ashmos, D.P., D. Duchon and R.R. McDaniel (1998), 'Participation in strategic decision making: the role of organizational predisposition and issue interpretation', *Decision Sciences*, **29** (1), 25–51.

Axelrod, E. (1999), *The Conference Method*, San Francisco, CA: Berrett-Koehler.

Bacharach, S.B. and E.J. Lawler (1980), *Power and Politics in Organizations*, San Francisco, CA: Jossey-Bass.

Banaji, M.R. and D.A. Prentice (1994), 'The self in social contexts', in L.W. Porter and M.R. Rosenzweig (eds), *Annual Review of Psychology*, **45**, Palo Alto, CA: Annual Reviews, pp. 297–332.

Barney, J.B. (2002), 'Strategic management: from informed conversation to academic discipline', *Academy of Management Executive*, **16** (2), 53–7.

Barney, J.B. and A.C. Stewart (2000), 'Organizational identity as moral philosophy: competitive implications for diversified corporations', in

M. Schultz, M.J. Hatch and M.H. Larsen (eds), *The Expressive Organization: Linking Identity, Reputation, and the Corporate Brand*, Oxford: Oxford University Press, pp. 36–47.

Barney, J.B., J.S. Bunderson, P. Foreman, L.T. Gustafson, A.S. Huff, L.L. Martins, R.K. Reger, Y. Sarason and J.L. Stimpert (1998), 'A strategy conversation on the topic of organization identity', in D.A. Whetten and P.C. Godfrey (eds), *Identity in Organizations – Building Theory through Conversations*, Thousand Oaks, CA: Sage, pp. 99–168.

Barr, P.S., J.L. Stimpert and A.S. Huff (1992), 'Cognitive change, strategic action, and organizational renewal', *Strategic Management Journal*, **13** (8), 15–36.

Barrett, F. and R. Fry (2002), 'Appreciative inquiry in action: the unfolding of a provocative invitation', in R.E. Fry, F. Barret, J. Seiling and D. Whitney (eds), *Appreciative Inquiry and Organizational Transformation: Reports from the Field*, Westport, CT: Quorum Books, pp. 1–23.

Barry, D. and M. Elmes (1997), 'Strategy retold: toward a narrative view of strategic discourse', *Academy of Management Review*, **22** (2), 429–52.

Bartlett, C.A. and S. Ghoshal (1990), 'Matrix management: not a structure, a frame of mind', *Harvard Business Review*, **68** (4), 138–47.

Bartlett, C.A. and S. Ghoshal (1993), 'Beyond the M-form: toward a managerial theory of the firm', *Strategic Management Journal*, **14** (Special Issue), 23–46.

Bartlett, F.C. (1932), *Remembering: A Study in Experimental and Social Psychology*, New York: Macmillan.

Baumeister, R.F. (1982), 'Self-esteem, self-presentation, and future interaction: a dilemma of reputation', *Journal of Personality*, **50**, 29–45.

Baumeister, R.F. and M.R. Leary (1995), 'The need to belong: desire for interpersonal attachments as a fundamental human motivation', *Psychological Bulletin*, **117** (3), 497–529.

Baumeister, R.F. and L.S. Newman (1994), 'How stories make sense of personal experiences: motives that shape autobiographical narratives', *Personality and Social Psychology Bulletin*, **20** (6), 676–90.

Bea, F.X. and J. Haas (2001), *Strategisches Management*, 3rd edition, Stuttgart: Lucius & Lucius.

Beaver, G. (2001), 'Editorial: strategy, management creativity and corporate history', *Strategic Change*, **10** (1), 1–4.

Bennis, W. and B. Nanus (1986), *Leaders: The Strategies for Taking Charge*, New York: Harper Perennial.

Bogner, W.C. and P.S. Barr (2000), 'Making sense in hypercompetitive environments: a cognitive explanation for the persistence of high velocity competition', *Organization Science*, **11** (2), 212–26.

Boje, D.M. (1991), 'The storytelling organization: a study of story performance in an office-supply firm', *Administrative Science Quarterly*, **36** (1), 106–26.

Boland, R.J. (1984), 'Sense-making of accounting data as a technique of organizational diagnosis', *Management Science*, **30** (7), 868–82.

Boland, R.J. and R.V. Tenkasi (1995), 'Perspective making and perspective taking in communities of knowing', *Organization Science*, **6** (4), 350–72.

Bood, R.P. and T.J.B.M. Postma (1997), 'Strategic learning with scenarios', *European Management Journal*, **15** (6), 633–47.

Bostrom, R.P., R. Anson and V.K. Clawson (1993), 'Group facilitation and group support systems', in L.M. Jessup and J.S. Valacic (eds), *Group Support Systems: New Perspectives*, New York: Macmillan, pp. 146–68.

Bouchikhi, H. and J.R. Kimberly (2003), 'Escaping the identity trap', *Sloan Management Review*, **44** (3), 20–26.

Bouchikhi, H., C.M. Fiol, D.M. Gioia, K. Golden-Biddle, M.J. Hatch, H. Rao, V. Rindova and M. Schultz (1998), 'The identity of organizations', in D.A. Whetten and P.C. Godfrey (eds), *Identity in Organizations – Building Theory through Conversations*, Thousand Oaks, CA: Sage, pp. 33–80.

Braybrooke, D. and C.E. Lindblom (1963), *A Strategy of Decision*, New York: Free Press.

Brewer, M.B. and W. Gardner (1996), 'Who is this "we"? Levels of collective identity and self representations', *Journal of Personality and Social Psychology*, **71** (1), 83–93.

Brown, A.D. (1997), 'Narcissism, identity, and legitimacy', *Academy of Management Review*, **22** (3), 643–86.

Brown, A.D. (2001), 'Organization studies and identity: towards a research agenda', *Human Relations*, **54** (1), 113–21.

Brown, A.D. and K. Starkey (2000), 'Organizational identity and learning: a psychodynamic perspective', *Academy of Management Review*, **25** (1), 102–20.

Bruner, J. (1990), *Acts of Meaning*, Cambridge, MA: Harvard University Press.

Bryson, J.M. (1995), *Strategic Planning for Public and Nonprofit Organizations*, San Francisco, CA: Jossey-Bass.

Burke, P.J. (1980), 'The self: measurement requirements from an interactionist perspective', *Social Psychology Quarterly*, **44**, 83–92.

Bushe, G. (2002), 'Meaning making in teams: appreciative inquiry with preidentity and postidentity groups', in R.E. Fry, F. Barret, J. Seiling and D. Whitney (eds), *Appreciative Inquiry and Organizational Transformation: Reports from the Field*, Westport, CT: Quorum Books, pp. 39–63.

Butler, D.L. and M.A. Kline (1999), 'Good versus creative solutions: a comparison of brainstorming, hierarchical, and perspective-changing heuristics', *Creativity Research Journal*, **11** (4), 325–31.

Cambridge Management Consulting (2001), 'Company change – transforming organizations: acting your way into a new way of thinking', www.celerantconsulting.com/perspectives/publications/Change_Feb_ 2001.pdf, 2 May 2005.

Chakravarthy, B., G. Mueller-Stewens, P. Lorange and C. Lechner (eds) (2003), *Strategy Process: Shaping the Contours of the Field*, Malden, MA: Blackwell.

Chatman, J.F., N.E. Bell and B.M. Staw (1986), 'The managed thought', in H.P. Sims and D.A. Gioia (eds), *The Thinking Organization: Dynamics of Organizational Social Cognition*, San Francisco, CA: Jossey-Bass, pp. 191–214.

Cheney, G. and L.T. Christensen (2001), 'Organizational identity at issue: linkages between "internal" and "external" organizational communication', in F.M. Jablin and L.L. Putnam (eds), *The New Handbook of Organizational Communication*, Thousand Oaks, CA: Sage, pp. 231–69.

Collier, N., F. Fishwick and F.S. Floyd (2004), 'Managerial involvement and perceptions of strategy process', *Long Range Planning*, **37** (1), 67–83.

Collins, J.C. and P.I. Porras (1994), *Built to Last: Successful Habits of Visionary Companies*, New York: Harper Business.

Conway, M.A. (1996), 'Autobiographical memory', in E.L. Bjork and R.A. Bjork (eds), *Memory*, San Diego, CA: Academic Press, pp. 165–94.

Cooley, C. (1902), *Human Nature and Social Order*, New York: Scribners.

Cooperrider, D.L. (1990), 'Positive image, positive action: the affirmative basis of organizing', in S. Srivastva and D.L. Cooperrider (eds), *Appreciative Management and Leadership*, San Francisco, CA: Jossey-Bass, pp. 91–125.

Cooperrider, D.L. and S. Srivastva (1987), 'Appreciative inquiry in organizational life', in W. Pasmore and R. Woodman (eds), *Research in Organizational Change and Development*, **1**, Greenwich, CT: JAI Press, pp. 129–69.

Cooperrider, D.L., P. Sorensen, D. Whitney and T. Yaeger (1999), *Appreciative Inquiry: Rethinking Human Organization toward a Positive Theory of Change*, Champaign, IL: Stipes.

Corley, K.G. (2002), 'Breaking away: an empirical examination of how organizational identity changes during a spin-off', unpublished doctoral dissertation, Pennsylvania State University, University Park, US.

Coyne, K.P. (1986), 'Sustainable competitive advantage – what it is, what it isn't', *Business Horizons*, **29** (1), 54–61.

Cyert, R.M. and J.G. March (1963), *A Behavioral Theory of the Firm*, Englewood Cliffs, NJ: Prentice-Hall.

Czarniawska, B. (1997), *Narrating the Organization: Dramas of Institutional Identity*, Chicago, IL: University of Chicago Press.

Czarniawska, B. (1998), *A Narrative Approach to Organization Studies*, Qualitative Research Methods, **43**, Thousand Oaks, CA: Sage.

D'Aveni, R.A. (1994), *Hypercompetition – Managing the Dynamics of Strategic Maneuvering*, New York: Free Press.

Daniels, K., L. Makóczy and L. de Chernatony (1994), 'Techniques to compare cognitive maps', in C. Stubbart, J.R. Meindel and J.F. Porac (eds), *Advances in Managerial and Organizational Information Processing*, **5**, Greenwich, CT: JAI Press, pp. 141–64.

Darragh, J. and A. Campbell (2001), 'Why corporate initiatives get stuck?', *Long Range Planning*, **34** (1), 33–52.

David, O. and J. Roos (2004), 'Constructing organizational identity', paper presented at Academy of Management Annual Meeting, New Orleans, US.

de Bono, E. (1992), *Serious Creativity: Using the Power of Lateral Thinking to Create New Ideas*, New York: Harper Business.

Diamond, M. (1993), *The Unconscious Life of Organizations: Interpreting Organizational Identity*, Westport, CT: Quorum Books.

DiMaggio, P. and W. Powell (1983), 'The iron cage revisited: institutional isomorphism and collective rationality in organizational fields', *American Sociological Review*, **48** (2), 147–60.

Dowling, G.R. (2001), *Creating Corporate Reputations: Identity, Image, and Performance*, Oxford: Oxford University Press.

Doyle, J.R and D. Sims (2002), 'Enabling strategic metaphor in conversation: a technique of cognitive sculpting for explicating knowledge', in A. Huff and M. Jenkins (eds), *Mapping Strategic Knowledge*, London: Sage, pp. 63–85.

du Gay, P., S. Hall, L. Janes, H. Mackay and K. Negus (1997), *Doing Cultural Studies – The Story of the Sony Walkman*, London: Sage.

Dukerich, J.M., R. Kramer and J.M. Parks (1998), 'The dark side of organizational identification', in D.A. Whetten and P.C. Godfrey (eds), *Identity in Organizations – Building Theory through Conversations*, Thousand Oaks, CA: Sage, pp. 245–56.

Dunford, R. and D. Jones (2000), 'Narrative in strategic change', *Human Relations*, **53** (9), 1207–26.

Dutton, J.E. and S.J. Ashford (1993), 'Selling issues to top management', *Academy of Management Review*, **18** (3), 397–428.

Dutton, J.E. and J. Dukerich (1991), 'Keeping an eye on the mirror: the role of image and identity in organizational adaptation', *Academy of Management Journal*, **34** (3), 517–54.

Dutton, J.E. and R.B. Duncan (1987a), 'The creation of momentum for change through the process of strategic issue diagnosis', *Strategic Management Journal*, **8**, 279–95.

Dutton, J.E. and R.B. Duncan (1987b), 'The influence of the strategic planning process on strategic change', *Strategic Management Journal*, **8**, 103–16.

Dutton, J.E. and W.J. Penner (1993), 'The importance of organizational identity for strategic agenda building', in J. Hendry and G. Johnson (eds) with J. Newton, *Strategic Thinking: Leadership and the Management of Change*, New York: Wiley, pp. 89–113.

Dutton, J.E. and J. Webster (1988), 'Patterns of interest around issues: the role of uncertainty and feasibility', *Academy of Management Journal*, **31** (3), 663–75.

Dutton, J.E., J.M. Dukerich and C.V. Harquail (1994), 'Organizational images and member identification', *Administrative Science Quarterly*, **39** (2), 239–63.

Dutton, J.E., S.J. Ashford, R.M. O'Neill, E. Hayes and E.E. Wierba (1997), 'Reading the wind: how middle managers assess the context for selling issues to top managers', *Strategic Management Journal*, **18** (5), 407–25.

Eden, C. and F. Ackermann (1998), *Making Strategy: The Journey of Strategic Management*, London: Sage.

Elsbach, K.D. and M.A. Glynn (1996), 'Believing your own "PR": embedding identification in strategic reputation', in J.A.C. Baum and J.E. Dutton (eds), *Advances in Strategic Management*, Greenwich, CT: JAI Press, pp. 63–88.

Elsbach, K.D. and R.M. Kramer (1996), 'Members' responses to organizational identity threats: encountering and countering the *Business Week* rankings', *Administrative Science Quarterly*, **41** (3), 442–76.

Erickson, E. (1959), *Identity and the Life Cycle*, New York: International Universities Press.

Ezzy, D. (1998), 'Theorizing narrative identity: symbolic interactionism and hermeneutics', *Sociological Quarterly*, **39** (2), 239–52.

Farjoun, M. (2002), 'Towards an organic perspective on strategy', *Strategic Management Journal*, **23** (7), 561–94.

Farjoun, M. and L. Lai (1997), 'Similarity judgements in strategy formulation: role, process and implications', *Strategic Management Journal*, **18** (4), 255–73.

Farmer, R.N. and B.M. Richman (1965), *Comparative Management and Economic Progress*, Homewood, IL: Irwin.

Fengler, J. (2000), *Strategisches Wissensmanagement: Die Kernkompetenzen des Unternehmens entdecken*, Berlin: Logos.

Fengler, J. (2003), *Strategische Prototypen: Neue Ansätze für das Strategie-Benchmarking*, Berlin: Logos.

Finke, R.A. (1995), 'Creative realism', in S.M. Smith, T.B. Ward and R.A. Finke (eds), *The Creative Cognition Approach*, Cambridge, MA: MIT Press, pp. 303–26.

Fiol, C.M. (1991), 'Managing culture as a competitive resource: an identity-based view of sustainable competitive advantage', *Journal of Management*, **17** (1), 191–211.

Fiol, C.M. and A.S. Huff (1992), 'Maps for managers: where are we? Where do we go from here?', *Journal of Management Studies*, **29** (3), 267–85.

Fiol, C.M., M.J. Hatch and K. Golden-Biddle (1998), 'Organizational culture and identity: what's the difference anyway?', in D.A. Whetten and P.C. Godfrey (eds), *Identity in Organizations – Building Theory through Conversations*, Thousand Oaks, CA: Sage, pp. 56–9.

Fisher, R.P. and R.E. Geiselman (1988), 'Enhancing eyewitness memory with the cognitive interview', in M.M. Gruneberg, P.E. Morris and R.N. Sykes (eds), *Practical Aspects of Memory: Current Research and Issues*, Chichester, UK: Wiley, pp. 34–9.

Fletcher, K.E. and A.S. Huff (1990), 'Strategic argument mapping: a study of strategy reformulation at AT&T', in A.S. Huff, (ed.), *Mapping Strategic Thought*, Chichester, UK: Wiley, pp. 165–93.

Floyd, S.W. and B. Wooldridge (2000), *Building Strategy from the Middle: Reconceptualizing Strategy Process*, Thousand Oaks, CA: Sage.

Ford, J.D. and L.W. Ford (1994), 'Logics of identity, contradictions and attraction in change', *Academy of Management Review*, **19** (4), 756–86.

Ford, C.M. and D.A. Gioia (1995), 'Multiple visions and multiple voices: academic and practitioner conceptions of creativity in organizations', in C.M. Ford and D.A. Gioia (eds), *Ivory Tower Visions and Real World Voices*, Thousand Oaks, CA: Sage, pp. 3–11.

Freeman, R.E. (1984), *Strategic Management – A Stakeholder Approach*, Marshfield, MA: Pitman.

Freeman, R.E. and J. Liedtka (1991), 'Corporate social responsibility: a critical approach', *Business Horizons*, **34** (4), 92–8.

French, J.R.P. and B. Raven (1959), 'The bases of social power', in D. Cartwright (ed.), *Studies in Social Power*, Ann Arbor, MI: Institute for Social Research, pp. 150–67.

Frost, P.J. and C.P. Egri (1990), 'Appreciating executive action', in S. Srivastva and D.L. Cooperrider (eds), *Appreciative Management and Leadership*, San Francisco, CA: Jossey-Bass, pp. 289–322.

Fry, R.E., F. Barret, J. Seiling and D. Whitney (2002), *Appreciative Inquiry and Organizational Transformation: Reports from the Field*, Westport, CT: Quorum Books.

Gabriel, Y. (1998), 'Psychoanalytical contributions to the study of the emotional life of organizations', *Administration & Society*, **30** (3), 291–314.

Gabriel, Y. (2000), *Storytelling in Organizations: Facts, Fictions, Fantasies*, Oxford: Oxford University Press.

Garud, R. and P. Karnoe (2001), *Path Dependence and Creation*, Mahwah, NJ: Lawrence Erlbaum.

Gedi, N. and Y. Elam (1996), 'Collective memory – what is it?', *History and Memory*, **8** (1), 30–50.

Genger, J. and J. Flottau (2002), 'Air Berlin folgt dem Trend zum Billigflieger', *Financial Times Deutschland*, 4 September, 7.

Ghemawat, P. (1991), *Commitment – The Dynamic of Strategy*, New York: Free Press.

Giddens, A. (1991), *Modernity and Self-identity*, Stanford, CT: Stanford University Press.

Gioia, D.A. (1998), 'From individual to organizational identity', in D.A. Whetten and P.C. Godfrey (eds), *Identity in Organizations – Building Theory through Conversations*, Thousand Oaks, CA: Sage, pp. 17–31.

Gioia, D.A. and K. Chittipeddi (1991), 'Sensemaking and sensegiving in strategic change initiation', *Strategic Management Journal*, **12** (6), 443–8.

Gioia, D.A. and J.B. Thomas (1996), 'Identity, image, and issue interpretation: sensemaking during strategic change in academia', *Administrative Science Quarterly*, **41** (3), 370–403.

Gioia, D.A., M. Schultz and K.G. Corley (2000), 'Organizational identity, image and adaptive instability', *Academy of Management Review*, **25** (1), 63–81.

Glasl, F. and B. Lievegoed (1996), *Dynamische Unternehmensentwicklung: Wie Pionierbetriebe und Bürokratien zu schlanken Unternehmen werden*, 2nd edition, Bern: Haupt.

Glynn, M.A. (2000), 'When cymbals become symbols: conflict over organizational identity within a symphony orchestra', *Organization Science*, **11** (3), 285–98.

Goffman, E. (1959), *The Presentation of the Self in Everyday Life*, Garden City, NJ: Doubleday-Anchor.

Golden-Biddle, K. and H. Rao (1997), 'Breaches in the boardroom: organizational identity and conflict of commitment in a non-profit organization', *Organization Science*, **8** (6), 593–611.

Gripsrud, G. and K. Gronhaug (1985), 'Structure and strategy in grocery retailing: a sociometric approach', *Journal of Industrial Economics*, **33** (3), 339–47.

Große-Oetringhaus, W.F. (1996), *Strategische Identität – Orientierung im Wandel*, Berlin: Springer.

Groys, B. (1992), *Über das Neue: Versuch einer Kulturökonomie*, Munich: Hanser.

Hambrick, D.C. and J.W. Fredrickson (2001), 'Are you sure you have a strategy?', *Academy of Management Executive*, **15** (4), 48–59.

Hambrick, D.C. and P.A. Mason (1984), 'Upper echelons: the organization as a reflection of its top managers', *Academy of Management Review*, **9** (2), 193–206.

Hamel, G. (1996), 'Strategy as revolution', *Harvard Business Review*, **74** (4), 69–82.

Hamel, G. (1997), 'Reinventing the basis for competition', in R. Gibson (ed.), *Rethinking the Future: Rethinking Business, Principles, Competition, Control and Complexity, Leadership, Markets and the World*, London: Brealey, pp. 77–91.

Hamel, G. (1998), 'Strategy innovation and the quest for value', *Sloan Management Review*, **39** (2), 7–14.

Hamel, G. and C.K. Prahalad (1994), *Competing for the Future*, Boston, MA: Harvard Business School Press.

Hammersley, M. and P. Atkinson (1995), *Ethnography: Principles in Practice*, 2nd edition, London: Routledge.

Hammond, S.A. (1998), *The Thin Book of Appreciative Inquiry*, 2nd edition, Plano, TX: Thin Book Publishing.

Hampden-Turner, C.M. (1993), 'Dilemmas of strategic learning loops', in J. Hendry and G. Johnson (eds) with J. Newton, *Strategic Thinking: Leadership and the Management of Change*, London: Wiley, pp. 327–46.

Hannan, M.T. and J. Freeman (1984), 'Structural inertia and organizational change', *American Sociological Review*, **49**, 149–64.

Hanssmann, F. (1993), *Einführung in die Systemforschung*, 4th edition, Munich: Oldenbourg.

Hanssmann, F. (1995), *Quantitative Betriebswirtschaftslehre: Lehrbuch der modellgestützten Unternehmensplanung*, 4th edition, Munich: Oldenbourg.

Hardy, C., T.B. Lawrence and D. Grant (2005), 'Discourse and collaboration: the role of conversations and collective identity', *Academy of Management Review*, **30** (1), 58–77.

Haslam, S.A., R.A. Eggins and K.J. Reynolds (2003a), 'The ASPIRe model: actualizing social and personal identity resources to enhance organizational outcomes', *Journal of Occupational and Organizational Psychology*, **76** (1), 83–113.

Haslam, S.A., T. Postmes and N. Ellemers (2003b), 'More than a metaphor: organizational identity makes organizational life possible', *British Journal of Management*, **14** (4), 357–69.

Hatch, M.J. (1993), 'The dynamics of organizational culture', *Academy of Management Review*, **18** (4), 657–93.

Hatch, M.J. and M. Schultz (1997), 'Relations between organizational culture, identity and image', *European Journal of Marketing*, **31** (5), 356–65.

Hatch, M.J. and M. Schultz (2000), 'Scaling the tower of Babel: relational differences between identity, image, and culture in organizations', in M. Schultz, M.J. Hatch and M.H. Larsen (eds), *The Expressive Organization – Linking Identity, Reputation, and the Corporate Brand*, Oxford: Oxford University Press, pp. 11–35.

Hatch, M.J. and M. Schultz (2002), 'The dynamics of organizational identity', *Human Relations*, **55** (8), 989–1018.

Hatch, M.J. and M. Schultz (eds) (2004), *Organizational Identity – A Reader*, Oxford: Oxford University Press.

Hayashi, S. (1990), *Culture and Management in Japan*, Tokyo: University of Tokyo Press.

Head, T.C. (2000), 'Appreciative inquiry: debunking the mythology behind resistance to change', *OD Practitioner*, **32** (1), 27–35.

Hickling, A. (1990), 'Decision spaces: a scenario about designing appropriate rooms for group decision management', in C. Eden and J. Radford (eds), *Tackling Group Problems: The Role of Group Decision Support*, London: Sage, pp. 169–77.

Higgins, J.M. (1994), *101 Creative Problem Solving Techniques: The Handbook of New Ideas for Business*, Winter Park, FL: New Management Publishing Company.

Higgins, J.M. (1996), 'Innovate or evaporate: creative techniques for strategists', *Long Range Planning*, **29** (3), 370–80.

Hogg, M.A. (1992), *The Social Psychology of Group Cohesiveness: From Attraction to Social Identity*, New York: Harvester Wheatsheaf.

Hogg, M.A. (1993), 'Group cohesiveness: a critical review and some new directions', *European Review of Social Psychology*, **4**, 85–111.

Hogg, M.A. (2000a), 'Social identity and social comparison', in J. Suls and L. Wheeler (eds), *Handbook of Social Comparison: Theory and Research*, New York: Plenum, pp. 401–21.

Hogg, M.A. (2000b), 'Subjective uncertainty reduction through self-categorization: a motivational theory of social identity processes', *European Review of Social Psychology*, **11**, 223–56.

Hogg. M.A. and D. Abrams (1988), *Social Identifications: A Social Psychology of Intergroup Relations and Group Processes*, London: Routledge.

Hogg, M.A. and D. Abrams (1993), 'Towards a single-process uncertainty-reduction model of social motivation in groups', in M.A. Hogg and

D. Abrams (eds), *Group Motivation: Social Psychological Perspectives*, New York: Prentice-Hall, pp. 173–90.

Hogg, M.A. and D. Abrams (1999), 'Social identity and social cognition: historical background and current trends', in D. Abrams and M.A. Hogg (eds), *Social Identity and Social Cognition*, Oxford: Blackwell, pp. 1–25.

Hogg, M.A. and B.A. Mullin (1999), 'Joining groups to reduce uncertainty: subjective uncertainty reduction and group identification', in D. Abrams and M.A. Hogg (eds), *Social Identity and Social Cognition*, Oxford: Blackwell, pp. 249–79.

Hogg, M.A. and D.J. Terry (2000a), 'Social identity and self-categorization processes in organizational contexts', *Academy of Management Review*, **25** (1), 121–40.

Hogg, M.A. and D.J. Terry (2000b), 'Identity dialogues: the dynamic, diverse, and variable faces of organizational identity', *Academy of Management Review*, **25** (1), 150–52.

Hogg, M.A. and D.J. Terry (2001), *Social Identity Processes in Organizational Contexts*, Philadelphia, PA: Psychology Press.

Hogg, M.A., D.J. Terry and K.M. White (1995), 'A tale of two theories: a critical comparison of identity theory with social identity theory', *Social Psychology Quarterly*, **58** (4), 255–69.

Huff, A.S. (1982), 'Industry influences on strategy reformulation', *Strategic Management Journal*, **3** (2), 119–31.

Huff, A.S. (1990), *Mapping Strategic Thought*, Chichester, UK: Wiley.

Huff, A.S. (2001), 'The continuing relevance of strategy', *Human Relations*, **54** (1), 123–30.

Huff, A.S. and M. Jenkins (2002), *Mapping Strategic Knowledge*, London: Sage.

Huff, J.O., A.S. Huff and H. Thomas (1992), 'Strategic renewal and the interaction of cumulative stress and inertia', *Strategic Management Journal*, **13** (8), 55–75.

Huff, A.S. and J.O. Huff with P. Barr (2000), *When Firms Change Direction*, New York: Oxford University Press.

Hultman, K. (1998), *Making Change Irresistible: Overcoming Resistance to Change in your Organization*, Palo Alto, CA: Davies-Black.

Hultman, K. with B. Gellerman (2002), *Balancing Individual and Organizational Values: Walking the Tightrope to Success*, San Francisco, CA: Jossey-Bass/Pfeiffer.

Humphreys, M. and A.D. Brown (2002), 'Narratives of organizational identity and identification: a case study of hegemony and resistance', *Organization Studies*, **23** (3), 421–47.

James, W. (1890), *The Principles of Psychology*, New York: Dover.

Jelinek, M. and J.A. Litterer (1994), 'Toward a cognitive theory of organizations', in C. Stubbart, J.R. Meindel and J.F. Porac (eds), *Advances in Managerial and Organizational Information Processing*, 5, Greenwich, CT: JAI Press, pp. 3–41.

Johnson, P., K. Daniels and R. Asch (1998), 'Mental models of competition', in C. Eden and J.-C. Spender (eds), *Managerial and Organizational Cognition: Theory, Methods and Research*, London: Sage, pp. 130–46.

Johnston, R.E. and J.D. Bate (2003), *The Power of Strategy Innovation – A New Way of Linking Creativity and Strategic Planning to Discover Great Business Opportunities*, New York: Amacom.

Jussim, L. (1986), 'Self-fulfilling prophecies: a theoretical and integrative review', *Psychological Review*, **93** (4), 429–45.

Jussim, L. (1989), 'Teacher expectations: self-fulfilling prophecies, perceptual biases, and accuracy', *Journal of Personality and Social Psychology*, **57** (3), 469–80.

Kato, K. and H. Markus (1993), 'The role of possible selves in memory', *Psychologia*, **36** (2), 73–83.

Kirton, M.J. (1994), *Adaptors and Innovators: Styles of Creativity and Problem Solving*, revised edition, London: Routledge.

Keleman, S. (1976), *Living your Dying*, New York: Random House.

Kemmerer, B. and V.K. Narayanan (2000), 'A cognitive perspective on strategic management: contributions and implications', paper presented at Strategic Management Society (SMS) 20th Annual International Conference, Vancouver, Canada.

Langfield-Smith, K. (1992), 'Exploring the need for a shared cognitive map', *Journal of Management Studies*, **29** (3), 349–68.

Larsen, E.R. and A. Lomi (1999), 'Resetting the clock: a feedback approach to the dynamics of organizational inertia, survival and change', *Journal of the Operational Research Society*, **50** (4), 406–21.

Leahy, R.L. (2000), 'Sunk costs and resistance to change', *Journal of Cognitive Psychotherapy*, **14** (4), 355–71.

Learned, E.P., C.R. Christensen, K.R. Andrews and W.D. Guth (1965), *Business Policy: Text and Cases*, Homewood, IL: Irwin.

Leary, M.R. and R.M. Kowalski (1990), 'Impression management: a literature review and two-component model', *Psychological Bulletin*, **107** (1), 34–47.

Leonard, D. and J.F. Rayport (1997), 'Spark innovation through empathic design', *Harvard Business Review*, **75** (6), 102–13.

Lester, R.K. and M.J. Piore (2004), *Innovation – The Missing Dimension*, Cambridge, MA: Harvard University Press.

Liebl, F. (1996), *Strategische Frühaufklärung: Trends – Issues – Stakeholders*, Munich: Oldenbourg.

Liebl, F. (1999a), ' "Babylon is Burning" oder: Postmoderne Zeiten verlangen eine entscheidungsorientierte Strategieauffassung', in O.G. Rughase, *Jenseits der Balanced Scorecard: Strategische Wettbewerbsvorteile messen*, Berlin: Logos, pp. 7–9.

Liebl, F. (1999b), 'Der Roberto-Blanko-Faktor', *brand eins*, **1** (3), 112–13.

Liebl, F (1999c), 'Schwächen schwächen', *econy*, **2** (1), 76–7.

Liebl, F. (2000a), 'Marketing-Apokalypse', *brand eins*, **2** (7), 128–9.

Liebl, F. (2000b), *Der Schock des Neuen: Entstehung und Management von Issues und Trends*, Munich: Gerling.

Liebl, F. (2001a), 'Die Implementierungsfalle', *brand eins*, **3** (1), 132–3.

Liebl, F. (2001b), 'Vision impossible', *brand eins*, **3** (10), 128–9.

Liebl, F. (2001c), 'Vom Trend zum Issue – Die Matrix des Neuen', in R. Gerling, O.-P. Obermeier and M. Schütz (eds), *Trends – Issues – Kommunikation*, Munich: Gerling Akademie Verlag, pp. 11–42.

Liebl, F. (2002a), 'Empathie als Dienstleistung', *brand eins*, **4** (3), 126–7.

Liebl, F. (2002b), 'Strategic knowledge management: towards a conceptual framework', paper presented at Strategic Management Society (SMS) 22nd Annual International Conference, Paris.

Liebl, F. (2004), 'Knowledge management for strategic marketing', in H.E. Spotts (ed.), *Developments in Marketing Science Volume XXVII – Proceedings of the Annual Conference of the Academy of Marketing Science*, Vancouver, Canada, pp. 48–57.

Liebl, F. and O.G. Rughase (2002), 'Storylistening', *gdi impuls*, **20** (3), 34–9.

Llewellyn, N. (2004), 'In search of modernization: the negotiation of social identity in organizational reform', *Organization Studies*, **25** (6), 947–68.

Magretta, J. (2002), *What Management Is: How It Works and Why It's Everyone's Business*, New York: Free Press.

March, J. and J. Olsen (1989), *Rediscovering Institutions*, New York: Free Press.

Margulies, W. (1977), 'Make the most of your corporate identity', *Harvard Business Review*, **55** (4), 17–55.

Markides, C. (2004), 'What is strategy and how do you know if you have one?', *Business Strategy Review*, **15** (2), 5–12.

Markus, H. and P. Nurius (1986), 'Possible selves', *American Psychologist*, **41** (9), 954–69.

Markus, H. and A. Ruvolo (1989), 'Possible selves: personalized representations of goals', in L.A. Pervin (ed.), *Goal Concepts in Personality and Social Psychology*, Hillsdale, NJ: Lawrence Erlbaum, pp. 211–41.

Markus, H. and E. Wurf (1987), 'The dynamic self concept: a social psychological perspective', *Annual Review of Psychology*, **38**, 299–337.

Martin, D.D. (2002), 'From appearance tales to oppression tales: frame alignment and organizational identity', *Journal of Contemporary Ethnography*, **31** (2), 158–206.

Martin, J., M.S. Feldman, M.J. Hatch and S.B. Sitkin (1983), 'The uniqueness paradox in organizational stories', *Administrative Science Quarterly*, **28** (3), 438–53.

Mason, R.O. and I. Mitroff (1981), *Challenging Strategic Planning Assumptions – Theory, Cases and Techniques*, New York: Wiley.

McAdams, D.P. (1993), *The Stories We Live By: Personal Myths and the Making of the Self*, New York: Guilford Press.

McGrath, R.G. and I. MacMillan (2000), *The Entrepreneurial Mindset*, Boston, MA: Harvard Business School Press.

Mead, G.H. (1934), *Mind, Self, and Society*, Chicago, IL: University of Chicago Press.

Mead, G.H. (1956), *The Social Psychology of George Herbert Mead*, ed. A.M. Strauss, Chicago, IL: Chicago University Press.

Mead, G.H. (1959), *The Philosophy of the Present*, ed. Arthur E. Murphy, La Salle, PA: Open Court.

Meier, D. (1999), 'McKinsey ist selber zum Restrukturierungsfall geworden', *SonntagsZeitung*, 31 January, Zürich, Switzerland.

Meyer, J.P., J.M. Bartunek and C.A. Lacey (2002), 'Identity change and stability in organizational groups: a longitudinal investigation', *International Journal of Organizational Analysis*, **10** (1), 4–29.

Mezias, J.M., P. Grinyer and W.D. Guth (2001), 'Changing collective cognition: a process model for strategic change', *Long Range Planning*, **34** (1), 71–95.

Milliken, F.J. and T.K. Lant (1991), 'The effect of an organization's recent performance history on strategic persistence and change: the role of managerial interpretations', in P. Shrivastava, A. Huff and J. Dutton (eds), *Advances in Strategic Management*, **7**, Greenwich, CT: JAI Press, pp. 129–56.

Mintzberg, H. (1987), 'Strategy concept I: five Ps for strategy', *California Management Review*, **30** (1), 11–24.

Mintzberg. H. (1990), 'The design school: reconsidering the basic premises of strategic management', *Strategic Management Journal*, **11** (3), 171–95.

Mintzberg, H. (1991), 'Learning 1, planning 0 – Reply to Igor Ansoff', *Strategic Management Journal*, **12** (6), 463–6.

Mintzberg, H. (1994), *The Rise and Fall of Strategic Planning*, New York: Free Press.

Mintzberg, H. and J. Lampel (1999), 'Reflecting on the strategy process', *Sloan Management Review*, **40** (3), 21–30.

Mintzberg, H. and J.B. Quinn (1996), *The Strategy Process: Concepts Contexts, Cases*, 3rd edition, Upper Saddle River, NJ: Prentice-Hall.

Mintzberg, H. and J.A. Waters (1985), 'Of strategies, deliberate and emergent', *Strategic Management Journal*, **6** (3), 257–72.

Mitchell, D.W. and C.B. Coles (2003), 'The ultimate competitive advantage of continuing business model innovation', *Journal of Business Strategy*, **24** (5), 15–21.

Mitchell, D.W. and C.B. Coles (2004), 'Business model innovation breakthrough moves', *Journal of Business Strategy*, **25** (1), 16–26.

Mitroff, I.I. and R.H. Kilmann (1975), 'Stories managers tell: a new tool for organizational problem solving', *Management Review*, **64** (7), 18–28.

Mitroff, I.I. and R.H. Kilmann (1976), 'On organization stories: an approach to the design and analysis of organisations through myths and stories', in R.H. Kilmann, L.R. Pondy and D. Slevin (eds), *The Management of Organization Design – Strategies and Implementation*, New York: Elsevier North-Holland, pp. 189–207.

Morgan, A.J. (1993), 'The evolving self in consumer behavior: exploring possible selves', *Advances in Consumer Research*, **20**, 429–32.

Morita, A. (1986), *Made in Japan – Akio Morita and Sony*, New York: Dutton.

Müller, M. and H. Sottong (2000), 'Die Koordinaten der Unternehmensidentität', in B. Hentschel, M. Müller and H. Sottong (eds), *Verborgene Potenziale – Was Unternehmen wirklich wert sind*, Munich: Hanser, pp. 147–64.

Mumford, M.D. and S.B. Gustafson (1988), 'Creativity syndrome: integration, application, and innovation', *Psychological Bulletin*, **103** (1), 27–43.

Munson, J.M. (1993), 'Perceptions of self: the effects of self-concept discrepancy, possible selves and dispossession', *Advances in Consumer Research*, **20**, 433–5.

N.N. (2003), 'Strategy process: shaping the contours of the field', *Work Study*, **52** (6/7), 324–5.

N.N. (2004), 'Billigfluglinie V-Bird stellt den Betrieb ein', *Handelsblatt*, 11 October, 11.

Nelson, R. and S.G. Winter (1982), *An Evolutionary Theory of Economic Change*, Cambridge, MA: Harvard University Press.

Nelson, T. and E. McFadzean (1998), 'Facilitating problem-solving groups: facilitator competencies', *Leadership and Organization Development Journal*, **19** (2), 72–82.

Nonaka, I. (1988), 'Toward middle-up-down management: accelerating information creation', *Sloan Management Review*, **29** (3), 9–18.

O'Brien, F. and M. Meadows (2000), 'Corporate visioning: a survey of UK practice', *Journal of the Operational Research Society*, **51** (1), 36–44.

Oakes, P.J. and J.C. Turner (1986), 'Distinctiveness and the salience of social category memberships: is there an automatic perceptual bias towards novelty?', *European Journal of Social Psychology*, **16**, 325–44.

Ogilvie, D.M. (1987), 'The undesired self: a neglected variable in personality research', *Journal of Personality and Social Psychology*, **52** (2), 379–85.

Olins, W. (1989), *Corporate Identity: Making Business Strategy Visible through Design*, London: Thames and Hudson.

Patton, M.Q. (2002), *Qualitative Evaluation and Research Methods*, 3rd edition, Thousand Oaks, CA: Sage.

Pavlik, L. (1997), 'Structured imagination in story creation', *Journal of Creative Behavior*, **31** (3), 180–200.

Perkins, D.N. (1981), *The Mind's Best Work*, Cambridge, MA: Harvard University Press.

Pitt, L.F. and M.T. Ewing (2001), 'Corollaries of the collective: the influence of organizational culture and memory development on perceived decision-making context', *Journal of the Academy of Marketing Science*, **29** (2), 135–50.

Polak, F. and E. Boulding (1973), *The Image of the Future*, Amsterdam: Elsevier.

Porac, J. and H. Thomas (1990), 'Taxonomic mental models in competitor definition', *Academy of Management Review*, **15** (2), 224–40.

Porac, J. and H. Thomas (1994), 'Cognitive categorization and subjective rivalry among retailers in a small city', *Journal of Applied Psychology*, **79** (1), 54–66.

Porac, J., H. Thomas and C. Baden-Fuller (1989), 'Competitive groups as cognitive communities: the case of Scottish knitwear manufacturers', *Journal of Management Studies*, **26** (4), 397–416.

Porac, J., Y. Mishina and T. Pollock (2002), 'Entrepreneurial narratives and the dominant logics of high-growth firms', in A.S. Huff and M. Jenkins (eds), *Mapping Strategic Knowledge*, London: Sage, pp. 112–36.

Porter, M.E. (1980), *Competitive Strategy: Techniques for Analyzing Industries and Competitors*, New York: Free Press.

Porter, M.E. (1985), *Competitive Advantage: Creating and Sustaining Superior Performance*, New York: Free Press.

Porter, M.E. (1996), 'What is strategy?', *Harvard Business Review*, **74** (6), 61–78.

Porter, M.E. (1997), 'Creating tomorrow's advantages', in R. Gibson (ed.), *Rethinking the Future: Rethinking Business, Principles, Competition, Control, Leadership, Markets and the World*, London: Brealey, pp. 48–61.

Postma, T.J.B.M. and F. Liebl (2005), 'How to improve scenario analysis as a strategic management tool?', *Technological Forecasting & Social Change*, **72** (2), 161–73.

Prahalad, C.K. and R.A. Bettis (1986), 'The dominant logic: a new linkage between diversity and performance', *Strategic Management Journal*, **7** (6), 485–501.

Pratt, M.G. (1998), 'To be or not to be? Central questions in organizational identification', in D.A. Whetten and P.C. Godfrey (eds), *Identity in Organizations – Building Theory through Conversations*, Thousand Oaks, CA: Sage, pp. 171–207.

Pratt, M.G. and J.E. Dutton (2000), 'Owning up or opting out: the role of emotions and identities in issue ownership', in N. Ashkanasy (ed.), *Emotions in the Workplace*, Westport, CT: Quorum Books, pp. 103–29.

Pratt, M.G. and P.O. Foreman (2000a), 'Classifying managerial responses to multiple organizational identities', *Academy of Management Review*, **25** (1), 18–42.

Pratt, M.G. and P.O. Foreman (2000b), 'Identity dialogues: the beauty of and barriers to organizational theories of identity', *Academy of Management Review*, **25** (1), 141–3.

Pratt, M.G. and A. Rafaeli (1997), 'Organizational dress as a symbol of multilayered social identities', *Academy of Management Journal*, **40** (4), 862–98.

Priddat, B.P. (2000), 'Menschen in Kooperation – Organisationen als Identitätslandschaften', in B. Hentschel, M. Müller and H. Sottong (eds), *Verborgene Potenziale – Was Unternehmen wirklich wert sind*, Munich, Germany: Hanser, pp. 21–43.

Ramírez, R. and J. Wallin (2000), *Prime Movers – Define your Business or have Someone Define it Against You*, Chichester, UK: Wiley.

Rappaport, J. (1993), 'Narrative studies, personal stories, and identity transformation in the mutual help context', *Journal of Applied Behavioral Science*, **19** (2), 239–56.

Ravasi, D. and J. van Rekom (2003), 'Key issues in organizational identity and identification theory', *Corporate Reputation Review*, **6** (2), 118–32.

Raynor, M.E. (1998), 'That vision thing: do we need it?', *Long Range Planning*, **31** (3), 368–78.

Reason, P. and J. Rowan (1990), 'Storytelling as inquiry', in P. Reason (ed.), *Human Inquiry in Action: Developments in New Paradigm Research*, London: Sage, pp. 79–101.

Reger, R.K. (1990), 'Managerial thought structures and competitive positioning', in A.S. Huff (ed.), *Mapping Strategic Thought*, Chichester, UK: Wiley, pp. 71–88.

Reger, R.K. and A.S. Huff (1993), 'Strategic groups: a cognitive perspective', *Strategic Management Journal*, **14** (2), 103–24.

Reger, R.K., L.T. Gustafson, S.M. Demarie and J.V. Mullane (1994),

'Reframing the organization: why implementing total quality is easier said than done', *Academy of Management Review*, **19** (3), 565–84.

Rindova, V.P. and C.J. Fombrun (1999), 'Constructing competitive advantage: the role of firm-constituent interactions', *Strategic Management Journal*, **20** (8), 691–710.

Rindova, V.P. and M. Schultz (1998), 'Identity within and identity without: lessons from corporate and organizational identity', in D.A. Whetten and P.C. Godfrey (eds), *Identity in Organizations – Building Theory through Conversations*, Thousand Oaks, CA: Sage, pp. 46–51.

Roos, J., B. Victor and M. Statler (2004), 'Playing seriously with strategy', *Long Range Planning*, **37** (6), 549–68.

Rosenthal, R. and D. Rubin (1978), 'Interpersonal expectancy effects: the first 345 studies', *Behavioral and Brain Sciences*, **3**, 377–415.

Rughase, O.G. (1999), *Jenseits der Balanced Scorecard: Strategische Wettbewerbsvorteile messen*, Berlin: Logos.

Rughase, O.G. (2001), 'Strategische Flexibilität in Organisationen: Ethnographische Methoden in der Strategieberatung', Paper presented at conference 'Das Innenleben der Organisation: Ethnographische Methoden in der Organisationsberatung', Department of European Ethnology, Berlin.

Rughase, O.G. (2002), 'Linking content to process: how mental models of the customer enhance creative strategy processes', in A. Huff and M. Jenkins (eds), *Mapping Strategic Knowledge*, London: Sage, pp. 46–62.

Rughase, O.G. and M. Schindl (2003), ' "I will do it my way" – Zum Rollenverständnis von Prozeßleitung und Unternehmensleitung in der Grassroots-Praxis', in T. Voigt, *Just Implement It? Strategische Kräfte im Unternehmen mobilisieren*, Berlin: Logos, pp. 149–63.

Sappington, A.A. and W.E. Farrar (1982), 'Brainstorming vs. critical judgement in the generation of solutions which conform to certain reality constraints', *Journal of Creative Behavior*, **16** (1), 68–73.

Sarason, Y. (1996), 'Identity and the baby bells: applying structuration theory to strategic management', Unpublished doctoral dissertation, University of Colorado, Boulder.

Sarason, Y. (1998), 'US West Inc.', in D.A. Whetten and P.C. Godfrey (eds), *Identity in Organizations – Building Theory through Conversations*, Thousand Oaks, CA: Sage, pp. 128–32.

Schank, R.C. and R.P. Abelson (1995), 'Knowledge and memory: the real story', in R.S. Wyer (ed.), *Advances in Social Cognition: Vol. 8 Knowledge and Memory: The Real Story*, Hillsdale, NJ: Lawrence Erlbaum, pp. 1–85.

Schein, E. (1985), *Organizational Culture and Leadership*, San Francisco, CA: Jossey-Bass.

Schendel, C.E. and C.W. Hofer (1979), *Strategic Management – A New View of Business Policy and Planning*, Boston, MA: Little, Brown and Co.

Schlenker, B.R. (1985), 'Identity and self-identification', in B.R. Schlenker (ed.), *The Self and Social Life*, New York: McGraw-Hill, pp. 65–99.

Schlenker, B.R. and M.F. Weigold (1989), 'Goals and the self-identification process: constructing desired identities', in L.A. Pervin (ed.), *Goal Concepts in Personality and Social Psychology*, Hillsdale, NJ: Lawrence Erlbaum, pp. 243–90.

Schoemaker, P.J.H. (1992), 'How to link strategic vision to core capabilities', *Sloan Management Review*, **34** (1), 67–75.

Schultz, M., M.J. Hatch and M.H. Larsen (eds) (2000), *The Expressive Organization – Linking Identity, Reputation, and the Corporate Brand*, Oxford: Oxford University Press.

Schuman, S.P. (1996), 'What to look for in a group facilitator', *Quality Progress*, **29** (6), 69–72.

Schütz, A. (1967), *The Phenomenology of the Social World*, New York: Northwestern University Press.

Schwarz, R.M. (1994), *The Skilled Facilitator: Practical Wisdom for Developing Effective Groups*, San Francisco, CA: Jossey-Bass.

Schwenk, C. and M. Tang (1989), 'Economic and psychological explanations for strategic persistence', *OMEGA International Journal of Management Science*, **17** (6), 559–70.

Schwub-Gwinner, G. (1993), *Strategische Unternehmensführung und kollektive Entscheidungsprozesse*, Munich: Kirsch.

Scott, S.G. and V.R. Lane (2000), 'A stakeholder approach to organizational identity', *Academy of Management Review*, **25** (1), 43–62.

Scott-Morgan, P. (1994), *The Unwritten Rules of the Game: Master them, Shatter them and Break through the Barriers to Organizational Change*, New York: McGraw-Hill.

Selame, E. and J. Selame (1975), *Developing a Corporate Identity – How to Stand Out in the Crowd*, New York: Lebhar-Friedmann.

Selznick, P. (1957), *Leadership in Administration: A Sociological Interpretation*, Evanston, IL: Row Peterson.

Senge, P. (1990), *The Fifth Discipline: The Art and Practice of the Learning Organization*, New York: Doubleday.

Shane, S. (2000), 'Prior knowledge and the discovery of entrepreneurial opportunities', *Organization Science*, **11** (4), 448–69.

Shaw, G.G. (2000), 'Planning and communicating using stories', in M. Schultz, M.J. Hatch and M.H. Larsen (eds), *The Expressive Organization: Linking Identity, Reputation, and the Corporate Brand*, Oxford: Oxford University Press, pp. 182–95.

Sherman, S.J., D.L. Hamilton and A.C. Lewis (1999), 'Perceived entitativity and the social identity value of group memberships', in D. Abrams and M.A. Hogg (eds), *Social Identity and Social Cognition*, Oxford: Blackwell, pp. 80–110.

Simon, B. (1999), 'A place in the world: self and self categorization', in T.R. Tyler, R.M. Kramer and O.P. John (eds), *The Psychology of the Social Self*, Mahwah, NJ: Lawrence Erlbaum, pp. 47–69.

Simon, B. and B. Klandermans (2001), 'Politicized collective identity – a social psychological analysis', *American Psychologist*, **56** (4), 319–31.

Simon, H. (1947), *Administrative Behavior*, New York: Macmillan.

Slywotzky, A.J. (1996), *Value Migration – How to Think Several Moves Ahead of the Competition*, Boston, MA: Harvard Business School Press.

Smith, G.F. (1998), 'Idea-generation techniques: a formulary of active ingredients', *Journal of Creative Behavior*, **32** (2), 107–33.

Smith, S.M. (1995), 'Fixation, incubation, and insight in memory and creative thinking', in S.M. Smith, T.B. Ward and R.A. Finke (eds), *The Creative Cognition Approach*, Cambridge, MA: MIT Press, pp. 135–56.

Smith, S.M., T.B. Ward and J.S. Schumacher (1993), 'Constraining effects of examples in a creative generation task', *Memory & Cognition*, **21** (6), 837–45.

Spradley, J.P. (1979), *The Ethnographic Interview*, New York: Holt, Rinehart & Winston.

Stapel, D.A. and W. Koomen (2001), 'I, we, and the effects of others on me: how self-construal level moderates social comparison effects', *Journal of Personality and Social Psychology*, **80** (5), 766–81.

Starbuck, W.H. (1985), 'Acting first and thinking later: theory versus reality in strategic change', in J.M. Pennings (ed.), *Organizational Strategy and Change*, San Francisco, CA: Jossey-Bass, pp. 336–72.

Stimpert, J.L.L., L.T. Gustafson and Y. Sarason (1998), 'Organizational identity within the strategic management conversation', in D.A. Whetten and P.C. Godfrey (eds), *Identity in Organizations – Building Theory through Conversations*, Thousand Oaks, CA: Sage, pp. 83–98.

Stoecker, R. (1995), 'Community, movement, organization: the problem of identity convergence in collective action', *Sociological Quarterly*, **36** (1), 111–30.

Stryker, S. (1980), *Symbolic Interactionism: A Social Structural Version*, Palo Alto, CA: Benjamin/Cummings.

Stryker, S. (1987), 'Identity theory: developments and extensions', in K. Yardley and T. Honess (eds), *Self and Identity*, New York: Wiley, pp. 89–104.

Sulzmaier, S. (2001), *Consumer-oriented Business Design: The Case of Airport Management*, Heidelberg: Physica.

Sveningsson, S. and M. Alvesson (2003), 'Managing managerial identities: organizational fragmentation, discourse and identity struggle', *Human Relations*, **56** (10), 1163–93.

Swann, W.B. Jr (1987), 'Identity negotiation: where two roads meet', *Journal of Personality and Social Psychology*, **53** (6), 1038–51.

Tajfel, H. (1972), 'La catégorisation sociale', in S. Moscovici (ed.), *Introduction à la Psychologie Sociale*, **1**, Paris: Larousse, pp. 272–302.

Tajfel, H. and J.C. Turner (1986), 'The social identity theory of intergroup behaviour', in S. Worchel and W.G. Austin (eds), *Psychology of Intergroup Relations*, 2nd edition, Chicago, IL: Nelson-Hall, pp. 7–24.

Taket, A. and L. White (2000), *Partnership & Participation*, Chichester, UK: Wiley.

Tanabe, H. (1940), *Rekishiteki genjitsu [Historical reality]*, Tokyo, Japan: Iwanami Shoten.

Tannenbaum, R. and R.W. Hanna (1985), 'Holding on, letting go, and moving on: understanding a neglected perspective on change', in R. Tannenbaum, N. Margulies and F. Massarik (eds), *Human Systems Development*, San Francisco, CA: Jossey-Bass, pp. 95–121.

Tannenbaum, R. and W.H. Schmidt (1958), 'How to choose a leadership pattern', *Harvard Business Review*, **36** (2), 95–101.

Taylor, D. (1996), *The Healing Power of Stories – Creating Yourself through the Stories of Your Life*, New York: Doubleday.

Taylor, G. (1996), *Cultural Selection: Why Some Achievements Survive the Test of Time – and Others Don't*, New York: Basic Books.

Tedeschi, J.T. and N. Norman (1985), 'Social power, self-presentation, and the self', in B.R. Schlenker (ed.), *The Self and Social Life*, New York: McGraw-Hill, pp. 293–322.

Tuckman, B.W. (1965), 'Developmental sequences in small groups', *Psychological Bulletin*, **63**, 384–99.

Turner, J.C. (1975), 'Social comparison and social identity: some prospects for intergroup behaviour', *European Journal of Social Psychology*, **5**, 5–34.

Turner, J.C. (1982), 'Towards a cognitive redefinition of the social group', in H. Tajfel (ed.), *Social Identity Intergroup Relations*, Cambridge: Cambridge University Press, pp. 15–40.

Turner, J.C. (1985), 'Social categorization and the self-concept: a social cognitive theory of group behaviour', in E.J. Lawler (ed.), *Advances in Group Processes: Theory and Research*, **2**, Greenwich, CT: JAI Press, pp. 77–122.

Turner, J.C. (1996), 'Henri Tajfel: an introduction', in W.P. Robinson (ed.), *Social Groups and Identities: Developing the Legacy of Henri Tajfel*, Oxford: Butterworth-Heinemann, pp. 1–23.

Turner, J.C., M. Hogg, P. Oakes, S. Reicher and M. Wetherell (1987), *Rediscovering the Social Group: A Self-categorization Theory*, Oxford: Blackwell.

Ulwick, A.W. (1999), *Business Strategy Formulation: Theory, Process, and the Intellectual Revolution*, Westport, CT: Quorum Books.

Union of International Associations (2005), 'Towards a new order of meeting participation', www.uia.org/uiadocs/contract.htm#reminder, 2 May.

van der Heijden, K. (1996), *Scenarios: The Art of Strategic Conversation*, Chichester, UK: Wiley.

van Knippenberg, D., B. van Knippenberg, L. Monden and F. de Lima (2002), 'Organizational identification after a merger: a social identity perspective', *British Journal of Social Psychology*, **41** (2), 233–53.

van Rekom, J. (2003), 'Linking being to doing – how does organizational identity influence what organizational members do?', Paper presented at Academy of Management Annual Meeting, Seattle.

van Rekom, J. and C.B.M. van Riel (2000), 'Operational measures of organizational identity: a review of existing methods', *Corporate Reputation Review*, **3** (4), 334–50.

van Riel, C.B.M. and J.M.T. Balmer (1997), 'Corporate identity: the concept, its measurement and management', *European Journal of Marketing*, **31** (5/6), 340–55.

Voigt, T. (2003), *Just implement it? Strategische Kräfte im Unternehmen mobilisieren*, Berlin: Logos.

Voigt, T. (2005), 'Strategic management as a mobilization process – what strategic management can learn from social movements', unpublished doctoral thesis, University of Witten/Herdecke, Germany.

Walsh, J.P. (1995), 'Managerial and organizational cognition: notes from a trip down memory lane', *Organization Science*, **6** (3), 280–321.

Walton, E.J. (1986), 'Managers' prototypes of financial firms', *Journal of Management Studies*, **23**, 679–98.

Ward, T.B. (1994), 'Structured imagination: the role of conceptual structure in exemplar generation', *Cognitive Psychology*, **27**, 1–40.

Ward, T.B. (1995), 'What's old about new ideas?', in S.M. Smith, T.B. Ward and R.A. Finke (eds), *The Creative Cognition Approach*, Cambridge, MA: MIT Press, pp. 157–78.

Ward, T.B. (2001), 'Creative cognition, conceptual combination, and the creative writing of Stephen R. Donaldson', *American Psychologist*, **56** (4), 350–54.

Ward, T.B., R.A. Finke and S.M. Smith (1995), *Creativity and the Mind: Discovering the Genius Within*, New York: Plenum Press.

Ward, T.B., S.M. Smith and J. Vaid (1997), 'Conceptual structures and processes in creative thought', in T.B. Ward, S.M. Smith and J. Vaid (eds),

Creative Thought: An Investigation of Conceptual Structures and Processes, Washington, DC: American Psychological Association, pp. 1–27.

Warihay, F.D. (1992), 'Are good facilitators born or can they be developed?', *Journal for Quality and Participation*, **15** (1), 60–63.

Watkins, J.M. and D. Cooperrider (2000), 'Appreciative inquiry: a transformative paradigm', *OD Practitioner*, **32** (1), 6–12.

Watkins, J.M. and B.J. Mohr (2001), *Appreciative Inquiry: Change at the Speed of Imagination*, San Francisco, CA: Jossey-Bass/Pfeiffer.

Watzlawick, P. (1997), *Vom Unsinn des Sinns oder vom Sinn des Unsinns*, 4th edition, Munich: Piper.

Weick, K.E. (1995), *Sensemaking in Organizations*, Thousand Oaks, CA: Sage.

Weisberg, R.W. (1995), 'Case studies of creative thinking: reproduction versus restructuring in the real word', in S.M. Smith, T.B. Ward and R.A. Finke (eds), *The Creative Cognition Approach*, Cambridge, MA: MIT Press, pp. 53–72.

Wernerfelt, B. (1984), 'A recourse-based view of the firm', *Strategic Management Journal*, **5** (2), 171–80.

Wheelen, T.J. and J.D. Hunger (2002), *Concepts in Strategic Management and Business Policy*, 8th edition, Upper Saddle River, NJ: Prentice Hall.

Whetten, D.A. (1997), 'Theory development and the study of corporate reputation', *Corporate Reputation Review*, **1** (1), 26–34.

Whetten, D.A. and P.C. Godfrey (1998), *Identity in Organizations – Building Theory through Conversations*, Thousand Oaks, CA: Sage.

Whetten, D.A. and A. Mackey (2002), 'A social actor conception of organizational identity and its implications for the study of organizational reputation', *Business & Society*, **41** (4), 393–414.

White, L.A. and A. Taket (1995), 'Changing faces: an investigation of guises for intervention', in *Proceedings of the 39th Annual Meeting of the ISSS: Systems Thinking, Government Policy and Decision Making*, Amsterdam, Netherlands, July, pp. 1088–97.

Whitty, M. (2002), 'Possible selves: an exploration of the utility of a narrative approach', *Identity*, **2** (3), 211–28.

Wilcox, D. (1994), *The Guide to Effective Participation*, Brighton, UK: Joseph Rowntree Foundation/Partnership Books.

Yip, G.S. (2004), 'Using strategy to change your business model', *Business Strategy Review*, **15** (2), 17–24.

Young, D.R. (2001), 'Organizational identity and the structure of nonprofit umbrella associations', *Nonprofit Management & Leadership*, **11** (3), 289–304.

Index

Aaker, D. 151
Abell, D.F. xiv, 8, 11, 13, 149–50, 194
Abelson, R.P. 103
Abrams, D. 18, 25
Ackermann, F. 6, 7, 12, 13, 35, 56, 64,
    69, 77, 79, 80, 85, 88, 96, 102, 105,
    106, 116, 117, 132, 170, 184, 189
Ackoff, R.L. xiv, 55, 58, 59–60, 62–3,
    64, 65, 66, 68, 69, 76, 115, 132,
    178, 180, 181, 187, 195
action plans 35
Adams, J.L. 139
adaptive instability 19
Adaval, R. 104
affiliation 17
aggregation, creating shared desired
    identity through 115–17
Air Berlin 46
airline industry 46
Albert, S. 11, 12, 15, 18, 19, 25, 40
Alvesson, M. 19, 21, 41, 68
analytical objectivity 7–8, 11, 55, 56
Ancona, D.G. 50
Anderson, R.C. 132, 139
Andrews, K.R. xiv, 6, 7, 8, 9, 10, 12,
    14, 46, 53, 55, 56, 57, 71, 77, 169,
    174, 182, 194
Ansoff, H.I. 7, 12, 14, 54, 56, 72, 85,
    170, 171
anthropology 104
anti-identities 37, 41
appreciative inquiry 58, 60–62, 178
    core principles and benefits of 62–7
Ashford, S.J. 56
Ashforth, B.E. 11, 15, 17, 18, 19, 25,
    28, 29, 33, 34, 35, 37, 38, 39, 40,
    41, 42, 49, 55, 66
Ashmos, D.P. 65
assumptions, scenarios based on 132
AT&T 28
Atkinson, P. 104
attributes

comparing with other attributes 109,
    111, 117
letting go of 70–71
past experiences related to 118
prioritization of 109–11, 114–15,
    116
stories portraying 111, 118, 119
see also core attributes; peripheral
    attributes
Axelrod, E. 62

Bacharach, S.B. 56
Balmer, J.M.T. 20, 37
Banaji, M.R. 49
banks, strategy making in 55, 170
Barney, J.B. 21, 29, 32, 34, 35, 37, 39,
    40, 41, 42, 46, 51, 115
Barr, P.S. xv, 42, 146
Barrett, F. 61
Barry, D. 19, 88, 118, 119
Bartlett, C.A. 12, 66
Bartlett, F.C. 103
Bate, J.D. 27, 129, 137
Baumeister, R.F. 17, 19, 49, 119
Bea, F.X. 54, 151
Beaver, G. 63, 72
beliefs
    shared 17–18, 21, 29, 34, 35, 39, 72,
        82, 172
    violation of 56–7
Bell Telephone 28, 51
Bennis, W. 187
Bettis, R.A. 18, 34
Bogner, W.C. 42
Boje, D.M. 19, 103
Boland, R.J. 70, 139
Bood, R.P. 52
Bostrom, R.P. 76
Bouchikhi, H. 49, 53, 57
Boulding, E. 49
bounded rationality 8
brainstorming 13